# The Group and
the Unconscious

The International Library of Group Psychotherapy
and Group Process

*General Editors*

Dr Malcolm Pines
Tavistock Clinic, London

Dr Earl Hopper
London School of Economics and Political Science

The International Library of Group Psychotherapy and Group
Process is published in association with the Institute of Group
Analysis (London)

# The Group and the Unconscious

Didier Anzieu
*Translated from the French by*
Benjamin Kilborne

**Routledge & Kegan Paul**
London, Boston, Melbourne and Henley

This translation first published in 1984
by Routledge & Kegan Paul plc
39 Store Street, London WC1E 7DD, England
9 Park Street, Boston, Mass. 02108, USA
464 St Kilda Road, Melbourne,
Victoria 3004, Australia and
Broadway House, Newtown Road,
Henley-on-Thames, Oxon RG9 1EN, England
Set in Times 10 on 12 pt by Columns of Reading
and printed in Great Britain by
Billing & Sons Ltd, Worcester
Originally published in
French under the title
Le groupe et l'inconscient © Bordas 1975
This translation © Routledge & Kegan Paul 1984
No part of this book may be reproduced in
any form without permission from the publisher,
except for the quotation of brief
passages in criticism

Library of Congress Cataloging in Publication Data

Anzieu, Didier.

The group and the unconscious.
(The international library of group psychotherapy
and group process)
Translation of: Le groupe et l'inconscient.
Bibliography: p.
Includes index.
1. Group psychoanalysis. 2. Group psychotherapy.
3. Social groups. 4. Group psychotherapy—Study and
teaching. 5. Subconsciousness. I. Title. II. Series.
[DNLM: 1. Psychotherapy, Group. WM 430 A637g]
RC510.A5913   1983        616.89'17        83-17631

ISBN 0-7100-0693-4

# Contents

# Chapter 1
# On the psycho-analytic method and the rules of its application in group situations

## General and applied psycho-analysis

The unconscious universally produces effects that men continually defend themselves against, wrongly interpret, or seek to manipulate by obscure means for a presumed gain. A scientific approach to these unconscious manifestations depends upon the establishment of a situation in which, governed by specific rules, the situation itself transfers what the unconscious produces and guarantees the accuracy of the interpretations. In this situation two beings, the psycho-analyst and the subject (analysand), made homologous by their psychical apparatus, occupy dissimilar positions. Certain rules apply to them both: that of abstinence, which prohibits any 'real' personal relationship inside or outside the analytic situation and dooms them to merely phantasized symbolic – as well as everyday social – relations. Other rules apply specifically to each of the two positions. The task of the subject is to express everything he thinks, imagines or feels in the situation, i.e., to 'symbolize' the effects it has on him. The task of the analyst is to understand – as transference or as resistance to transference – everything the subject tries to express in the situation, and to intervene (by providing interpretations) only to make him aware of what he is expressing. It is in this way the psycho-analyst affects the situation from the inside.

Complementary rules lay down the respective positions of the body in space during the sessions, the frequency and duration of the sessions, and determine the symbolic activities required of the subject (speaking, drawing, playing with certain materials, relaxing, gesturing, mimicking, assuming certain body positions or reacting to them, having bodily contact, improvising roles, producing or interpreting a certain kind of document) and the financial demands placed upon him. However, this brings us into the realm of applied psycho-analysis.

In fact, the method defined above, long confused with the individual treatment of neuroses, which constituted the original ground upon which it was discovered and to which it was first applied, belongs to the discipline we shall call 'general psycho-analysis.' 'Applied psycho-analysis', on the other hand, is defined as the corpus of open-ended, continually evolving concrete applications of this general method. The now well-advanced task of general psycho-analysis is to construct a theory of the psychical apparatus (its origins, its functioning and its changes) on the basis of observations that psycho-analysts, beginning with Freud, have made and continue to make. The task of applied psycho-analysis is to discover the specific effects of the unconscious in a given field and the necessary transpositions of the general method when applied specifically to this field. These depend, for example, on the type of analysand ('normal', neurotic, narcissistic, psychotic, or psychosomatic; adult, adolescent or child; individual, group or institution) or the type of goal aimed at by the analysis (diagnostic, therapeutic, training, impact on the real social situation).

For the time being, only in psycho-analysis are unconscious effects created by and treated under scientific conditions. As a general rule the psycho-analytic method may be applied to all areas in which the effects of the unconscious are discernible, even if the unconscious resistance which these effects elicit from psycho-analysts themselves still obscures their origin and treatment.

Notwithstanding such exceptional circumstances, the general conditions for the application of the psycho-analytic method to a given field are the following:

(i)   the psycho-analyst who works in the field of applied psycho-analysis can do so only within a personal practice, which is indispensable for the treatment of individual adult patients;

(ii)   the 'interpreter' must not only make the rules governing the psycho-analytic situation explicit from the outset, but must above all observe them himself if they are adequately to fulfil their regulatory function. If the psycho-analyst exempts himself from the rules he imposes on the subject he provokes an unanalysable sado-masochistic or perverse relationship;

(iii)   like all other elements of the psycho-analytic situation, the rules are cathected – and defensively counter-cathected – in phantasy. This cathexis needs to be interpreted.

(iv)   the psycho-analyst who upholds the rules once they have been rendered explicit must not censor their application by the subject or subjects, but rather seek to understand and to interpret those occasions upon which the rules are broken or put into practice with difficulty;

(v)   the situation comes to an end when the psycho-analyst, no longer treated as the object of transference, is recognized by the subject(s) as equally human, when the operative character of the rules has been assimilated, when the resistance to terminate the situation has been analysed and when the end has been recognized as such.

Following these general considerations we can investigate concrete applications of psycho-analysis to group situations, particularly to training groups. I shall try to define three sorts of rules: those that constitute the basis of the psycho-analytic method applied to group phenomena, those that establish the psycho-analytic process in a group situation, and those that govern the psycho-analytic interpretation in this situation.

## The psycho-analytic method applied to groups

The psycho-analytic method is first of all a method of scientific reasoning. Whatever the area to which the psycho-analyst applies this method, his hypotheses concerning the unconscious processes specific to this area are assessed in terms of three criteria:

(i)   for each type of clinical fact there must be a corresponding hypothesis that accounts for it, and each hypothesis must be grounded in specific and significant clinical material; for example, the obstinate silence of certain participants in non-directive discussion groups can be explained with reference to the phantasized representation of the group as devouring mouth and breast. The existence of this representation has been confirmed by subsequent individual interviews with group members; timely interpretation may modify their attitude (see p. 171);

(ii)   each hypothesis must be congruent with those hypotheses specific to its field, and must also be able to be related to or deduced from already-established hypotheses in general psycho-analysis; for instance, Kaës's hypothesis, that ideas in group situations are produced by the defensive negation of a primal phantasy, is an application to the group of observations concerning primary processes and infantile sexual theories brought to light by individual psycho-analysis (Kaës, 1971b, 1973b, 1974b; Gori, 1973b);

(iii)   the validity of each hypothesis must be confirmed by the fruit it bears in an area other than the one for which it was originally conceived; for example, the hypothesis that the non-directive large group situation (30 to 60 persons) causes split transference and intensified negative transference helps us to understand from an economic point of view why large, 'real' social groups composed of several thousands of persons frequently resort to violent, archaic expressions of aggressiveness (e.g. war).

The psycho-analytic method applied to group phenomena depends equally on certain more specifically psycho-analytic criteria. The first of these concerns vocabulary. The psycho-analyst carrying out research on groups is limited to psycho-analytic jargon when he writes about them (in interpretative practice, on the other hand, he expresses himself as much as possible in everyday language). Indeed, although description of facts is rich, diversified and polyphasic, scientific explanation is monophasic. By psycho-analytic jargon is meant not only Freud's own concepts, but also the conceptual contributions of his successors, the validity of which has been established in particular areas of psycho-analysis.

The analogy between the group and the dream, which I developed in an article of 1966 (*infra*) (the group, like the dream, is the imaginary fulfilment of a repressed wish), refers back to early Freudian theory, i.e. to the first topography. Since then psycho-analytic group theory has progressed by systematic recourse to the second topography. This, moreover, is an appropriate turn of events, for Freud discovered the latter by associating hypnosis and crowds, on the one hand, and ambivalence towards paternal imagos and group psychology, on the other. The second topography draws on an analogy between inter- and intra-systemic conflicts and inter-individual tensions within a group, where the individual psychical apparatus is to be explained with reference to the internalization of a group model. But the analogy is reversible; there is a group psychical apparatus resembling that of the individual, but differing in function, homologous but not isomorphic. Missenard (1971, 1972, 1976) has shown that the principal effect of training group methods on subjects is the destruction of certain imaginary (phantasized) identifications, on the one hand, and the progressive establishment of stabilizing narcissistic identifications, followed by innovating symbolic identifications, on the other.

The contribution of Freud's successors has proved every bit as rich. In 1950 the British Kleinian school recognized that the anxiety level in groups was psychotic, and has since observed that persecutory and depressive anxiety are intensified by a group's non-directive character. In France, Angélo Béjarano, also influenced by Melanie Klein, discovered in 1968 that the seminar situation, in which participants work alternately in small groups and as a body, triggers off split transference: positive transference directed generally to the small group and negative transference directed to the group as a whole (Béjarano, 1971, 1976).

Psycho-analysts interested in training group methods have so far failed to take into account the criticism that Lewin, Rogers and their followers have directed at the psycho-sociological jargon, nor have they stated with sufficient clarity and conviction the fact that monitors of training groups resort to this jargon essentially as counter-transference. Psycho-sociological concepts used in group dynamics reflect a defensive attitude towards unconscious group processes. Psycho-sociology, for instance, has stressed leadership, making it a key process in the functioning and progress of the group. A psycho-analytic understanding of groups leads one to a rather different conclusion, as Béjarano (1972) has noted: the phenomena of leadership and splitting into groups constitute the *specific* form that resistance in non-directive training group situations usually takes; the spontaneous leader is the spokesman of the unconscious resistance of the group at a given time and if the group is not provided with a relevant interpretation (or if the group itself doesn't come up with one) its underlying phantasies remain repressed and its progress impaired.

In 1971, taking as our point of departure Winnicott's concept of 'illusion', we gave a more precise meaning to the hypothesis of the group illusion (see Chapter 3). In the course of staff discussions Schilder's notion of the body image enabled my colleagues and myself to realize that the 'large' group situation induces both a phantasized wish to explore the inside of the mother's body and its correlative anxiety (see section 3 of Chapter 4).

A second type of more specifically psycho-analytic criteria concerns the concept of determination rather than vocabulary. Psycho-analytic explanation is, in fact, multi-dimensional. All unconscious processes discovered to operate in a given field need to be explained from a number of perspectives: dynamic, economic, topographical, genetic, phantasmic. Take, for instance, one of the phenomena we have just mentioned, the group illusion, which designates certain moments of symbiotic euphoria during which all group members feel at ease together and happily consider themselves a good group. Dynamically, the group illusion is an attempt to resolve the conflict between a desire for security, on the one hand, and the anxiety of body fragmentation and the threat of loss of personal identity in the group situation, on the other. Economically, it constitutes a particular instance of split transference: the positive transference is concentrated on the group as libidinal object. Topographically, it demonstrates the existence of a group ideal ego. From the point of view of phantasy, it requires the introjection of – and narcissistic identification with – the good breast as part-object to compensate for the damage wrought by the destructive phantasy (induced specifically by the small group situation) of children who tear one another apart in the womb of the bad mother. Genetically, the illusion is, as we know from Winnicott (1953), a necessary stage in the child's conception of the external world, which the child represents as an extension of maternal omnipotence: the group illusion enables the group itself to function as transitional object.

A third psycho-analytic rule concerns the interaction of the subjects' unconscious and the unconscious of the interpreter(s) (where the seminar situations require a number of psycho-analysts acting as a team of interpreters). One of the formulations of this rule is the following: for every unconscious effect, in whatever field, there is a corresponding and opposed resistance. A psycho-analytic explanation of a group phenomenon necessarily takes into account the unconscious epistemological resistance to this phenomenon.

Thus the team of psycho-analysts with whom I have worked for the past fifteen years on training seminars did not readily admit that the rules of the 'small group' (diagnostic group, T group) were transposable in their entirety to the seminar as a whole. We went on trying to 'organize' these meetings – by assigning a theme in advance and by using directive and semi-directive methods (report followed by discussion, statement at the beginning and at the end, collective practical exercises, panel, Phillips 66), by instituting a day of review, by distributing notes of previous meetings to participants – until an internal process of collective working-through led us to recognize the defensive nature of these attempts at organization. What dangerous drive was this defensive mechanism directed against? The danger, resulting from split transference, of finding oneself exposed to the particular intensity of the death drive induced by the 'large' group. The removal of the defence (the 'organization' of the meetings) and a recognition of the form and strength of the repressed drive (split negative transference) went hand in hand. Knowledge of a specific interaction between a defence and a drive opens up the possibility of practical and scientifically grounded applications. For example, if one wants to allow a group to control the destructive drive within its own ranks, one must help it organize itself; if one wants to free this drive, for instance with a view to therapy or training, it is necessary to put the group in a situation governed by the rules of non-omission and of abstinence, and to preclude any other organization.

Another type of interaction, equally important from the triple standpoint of epistemology, technique and practice, is that of the phantasizing of subjects in group situations, and of the phantasizing of interpreters acting as a team. The former, that of the subjects, can only be apprehended to the extent that it triggers off the latter, that of the psycho-analysts', making them aware of it among themselves. In the case cited by Biffe and Martin (1971) of the 'psychotic' group, the phantasizing induced among the participants by a psycho-analytic group situation was evidently not picked up by the two interpreters, themselves preoccupied with their theoretical and technical differences, i.e., their own phantasized disagreement, which the group gave them the opportunity to air. Another case is that in which group monitors, who generally have psycho-sociological but not psycho-analytic training, let themselves be hoodwinked by the phantasizing of the subjects and 'fuse' with their group by, for example, sharing the group illusion instead of interpreting it. A third case has been described but not analysed by the school of Lewin under the concept of resistance to change: psycho-analytic experience in groups has shown that in a seminar to which participants come in order to 'change', resistance to change is a reaction to an unspoken phantasy unconsciously shared by the team of interpreters and known as the 'breaking apart' phantasy.

## The psycho-analytic group situation

All psycho-analytic situations, be they individual or group, therapeutic or training, are based on two basic rules: that of non-omission and that of abstinence. Naturally these rules need to be adapted to the particular areas in which they are applied.

The rule of non-omission does not mean that each member says *everything* that comes into his head – otherwise the result would be chaotic. In its application to groups this rule has three phases. First, group participants speak among themselves about any subject they wish. This encourages freedom and arouses anxiety over transgressing what is forbidden by verbalizing repressed wishes; hence the collective equivalents of the dream that unite group members together; hence, above all at first, inhibition, paralysis, silence. For the rule of free speech is also a command to speak: participants and monitors must discuss together what they have to say; they have no choice but to do so (which is already the rule of abstinence). Finally, this rule gives group members an opportunity of making public during the session conversations held in private, in so far as these conversations concern the group as a whole (implicit rule of restitution).

These three stages apply above all to small non-directive discussion groups. Groups involving psychodrama, relaxation or bodily expression, and large, non-directive groups need to be handled differently, depending on the purpose and size of the group. For example, in a large group, it is suggested that group members:

(i)   express what they feel here and now;
(ii)  address all group members when speaking about the seminar as a whole (on the other hand, matters of concern to small

diagnostic groups or psychodrama groups should be dealt with in those groups).

In fact, the seminar situation calls for a distinction between three orders of reality, as each problem is related to its corresponding level:

(i)  that of small groups (diagnostic, psychodrama or body exercise groups);
(ii)  that of large groups (full sessions of participants and monitors);
(iii)  that of groups of monitors.

In each situation the rule, together with its applications, is made explicit from the outset by the person responsible for interpreting it. The monitor-interpreter identifies himself as such at the same time as he lays down the rules. He intervenes only to see that the rules are followed, to encourage transference on to him and on to the group and to communicate his interpretations of what is happening.

The rule of abstinence is often omitted or broken by monitors who have not had psycho-analytic training. This is why such members fall victim to the group illusion and even believe the goal of the training experience is symbiotic euphoria or making new acquaintances. For the psycho-analyst all such behaviour is counter-transferential. The absence of *real* personal relations between the monitor and the participants, whether within or outside the session, is a *sine qua non* condition of establishing an interpretable transference. The rule has several phases: the monitor does not take part in verbal exchanges in the group when they relate to anything other than the *hic et nunc* group experience; he abstains from speaking of this experience outside the sessions (except in cases where a member needs an individual psychotherapeutic consultation). Naturally, he refrains from all aggressive or sexual acts with participants during the duration of the course of treatment. But the abstinence does not imply rigidity, nor does it preclude ordinary social, spontaneous relations or physical contact required by certain kinds of group activity. As for the participants, they are encouraged to be discreet about discussing with outsiders what goes on during the sessions.

Although psycho-analytic work with more complex units (e.g.

medical or social institutions or business concerns) is in its early stages, it is clear that certain kinds of educational or institutional psychotherapy that rely on group experiences – while doing away with anything resembling a basic rule and by refusing to define in advance the role of the interpreter – lead at best to collective versions of wild psycho-analysis and at worst to perverse manipulations of unconscious processes.

# Chapter 2

# The system of rules in diagnostic groups: structure, internal dynamics and groundwork

The rules of diagnostic groups or (T groups, development groups, sensitivity groups, encounter groups, etc.) are organized in an internally coherent symbolic system composed of polar opposites. The operational efficiency of this system for any individual psychological training and psychotherapy is derived from its resemblance to the social system and the system of the individual unconscious.

## The rules of diagnostic groups

Depending upon his personal style and the specific features of the group, the monitor lays down five basic rules at the beginning of the course:

  (i)   the rule of verbalization ('What we do is speak'), comple-
        mented by that of free speech ('say what you like');
 (ii)   the rule of here and now;
(iii)   the rule of abstinence ('outside sessions, the monitor does
        not take part in the conversations or activities of the partici-
        pants');
 (iv)   the rule of restitution ('it may be useful for what participants
        say outside the session to be repeated during the session');
  (v)   the rule of discretion ('what is said in the sessions is not to be
        repeated outside'), complemented by the rule of anonymity
        ('the names of the participants are not divulged by the
        organizers; however, the participants themselves may reveal
        their own names when the occasion arises; to facilitate con-

tact, you may if you wish call one another by your first names').

The monitor defines his role: he is present among the others, neither proposing subjects for discussion nor organizing conversations; he tries to understand what is going on here and now and talks about it. He also defines the roles of the observer(s) (taking notes at meetings; helping the meetings; helping the monitor to understand) and their requirement to respect the rule of discretion.

Another rule is formulated 'in practice' by the monitor, who sets an example by changing seats at the beginning of each session.

## Rules of psycho-analysis and rules of diagnostic groups

Rules introduce individuals into the symbolic dimension and it is only through such rules that individuals can be introduced into that dimension. For a rule never exists independently, but belongs to a coherent set of rules of which it is a part. None the less, this set of rules generally remains implicit, its coherence implied and any complete list of rules incomplete. Such – despite the work of grammarians and structural linguists – is the case of language. The rules of diagnostic groups have gradually emerged out of a long, insufficiently understood experience of groups. This experience has validated these rules, but cannot provide an adequate foundation for them. The purpose of a rule is to be sought not in its efficacy, but in its articulation within a symbolic system that gives it a specific function. For diagnostic groups psycho-analysis serves as a point of departure.

The psycho-analytic method – in the typical case of a neurotic adult – defines a situation and the rules to which the partners will function. The situation is located in space (the psycho-analyst's office, the couch on which the patient is lying, the armchair in which the psycho-analyst is sitting) and in time (the regular frequency of the sessions in the week, their fixed duration, the total number of sessions, which cannot be fixed in advance). There are two parties: the psycho-analyst and the patient. Any third party is excluded. The patient must follow two rules: the rule of non-omission and free association (speak freely of whatever comes to mind, trying to omit nothing), and the rule of abstinence (abstain from any other kind of relation to the psycho-analyst, whether acting out or any relation in real life, outside the sessions). The psycho-analyst must obey two similar rules: he must react to the patient's free associations by letting his concentration float free and, when the time is ripe, speak freely of what he has understood; during the sessions, he must refrain from deriving personal satisfaction from the counter-transference of the patient and, outside the sessions, must not speak of him (except to analyse his own counter-transference with a colleague, or, for scientific purposes, to write up the case material, in which case he must respect the patient's anonymity). Agreement concerning fees seals the pact between the two parties, and symbolically represents in the mind of the patient the price to be paid for a cure. Psycho-analytic practice involves a number of particular rules, depending on the case, the time and the difficulty of implementing them – but which none the less conform to the spirit of the basic rules.

It is difficult to discover the system of rules governing a specific domain for two reasons: the symbolic is the very element in which the mind functions and can therefore be grasped only awkwardly, uncertainly, for knowledge of symbolic systems block the way to the discovery of new systems. Moreover, as long as the symbolic organization of an activity or object remains in the dark, phantasies preclude understanding. Knowledge of a symbolic system requires that phantasies be known, otherwise each person continues to use the others for the satisfaction of his own wishes.

Freud invented the psycho-analytic rules by breaking medical habits (letting the patient speak rather than asking him questions, frustrating him by refusing to guarantee a cure by pills or hypnotism). But Freud did not invent these alone. Conversations first with Breuer then with Fliess, in addition to his self-analysis, made it possible for him to separate phantasy from knowledge and to define the rules of a new symbolic system whose area of operation is the unconscious.

The symbolic system of the rules of diagnostic groups emerged in the course of a similar process. Discussions inside the team to which I belong, the exchange of questions studied and comparing experiences with colleagues led us to discern the rules formulated at the beginning of this chapter.

These rules are articulated in terms of an overall structure that will emerge in due course. This structure determines the relations between the rules, the situation here and now and a number of participants. It determines the way in which the two fundamental rules, free association and abstinence, function with respect to the persons in this situation. It is thus possible to say that this structure is 'generative', in the sense used by mathematicians or linguists (e.g. 'generative grammar').

## The size of the groups

It varies between seven and fifteen. Eight is the optimum for a group in psychotherapy and ten to twelve for a training group. The logic behind these numbers reflects an old law: beyond a certain point, quantitative variation produces qualitative changes. In human (and animal) groups, the quality of the psychological processes varies with the number of individuals assembled. The total number of inter-individual relations possible between $n$ individuals is provided by the formula: $n(n-1)/2$. If $n$ is equal to or below 6, the total number of interrelations is equal to or below fifteen: in this case, it is easy for each individual actually to develop all the interrelations theoretically possible (five at most) and to recognize the development of all the interrelations among the others (ten at most). If $n$ is equal to or above fifteen, the total number of possible interrelations exceeds 100; in this case, it is no longer feasible for an individual to enter into the fourteen interrelations theoretically possible for him, nor to recognize the innumerable interrelations proliferating among the others. A group of between seven and fourteen members gives each a chance to develop a maximum of from six to thirteen different interrelations and to perceive among the others a theoretical maximum of fifteen (for seven members) and 78 (for fourteen members).

The diagnostic group situation is not a group situation from the beginning as is often believed. During the course the participants may feel they are part of a group, but this is neither a goal to set before them nor necessary for them to get something out of the experience.

Group members generally do not know one another beforehand. They call each other by their first names and are encouraged to disguise their social identities in order to appear more personal. For the implicit task is to seek to communicate part of one's subjectivity and, in turn, to understand that of others.

The size of the diagnostic group is determined by a double analogy: an analogy with socio-occupational life in which one is confronted with a limited number of colleagues, against a background of social life; and an analogy with the individual unconscious where a number of levels, drives and important identifications are continually interacting: the small group situation gives each individual an opportunity of projecting that level, that drive, that identification on to another member of the group.

## The space and time of meeting

These interrelations develop in a here and now situation different from that of an individual psycho-analysis. The 'here' is the place where the group meets, the place that it makes its own, encloses, just as animal bands delimit a territory, generally by their excrement, and protect it against enemy incursions. In the enclosed space of the diagnostic group, people are seated, with or without a table. The theoretical line that links them together varies from the circle to the regular polygon. Mathematicians were asked to calculate a curve such that group members, while situated at regular intervals along this curve, should be as close as possible to one another (the ideal in this case is a straight line) and as visible as possible to each other (the ideal in this case is a circle); such a form is an oval. Certain monitors have even had egg-shaped tables built for their diagnostic groups.

Group phenomena vary according to the way participants are arranged, e.g. in rows (as in school) or lying down (as in psychoanalysis). The latter arrangement is used for certain relaxation groups in which problems of individual body image are foremost.

Having neither the regularity nor the indefiniteness of individual psycho-analytic practice, the diagnostic group situation is located in time in a concentrated form. A diagnostic group functions on the basis of ten to twenty sessions concentrated in a short space of time: a minimum of three days and a maximum of fifteen. In other words each day there are at least one and at most four sessions of between one and a quarter to two hours each.

The team to which I belong (in common with other teams) has run long, cyclical diagnostic groups which meet, for example, once a week for one or two years. These experiences are too recent to allow us to draw any conclusions. This is particularly the case with the weekly 'slow open groups' of unlimited duration in which new members replace old members, who, considering themselves to be well enough trained, withdraw, with the agreement of the group. These are new experiences the psycho-therapeutic dimension of which overrides the training dimension.

In a diagnostic group lasting three or four days, time is experienced as a continuity broken only by nights. Other interruptions are not readily accepted by the participants, who often meet during the breaks, at noon and in the evening in a café or restaurant or at the home of one of them, to continue the session. The features of this diagnostic group time are based on what I call 'the intense ephemerality of brief encounters'. This involves strong and rapid, libidinal arousal in participants whose defences are not too rigid. The all-out striving after this concentration has led to marathon groups meeting eighteen hours on end, or over an entire weekend, with sleep reduced to a minimum. Keeping sessions distinct is, we believe, necessary, however flexible their overall duration may be.

René Kaës (1972) has pointed out that space and time in diagnostic groups have their own organization and differ from both the social organization of space and time and the particular organization of those categories in the unconscious. The spatio-temporal structure of the diagnostic group mediates between social organization and unconscious organization: one might compare it to a two-sided membrane, one side of which faces the social and the other the primary psychical processes.

The diagnostic group 'brackets-out' social space-time. The participants 'retreat' into a 'seminar'. By contrast to real, profane social space-time, the group space takes on a symbolic, sacred character; as Kaës (1972) remarks, the group space is at once an enclosed place (*huis clos*), from which ordinary social life is excluded, and a laboratory in which the participants experiment on the seething life of a society in miniature. They are not completely cut off from the outside: they can telephone, go home, eat in town, buy newspapers. They know that afterwards they will return to their usual family, social and professional routines, about which perhaps they will feel differently. The group space is thus not a 'hell' from which there is no escape, as in Sartre's play *Huis clos*, nor a desert island on which shipwrecked survivors seek shelter, as in William Golding's *Lord of the Flies*, nor a *Raft of the*

*Medusa*, cut off from all contact with the human world, where the struggle for survival becomes primordial and tragic. Society continues to nourish and protect the participants of a diagnostic group. Group space, is, in effect, a figure against the background of everyday social space. Often, however, a diagnostic group tries to represent another society, a society yet to be born; it strives for a social Utopia.

In fact, group space, by virtue of its temporary enclosure – and this is its other side – tends to be not a real or ideal society, but rather a phantasized space of unconscious repressed wishes. Each member anxiously tries to defend himself against the desire of others, who try to treat him as an object (a point on which there is a clear divergence with individual psycho-analysis). The diagnostic group helps its participants to extricate themselves not only from their social roles, but also from the roles in which the unconscious wishes of their professional and family milieux have frozen them. It can help them find their places as subjects.

Let us now examine the time of diagnostic groups. It is outside that of usual social relations. It may be vacation time, or quite simply time on one's hands. Above all, it is a time that gives the individual an opportunity of moving from one stage in his life to another. This theme – of passing to the other side, of crossing a threshold, of walking through a mirror – arises in a more explicit way in training groups using psychodrama than in diagnostic groups.

The participants in a diagnostic group lose their usual sense of time: they have all the time in the world and anyone who cannot stand waiting and tries to get the others to do something is promptly put in his place. Sessions run for varying lengths of time, and generally end unexpectedly, except when they coincide with periods of tension or boredom; occasionally, time itself seems to stand still: this is the time of immobility, of death, or the time before birth; at other moments the density of time is such that it seems to burst, hurtling the participants towards some possible new life. One might posit a symmetrical relation between the 'utopic' character of group space and, to use Renouvier's neologism, the 'uchronic' character of group time.

The reader will have noted in these descriptions made by participants of their experience the mark of Freud's 'unconscious time'. Unconscious time is the time of repetition, of the return of the repressed, of the automatism that drives the psychical apparatus to find again the first lost object; it is, in Proustian terms, the search for lost time. It is a phantasized, imaginary time, then, that abolishes real, profane time as the phantasized space abolishes social space. But in groups, as in individual psycho-analysis, the lost object is recovered in phantasy only so that it can be lost consciously and become the object of wishes. Each participant is born again in time, constituted, between his birth and the horizon of his death, as a horizon of his temporary partial subject, is driven to the dynamism of the repetition compulsion. There is, none the less, a considerable difference between psycho-analytic time, bearing the stamp of regression to childhood, of personal reconstruction of the past, of recovering lost memories, and this time without a past, which is that of the diagnostic group. The participants say little about their personal pasts. When the group begins, it is in a sense a-historical: it has no previous existence and, with a few exceptions, does not continue beyond the agreed duration. The desire to last as a group is one of the aspects of the group illusion. Thus, the time of the diagnostic group operates on three registers: the time of repetition, the time of returning to origins and the time of new beginnings.

When a diagnostic group has been able to live through these three phases, the prospect of the group's coming to an end no longer arouses anxiety. The last session no longer has an atmosphere of mourning in which silence alternates with funeral orations for the still-present departed. Early in our experience everyone analysed the role that each person had played in the group. This series of Rogerian analyses, so many mirrored reflexions of the participants' feelings for one another, ended in mutual panegyric. Separation anxiety prompted promises to get together again, the exchange of names and addresses, the request that the monitor disclose the ultimate meaning of their experience, etc. As we became more psycho-analytically oriented, we gave up our crutches (summarized explanations, a day of summing up and a questionnaire on how satisfied participants were). Naturally, those participants who wanted to extend their friendship in reality are perfectly free to do so, but the artificial need for the survival of the group as such had to be interpreted.

The principal theory on which the termination of a diagnostic group is based is diametrically opposed to the group illusion. It may be summarized as follows: the aim of group training methods is the more complete fulfilment of individual potential. An ephemeral, gratuitous group – the primary group of the sociologists – is no more than a mock goal for people who do not know one another at the outset and who have scarcely any chance of working together after the group is disbanded. The unfortunately ambiguous term 'group' refers here only to a group situation – its own place, its own duration, its own rules of the game – which enables the participants to come close to realizing their individual goals. Attaining such goals is impossible, of course, since a diagnostic group cannot of itself provide sufficient training, but, for some participants, it may represent a decisive turning-point in their lives. Individuals generally feel the effects of the experience *ex post facto*. The diagnostic group un-freezes defensive positions, removes counter-cathexis, gives greater mobility to the libido. Ending a diagnostic group on time, without drawing conclusions or promising to send a summary explaining everything, forces each participant to 'translaborate' – to use Melanie Klein's expression – what has been experienced collectively in what is inappropriately called a group. The death of the group may be agonizing only if participants, with the tacit consent of the monitor, take as their goal the emotional experience of a symbolic group. However, if participants are not victims of the group illusion, the termination of the course has a rather different sense. The enclosed space opens and its imaginary reality fades away. It becomes no more than a memory, a symbol of changes in the way each participant will place himself in relation to his social role, to others and above all to his wishes. The rule of not sitting in the same place at every session functions in this sense as a symbolic prefiguration. Group time comes to an end; individual time begins, a time more personal and freer both of social time and of the repetition of the unconscious.

We can now attempt to understand the functioning of the space-time rule as it applies to training groups ('sessions are here and now, not anywhere else, and they take place each day at fixed times'). As we noted in the preceding chapter, this rule recalls the famous rule of the three unities of space, time and action in classical tragedy. Drama is, in fact, the staging of a phantasy, itself the staging of a defensive conflict; it requires that the phantasy be summoned, as it were, to a certain place, at a certain time. But we eventually realized that it is a mistake to draw a parallel with classical tragedy. For the dramatic principle of the unity of action is purely aesthetic and quite inappropriate to the diagnostic group,

where there is never a unity of action – a shared phantasy – except
at the moment of the group illusion. In diagnostic groups, each
participant tries, unconsciously, at various times, to impose his
individual phantasies on the rest of the group. The resonance of
these phantasies in the unconscious of some – never all – of the
other participants corresponds to the phenomenon of leadership.
If there is no resonance, if each participant who exposes himself
waits for an echo that does not come, the group stagnates and is
experienced as a dismemberment. In which case, instead of
individual phantasies, the group attempts to organize itself around
an imago or a shared primal fantasy. One of the goals of the
diagnostic group is to enable participants to grasp the specific
character of the trans-individual circulation of phantasies. This
goal is obscured if the unity of action, or, what amounts to the
same thing, the constitution of a (united) group becomes the
overriding imperative.

We have seen the relation between the rule of spatio-temporal
unity and the unconscious. We shall now examine its relation to
human and social reality. Families and individuals do not choose
to be born. From birth there are others with whom one must live;
life at work follows life at school, and both repeat this limitation;
this dimension of family and social existence is reproduced by the
diagnostic group enclosed in a space in which participants who did
not know one another beforehand are obliged to communicate. So
much for the rule of spatial unity.

The fact that participants cannot decide when either the sessions
or the series of sessions as a whole begin or end refers to another
dimension of the human condition: no individual knows the hour
of his birth nor that of his death. This, we believe, is the basis of
the rule of temporal unity.

## The rule of free association

In diagnostic groups, as in psycho-analysis, there are two and only
two rules: that of free association (i.e., non-omission) and that of
abstinence. Depending on the group situation (size, place, time),
these rules are applied differently to (a) a participant considered as
an individual, (b) the group participants, (c) the monitor and (d)
the observers.

Let us begin with the rule of free association. It invites

participants to speak of whatever they want during the sessions (i.e., inside the situation). This 'invitation' is two-sided: it involves, on the one hand, obligation and, on the other, freedom. This reflects the two aspects of this rule: non-omission stresses obligation, free association stresses freedom. The participants are therefore morally obliged to communicate; they are not allowed, at least until the end of the series of sessions, to act together; they are condemned to freedom. This obligation is dual: they must speak and can only speak. On the one hand, they have to speak 'freely'; in other words, it is preferable for them not to decide on subjects for discussion that might predetermine the direction that discussion might take; there is no particular reason to choose certain subjects rather than others. What then is communicated? The only thing the participants have in common, the only subject immediately meaningful to all, is their experience of here and now. This experience is also a personal experience, and refers each individual to his own past, his childhood, his character, his private, occupational and social commitments. Each person is thus led to communicate to the others his personal manner of experiencing the group.

Where a number of individuals are involved, can one really use the expression 'non-omission'? In individual psycho-analytic treatment, the patient must not consciously or voluntarily leave out any of the affects and representations that come to mind during the session. This rule is, however, an ideal, an inaccessible goal. No patient, particularly at the beginning of psycho-analysis, can respect it fully. To be scrupulous in trying to do so is itself an obsessional defence. What is instructive and needs to be analysed is the way the patient behaves with respect to this rule. If several persons speak out at the same time, the result would be cacophonous, like the collective monologue Piaget describes among nursery school children or the myth of the Tower of Babel, often used as a metaphor in diagnostic groups. A defensive rationalization is often resorted to by some participants: they call for a 'chairman' who would control the discussion in an orderly fashion, calling not only on those who ask to speak, but also those who have something to say and don't dare to speak up. This defence mechanism is analogous to the self-imposed censorship encountered in individual treatment ('what's the point of telling the analyst that? It's unimportant, absurd, or won't get us any further'). In both cases, it amounts to an attempt to prevent the drives from expressing themselves freely, in a disorderly fashion. This defence mechanism seeks to impose on the id the 'order' of the super-ego.

During the sessions some participants keep quiet because others speak to them, faster or better than they are capable of doing. Certain participants do not verbalize their experience before finding a partner, an ally, who feels things as they do, whose former remarks they can rely on and on whom they rely for encouragement. The rule of non-omission means the same thing as in individual analysis, namely that what happens within the situation is spoken about: in this case several individuals are involved, so nothing pertaining to the way in which various participants experience this plural situation is to be omitted.

Is it enough for the monitor to define from the outset the rule of non-omission (or of free association) by restricting the freedom of saying what comes to mind to the here and now? Certain psycho-sociologists, stressing the 'obligation' side of the rule (the obligation to say whatever comes to mind), rather than the 'freedom' side (freedom to speak as one wishes), tell the participants to speak and speak only of what they feel in the *hic et nunc* situation. They thus aggravate the anxiety of the participants, without either theoretical or technical justification, causing long collective silences and, occasionally, breakdowns. Participants feel manhandled, forced, treated sadistically. In training, as in psycho-analysis, there cannot be birth without pain. But such a rule means a birth with forceps. Indeed it is often accompanied, on the part of its adherents, by the 'manipulation' of individuals behind the scenes and even the manipulation of the group during the sessions. True, diagnostic groups, if they progress, incite participants to concentrate increasingly on working out what they feel in the situation: thus in the end the group creates an authentic discourse on itself and, simultaneously, the collection of participants becomes a group in the sense that it is a place where symbols are traded and no longer where wishes are fulfilled in phantasy. To assign as a rule from the outset what must crop up in practice as the analysis of resistances and of the phantasized fears bolstering them is to put the cart before the horse. In individual analysis, the analyst does not order the patient, as during the early heroic period when hypnotic suggestion was still used, to 'speak of your symptoms, your traumas, of your childhood memories' or even 'speak of your transference on to me'. He states the rule as openly as possible: 'speak'. He does not stipulate in advance what must happen. Requiring that a patient, or individuals in a diagnostic group, formulate instantly what they feel (i.e. become directly conscious of the unconscious), underestimates the need for working through. And it is this working through that makes psycho-analysis and training analysis at once personal and inter-subjective. The latent content of dreams, symptoms, witticisms, or scientific or artistic creation can only be understood through manifest discourses that at once transpose and distort it. The processes of this transposition – displacement, condensation, symbolization, reversal into the opposite – were described by Freud in the self-analysis of his dreams. The individual patient or the members of a diagnostic group must be left free to produce the manifest contents from which the latent content can drawn. This is, in the strictly etymological sense, what analysis means. No recommendation can immediately solve the essential metapsychological problem inherent in human communication: primary process thinking cannot be explained by secondary process thinking. Such is the problem with which participants of a diagnostic group are faced.

## The rule of abstinence

When one tries to apply this rule to groups a doubt arises. Does abstaining from acting during sessions fall under the rule of non-omission or that of abstinence? Obviously, participants cannot choose to go off together to the movies instead of to one of their sessions under the pretext that they will then have something to discuss during the next session. Nor can they decide to indulge in such activities as cutting out paper birds or organizing a ping-pong match. Such *passages à l'acte*, when they occur, must be interpreted as escapes. On the other hand, those collective activities in which verbal expression retains an essential place, such as comments on a drawing on the blackboard, a collective poem, a sequence of psychodrama, even a mime, providing the drawing, poem, psychodrama and mime symbolically represent the here and now experience, do conform to the rule.

In fact the rule of abstinence revolves around something else; it requires participants to abstain from personal relationships with the monitor or observers during the course. Thus formulated, this rule is indispensable, for it defines what is forbidden. For this reason some monitors minimize or ignore it so as not to have to respect it themselves. Like any human being, monitors tend to try to get around what is forbidden. They, most of all, need to be lucid and firm, for they must impose the frustration and, at the same time, arouse the castration anxiety or narcissistic injury implied by the formulation of what is forbidden.

With the exception of everyday social relations, especially those required by the material needs of communal life in the case of 'live-in' seminars, the rule of abstinence lets participants believe that the monitor will abstain from all individual relations with them. This rule does not imply only that the monitor will avoid discussing, outside sessions, what goes on in the seminars with any participant, though this is the simplest and most natural way of formulating the rule at the opening of the course. Nor can this rule be reduced to a repudiation of favouritism by the training group's father, who loves all his children equally and therefore has no favourites. Like the analyst in individual treatment, the monitor frustrates all the drives, particularly the libidinous ones, which, consciously or unconsciously, participants project on to him. This is the fundamental meaning of the rule of abstinence. The monitor does not behave like a real object for the satisfaction of participants' wishes. At the same time, by frustrating them, he becomes the object of participants' phantasies. This is the technical condition that allows him, as a psycho-analyst, to work with the unconscious processes in and among several participants that are transferred on to him.

The rule of abstinence thus gives rise to pregenital or Oedipal prohibition. This does not always appear clearly in a diagnostic group of short duration in which most participants go home for lunch and in the evening. On the other hand, in seminars of a week's living-in, the Oedipal character comes out explicitly during the sessions of psychodrama or plenary meetings.

In a diagnostic group, libidinal or aggressive cathexis on other participants is as marked as it is on the monitor. The most obvious manifestation of this cathexis is the network of affinities between members, relationships which, together with their variations from session to session, may eventually be recorded using techniques of sociometry. But the participants understand, although they are never told, that even outside the sessions these relationships must not go beyond the spoken word. Sexual or violent physical relationships are understood to be forbidden. The temptation or the occasional act arouses intense guilt feelings. Only one physical activity is not only allowed but highly valued: communal meals, involving conversation among all or practically all group members. These meals have the effect of intensifying the group illusion.

At this point it is appropriate to wonder, as psycho-analysts have done, how to differentiate between the rule of free association and the rule of abstinence. Is there not rather one rule with different facets? Before being able to speak together of their phantasies, participants must refrain abreacting. In psycho-analysis, not abreacting is the necessary (but not sufficient) requirement needed to verbalize. This condition is generalized in diagnostic groups where each participant is the potential co-analyst of the others. At the same time any participant is the potential cathected object of any other. Each participant is thus expected to obey the same rules in his relation to other participants that he obeys in his relation to the monitor as analyst.

All this would seem to confirm Freud's position in *Totem and Taboo* (1912-13): the Oedipus complex is the basis of collective as much as of individual life. The prohibition against killing members, or having sexual relations with women or girls of one's own group is the beginning of morality and of a symbolic order that governs human relations. The power of Freud's myth – the murder of the father by sons who, at the totemic feast, eat him, not as representation of omnipotence, but as a regulating law – is borne out in diagnostic groups. The dual prohibition against murder and incest functions from the outset, and is encountered during meals eaten together. In diagnostic groups the monitor (or a substitute participant) is taken to pieces and the rules are gradually reinvented, thus allowing each member to recognize and to be recognized by the others (A. Missenard, 1972). However, as we will see later (p. 253), such group phenomena, whose existence is unquestionable, derive more from the central presence in the group of an unconscious imago than from a group effect of the Oedipus complex (see Anzieu, 1976a).

The frustration of the wish to know is even more difficult to tolerate for group members than the frustration of the wish for power (sexual or social). Most participants hope to acquire greater knowledge of themselves, of others and of groups. To them, the monitor is omniscient; they hope he will transfer his knowledge to them if he thinks them worthy, but fear that their mediocrity (their phantasized castration) will be exposed and prevent him from doing so. The monitor, in fact, helps participants to understand what is going on within and among themselves in the situation; he refuses to teach or to let participants believe that there are secrets, a knowledge of which would give greater power to those who knew them.

However, this refusal is different for the psycho-sociologist and for the psycho-analyst. For the psycho-sociologist, participants learn not from the monitor but from the group experience. A group that is beginning is an adventure. This group may, by a sort of collective self-analysis, acquire specific knowledge of itself and general knowledge of groups. The optimism of Lewin or Rogers leads to the conclusion that, put in an adequate situation, any individual will discover by himself what he needs to know. The psycho-analytic monitor frustrates the wish to know precisely because it is the only way of exposing the phantasized dimension of such a desire for knowledge.

The wish to know is rooted in what Freud called infantile sexual curiosity and Klein the 'epistemophilic' drive. The desire to see the difference between the sexes, to see the 'primal scene', to know the mysteries of sex, of procreation, and by the same token of one's own birth is accompanied by phantasies and guilt. The diagnostic group situation arouses in each participant the wish to know his or her 'difference' from the others, to 'see' the monitor 'function' in the group.

For a psycho-analytic monitor, it is of the utmost importance to elucidate these phantasies associated with the wish to know. It then becomes possible to bring to light the resistance hidden behind this wish: I came to look around, not to expose myself and certainly not to change. Once the anxiety aroused by the primal scene (which freezes the participants, fascinated and mute, on the spot) is partially cleared away, they can listen to their unconscious, i.e. to their repressed wishes. These wishes, in turn, become available to them once again. Generally speaking, any accurate analysis of a phantasy shared by several participants (practically never is one shared by all) liberates individually in each participant deep resources previously inaccessible. The monitor's refusal to give in to the demand to know and to be taught situates the diagnostic group in its true dimension: that of changing the relation to wishes. The same resistance is well known to so-called training psycho-analysts: patients who come supposedly to learn psycho-analysis often defensively resist analysis by pretending to learn it.

## The system of rules

We must now examine the ways in which the two basic rules apply to the various protagonists in the situation.

### For participants taken singly

As we have seen, the rules of non-omission and of abstinence govern relations between the participants and the monitor. Such relations are a transposition of the relation between individual patient and psycho-analyst.

### For participants taken together

These two basic rules establish dynamically antagonistic relations between the individual and the group as a whole, and between this group and the outside. The dynamically antagonistic character of the system of diagnostic group rules was first recognized by Kaës. Non-omission was taken by participants to mean the discussion in the group of private conversations pertaining to the group experience. Its counterpart is the principle of discretion or respect for anonymity: participants must refrain from revealing outside anything they may have learnt during the sessions about the inner life, personal history, important behaviour, or even the name of any of their number. Other aspects of this dynamic antagonism are the following: each person speaks, if not to all members, at least in front of them, and not to one privileged listener, even if he be the monitor; each person is led to reveal to the group aspects of himself that he conceals or insufficiently understands in the outside world; each person speaks to the group not of what he is or what he does outside, but rather of what he thinks and feels in the group situation.

*For the monitor*

The rule of non-omission applies differently to the monitor, in his relations both with the participants and with the observers. In the first case, the monitor does not keep what he knows of the group experience to himself; he shares it with the participants as a whole. The rule of non-omission here becomes the rule of interpretation. Interpretation in a diagnostic group has in turn its own rules, analogous to the rules of psycho-analytic interpretation in individual therapy. The monitor speaks when he thinks the moment is ripe, not when he is asked to speak (he abstains from speaking at the wrong time). Sooner or later he tells the participants what he has to say, or at least what can be understood (he abstains from giving 'wild' interpretations). Whenever possible, he speaks in such a way as to prepare the ground for the participants to discover for themselves the meaning of the group's experience; he hints, he allows them to glimpse, rather than presenting abruptly his insights, even if justified (though in certain situations such a procedure is necessary to remove some major obstacle). But as he is dealing with a number of participants, the monitor's interpretations in a diagnostic group don't follow the same rules as in individual analysis. As a general rule, the monitor communicates his insights concerning group behaviour to participants as a group. Only exceptionally does he communicate his understanding of an individual participant to him (he abstains from carrying on individual psycho-analysis). If he speaks of the reactions of a single participant, it is to illustrate a general group process and is related to shared experiences and the interrelationships between the single participant and the group as a whole. Similarly, interpretations are in a sense a-historical (the monitor abstains from any working through of an individual's past), as Ezriel has noted for group psycho-analysis. They are centred on the here and now, which does not exclude a consideration of the group's past as it has evolved during the course or been phantasized by the participants.

The rule of non-omission applies differently to monitor and observer. Everything the monitor privately feels about the shared experience and which it would be inappropriate, indiscreet or ill-advised to communicate to the group – in short, his counter-transference – is told to the observer. This is the rule of clarifying the counter-transference. An observer, preferably with psycho-analytic and diagnostic group training, is needed to put the rule into practice. The team of monitors with which I work has become convinced of the need for a competent observer.

The rule of abstinence applies to the monitor as it does to any member of the diagnostic group. In addition, this rule assumes certain forms on account of the monitor's role. He abstains from proposing a theme or topic for discussion. He abstains from any aside with a participant, even outside sessions, except for everyday social relations or if a participant who is shaken by the experience needs an individual meeting.

But all this constitutes only a secondary aspect of the rule of abstinence.

This rule demands more from the monitor than from the other group members. Not only is he bound to refrain from all emotional aggressive or sexual relations with participants, he must also control the inevitable – even indispensable – phantasized fulfilment of these wishes, not only with respect to each participant but above all with respect to the 'group' considered as his cathected 'object' (it is this object that provokes the most insidious phantasies). Here one finds the equivalent of the analyst's counter-transference on to his patient. Very often this counter-transference leads to the group illusion.

We can now define the dynamic antagonism of the two basic rules as they apply to the monitor, once it is agreed that he interreacts not with each individual participant but with the group as a whole. The monitor abstains from realizing his counter-transference, i.e. his phantasized relation to the group; however, on the symbolic plane, he tries to omit nothing of what he knows of the shared experience when he speaks to the group.

## For the observer(s)

The rule of abstinence is even more imperative for the observers than for the participants or the monitor. Apart from note-taking or recording, they not only abstain from doing anything physical, but also abstain from speaking during the sessions, whether to the group, to the monitor or to an individual participant. Outside the sessions, they don't speak with participants of the experience they have witnessed, and are obliged to be as discreet as the others.

The rule of free speech comes into play in the relation between observers and the monitor. There is no question of 'imposing' this rule on observers. It is enough to warn them, before the beginning of the course, and to repeat if necessary, that their position is uncomfortable: they share the experience with the same intensity as do the participants, but are not able to externalize their reactions during the sessions; they may, however, do this with the monitor outside the sessions. Observers also need to be warned that participants sometimes try to use them as intermediaries between themselves and the monitor: in such cases observers must be very reserved; but if the observer learns something from the participant that could further the understanding of the shared experience, it is important that he tells the monitor as soon as possible. Here is an example which will be taken up again in the chapter 'The Group Illusion' in which the unconscious of certain participants prevented this very thing. I was monitoring a diagnostic group in the east of France. During a meal we had together between the tenth and the eleventh sessions, I was sitting at one end of the table and the two observers, one responsible for recording what was said, were at the other. Participants at the observer's end of the table spoke openly about problems that arose in their professional life with members of the opposite sex: the wish to be free of certain taboos and guilt feelings. Their conversations confirmed precisely the interpretations that until that time I had proposed, in vain, during the sessions, concerning the flight from heterosexual relations. The paralysis of the eleventh session was aggravated by the fact that none of the participants involved in this conversation mentioned it during the session. The observers, cornered by the participants who drove them there just in time, for the beginning of the next session, thus unconsciously severing the relations between them and myself (the monitor), were not able to speak with me until after the twelfth and last session, by which time it was too late. The information could no longer be circulated, the paralysis of the group, when faced with a primal seduction phantasy, could no longer be analysed.

The observer fully shares the group experience. The error of the monitor would be to 'omit' this fundamental fact and its consequences. As for the observer when he speaks with the monitor, he is encouraged to omit as little as possible of his reactions to the shared experience. Such are the demands the rules make upon the observer. It obliges him to interact with the monitor, who helps him elucidate his counter-transference and abstain from any *passage à l'acte* that might disturb the functioning of the diagnostic group.

   The following is a specific example of this. During a meal on the first day of the diagnostic group (which was taped), I spoke with the observer of our fear that participants might tear out the microphone or cut the recording. From the second day on, we were relieved: everyone had forgotten that the sessions were being recorded. However, the rather sharp reactions of the person making the recording – the observer and I had asked him to join us at our table – to the inertia of the group and the stupidity of the discussions, led us after he had left the table to elaborate the following daydream: the observer, driven mad by what he was hearing from behind his glass screen, and being unable to intervene, set about smashing the equipment and trampling it underfoot. I recognized that this phantasy was an alarm signal. From then on I was more careful to develop personal contact with him during breaks, explaining the meaning of the session and getting his feedback. The recording was thus able to continue without problem to the end.

## The structure of the system

So far I have tried to analyse the complex symbolic system of rules that governs the diagnostic group. But sometimes one cannot see the wood for the trees. So I shall now present this system in simpler terms, with a view to bringing out its dynamic aspects:

   (i)   relations between participants and monitor are governed by the rule of abstinence;
  (ii)   relations among participants are governed by the rule of free speech;
 (iii)   relations between each participant and the group as a whole are governed by the rule of restitution;
  (iv)   relations between the group (including participants, monitor(s) and observer(s)) on the one hand, and the outside world, on the other, are governed by the rule of discretion.

   I do not believe that relations between monitor and observer call for any additional rules: in relations with the observer, the monitor applies the rule of free speech; in his relation with the monitor, the observer applies the rule of restitution.

To this may be added another an idea of my own: the rules of free speech and of restitution are applications of the same psycho-analytic principle to different elements of the situation. Similarly, the rule of discretion is a variant of the rule of abstinence.

To speak in terms of structural theory, the rule of abstinence introduces a discontinuity between the monitor and the participants, on the one hand, and the group and the external world on the other. The rule of non-omission, however, binds the participants to one another, on the one hand, and the monitor to the group on the other. In the final analysis, the internal dynamics of this symbolic system of rules rests on this opposition of continuity and discontinuity and on the distinctions between the monitor, the group and the outside world among whom various breaks and bonds operate.

## The bivalence of the rule: transgression

We should insist on one characteristic of the rules, one already stressed by numerous writers in other areas but which is particularly clear here. The rules are bivalent. They have two symmetrical, opposite 'sides'. The dynamic tension that circulates within a system of rules exists also within each rule. These two sides concern, respectively, what is permitted and what is forbidden. The rule of free speech in the psycho-analytic or the diagnostic training group situation offers greater freedom than in everyday life, where this freedom is curtailed. The same rule requires that, during the sessions, acting out and certain forms of gratification be eliminated: the reverse holds true for the rule of abstinence, which stresses the forbidden. Participants unconsciously feel the impossibility of having a personal relationship with the monitor as a guarantee against the emergence of individual Oedipal wishes and an invitation to pregenital regression: the monitor will not marry the group and the group will not kill the monitor. The negative is this time 'face up', and it is in the other side of this rule that the positive is to be found: the forbidden is what allows the individual to function differently. To speak in structuralist terms, a renewed field of possibilities opens up before those who observe the principles of continuity and discontinuity. In psycho-analytic terms, the subject accedes to internal freedom only by freeing himself from the anxiety of narcissistic wounds and phantasized castration, and by accepting limits on his phantasized omnipotence, i.e. his own symbolic castration.

The bivalent status of the rule, coupled with the fact that in the diagnostic group, as in psycho-analysis, failure to respect the rules is not punished but interpreted, leads to transgression.

Psycho-analysis has taught us to distinguish between two modes of transgression: that of acting and that of knowing. Sometimes a neurotic patient in psycho-analysis breaks a rule by acting outside the session (*passage à l'acte*) or during a session (acting out). In the final analysis such acts mask a transgression of sexual difference (the fundamental, 'anatomical' law, which has as a consequence the procreation of children by relations between these two sexes) and a denial of the correlative castration anxiety. Perverse patients (and such patients may not always require analysis) may find pleasure only in concrete transgressions of this law and certain of its corollaries. The psycho-analyst is, in another sense, he who transgresses, that is to say, he who goes beyond the limits: his transgression lies in the order of knowledge. He knows and leads his patient to recognize the psychical processes underlying sexuality (pleasure included) and also the unavoidable character of symbolic castration, in other words, the need to accept not having one's wishes fulfilled.

Let us examine from this point of view what was going on in the diagnostic group in eastern France referred to above. A number of participants applied the 'rule' of informality (*tutoiement*) from the outset, whereas the monitor deliberately did not say anything on the matter. (I explained why at the beginning of this chapter.) This 'rule' functioned throughout the course by tacit agreement, the meaning of which ('We the participants attach more importance to our own rules than to those of the monitor') was never made explicit. A clear transgression of one of the rules also appeared during the first session. When each participant introduced himself or herself, one of them broke the rule of anonymity by divulging his surname. Most of the participants, who knew this surname, were embarrassed by this indiscretion, but the transgression as such was neither picked up by them nor analysed by the monitor. Thus the idea was allowed currency that this group was protected against transgression.

As a result, two more important transgressions followed at the end of the course: a veiled violation of the rule of abstinence, followed by an overt transgression of the rule of restitution.

On the morning of the third and last day, during a pause between the 9th and the 10th sessions, the participants persuaded the monitor to go with them to a café. It is clear that they wanted to integrate the monitor in the group, to talk to him in a more direct, simpler, more spontaneous way. The monitor (myself) decided to go in the hope that the pause would be a sort of supplementary session in a more relaxed atmosphere, where certain resistances might be overcome; he felt a certain urgency as the course was drawing to a close. At the café, he was the first to break the ice.

A lively, fairly general conversation concerning problems of recording and transcription followed. Then one participant raised the question of techniques of intervention used by teachers in 'self-governing' groups of pupils in their classes. The monitor ended the conversation when time was up and it was noticed that one participant was missing.

When the group gathered together for the 10th session, nobody filled the missing participant in on what had been discussed at the café. Nor did the monitor encourage participants to think about the meaning of their invitation to join them at the café, believing this would come out of itself. The monitor transgressed the rule of abstinence: the participants transgressed the rule of restitution. These two, apparently minor transgressions were nevertheless to have wider effects.

At 1.00 pm, at the end of the 10th session, the suggestion to go off and eat sauerkraut together was enthusiastically accepted. The monitor and the observers thought it difficult to refuse. One of the results was, as we observed above, to prevent the participants from speaking as they were used to doing. When the 11th session began, not only was there no restitution of conversations held at opposite ends of the table, but it was hinted that there would be no more restitution. The session got nowhere. The participants digested both sauerkraut and the monitor, whom they had introjected and disarmed by having managed to bring him to their table. Prisoner of the general atmosphere, pleased at being able to get a complete recording of a course, tired by three consecutive days of group meetings, the monitor did not think of interpreting the participants' failure to obey the rule of restitution, or his own failure to obey the rule of abstinence, or the meaning that the closing meal had assumed in the dynamics of the course.

Thus, failure to interpret repeated transgressions in the diagnostic group led to the inclusion of the monitor in the group and strongly fostered the establishment of the group illusion.

This blinding fascination with transgression also brought to light the tendency of group members, monitor and observers included, to take pleasure in the group, rather as certain neurotic patients take pleasure in their phantasies during individual analysis. Psycho-analysts are familiar with the various attitudes of different types of neurotic patients towards their phantasies. The obsessional, for example, is fairly lucid with respect to his phantasies, contemplation of which give him an intellectual pleasure from which the body is excluded. For the hysteric, on the other hand, the body is the principal source of pleasure, and comes between him and his phantasies, thus preventing him from being conscious of them. The group illusion holds sway when the group is used by participants as a phantasized object of pleasure. A study of the phantasized relationship of participants and monitors towards the group-object would show how far it is possible to push the analogy with the relationship of individual neurotics to their phantasies.

## The origin of the rule

Where does the rule come from? At times the texts of sessions reads like a manifest – and disguised – discourse on this latent question. The symbolic system of rules establishes the specific experience of the diagnostic group. But who sets up these rules? Inevitably there is a time when the group wonders who set it up.

The monitor opens the course by stating the rules, but he does not invent them: they are not the result of his own arbitrary wishes, for if they were they might lead to the technique of 'brainwashing', 'confession', 'moral rearmament', etc.

The monitor does not impose his own law on the assembled group: he explicitly states that he will not direct conversation, that he will not plan what is to be discussed, that he will not lead the course towards some goal decided on in advance. The monitor's repressed will to power may nevertheless get around the rules of the game and, using his counter-transference, make him give disguised directives behind a non-directive façade. The monitor applies the same rules to himself as he applies to others. Where does he get them? On this point there is a difference between psycho-analytic work with individuals and the diagnostic group. The request for psycho-analysis comes from the patient. The offer of a diagnostic group comes, if not from the monitor, from a member of his team.

It might be objected that people who already know one another may ask for a monitor who would enable them to form a non-directive group. This bears some resemblance to the diagnostic group experience, but is actually different. There are three cases of this type. First, the people who meet as a group belong to a particular organization and have a problem: the person requested is expected to act as psychologist-adviser and cannot function as training monitor. It is not even clear whether the method of the diagnostic group is appropriate in such cases. Second, these people want the training experience of a non-directive group: it is possible to distribute such people in different diagnostic groups. Third, a socio-occupational organization may want to give a particular mission to the group. This is a particular variant of the diagnostic group, the purpose of which is now to test the ability of its members to live and work together. It is an interesting and fruitful variant, but it cannot be examined in detail here.

The only way for people who do not know one another to get together in a diagnostic group is for the organizer to take the initiative to get them together. The organizer is never an isolated individual, but rather an association, a team, an organization, in short, a group. When occasionally an individual successfully takes such an initiative, he always has behind him a scientific body or institution to which he belongs.

The rules that a monitor gives to a diagnostic group are the rules recognized by his organizing team. Thus the rules that institute a group are themselves instituted by a group. This does not mean simply that any rule must be collective to be valid. Although Freud individually invented the fundamental rule of psycho-analysis, psycho-analytic practice has been able to develop and spread because a psycho-analytic association – at first Viennese, then international – took upon itself the responsibility for this rule and made it more or less respected.

The history of the diagnostic group bears witness to what we might call a group genealogy of its rules, beginning with its invention in the US between 1946 and 1949 by the team of Kurt Lewin's disciples. It then spread to different countries in the form of more or less competing groups of monitors who have developed numerous theoretical and technical versions (see Anzieu, 1976a).

In psycho-analysis, the origin of the rule, like all problems of origin, is related to a phantasy of the primal scene. Seeing or hearing adults having sexual relations, the child is confronted with a fundamental law of the biology of mammals: a man and a woman must mate to produce a child. This law is hidden from the child by his phantasy 'projections' on to this scene, glimpsed or overheard, and from which he feels cruelly excluded. These projections organize the child's perception not in symbolic explanation but in an anxiety-grounded phantasy. By instructing the patient to 'speak', the psycho-analyst invites him implicitly to speak of the primal scene. In formulating the rule of abstinence the psycho-analyst adds a fine point: the primal scene, which the patient will re-live, cannot be realized with the psycho-analyst; the patient can only *speak* of it. In fact it is only possible to speak of the unconscious if what is unconscious is not realized in action. Thus, in individual analysis, the primal scene may be both analysed as a phantasy and recognized as the symbolic basis for all rules. To re-live the primal scene under these conditions is to be reborn. What is at work in psycho-analysis is not only a cure or a change, it is going back to beginnings and beginning again. Let us not forget that the phantasy of origins is reconstructed *ex post facto* by the child during the Oedipal phase.

What is the relation of the diagnostic group to the primal scene? In the diagnostic group in eastern France described above, the phantasy of the primal scene was present but implicit. Unvoiced questions circulated among the participants: what are the relations between monitor and observer (a woman), and between observer and recording operator? All these phantasy relationships had one point in common – they provided a response to the question: by what law were we engendered? But whereas the *ex post facto* reconstruction of the primal phantasy satisfies the child's questions (i.e. those of the individual), this reconstruction takes a different form in response to the questionings of the group. All diagnostic groups develop at the right time, myths of their origins: the myths answer the question concerning the origin of the rules that make the group function as it does. The timing of this myth in a diagnostic group is significant as an indication of the movement away from the phantasized reality prevalent until then. At first, a diagnostic group sees itelf unconsciously as a proliferation of unborn children in a mother's womb. As with the child, the oldest primal phantasy in a group is parthenogenetic. It indicates the level of regression induced in participants by the non-directive group situation: regression to the symbolic relationship of infant with the all-powerful mother. During the early phases of the Oedipus complex the child's reconstruction of the primal phantasy – on the model of a scene of sexual intercourse between two adults from which the child to be born is excluded – marks an important psychical alteration: giving up the primary narcissicism of the dual relationship involves the triangulation of relations and the discovery of prohibitions.

In a diagnostic group, the reconstruction after the event is oriented towards the creation myth, which explains the genesis not of an individual but of a community. In the group in eastern France, this myth appeared during the seventh session. Creation myths in contemporary French diagnostic groups – no doubt because of our cultural heritage – are of limited number. I know two: a three-sided biblical myth (Babel, Pentecost, Paradise Lost), on which Kaës (1970b) is working and on which we have written together (Kaës and Anzieu, 1976), and a secular 'Jacobin' myth. It was the second that arose in the diagnostic group in eastern France. The choice of this myth was due no doubt to the presence of secular educators among the participants and of a majority of 'heartland' Frenchmen, who were rather critical of aspects of the local culture. For example, the Concordat with the Vatican is still in force in Alsace and Lorraine, the only regions in France where religion is still an official activity and where clergy and religious education are paid for by the state. In this light, the conflict which, throughout the course, brought an Alsatian Christian into opposition with the rest of the group brought deep 'mythic' references into play. By opposing him, the others opposed the 'biblical' reference, making it impossible for him to develop it. At the same time, they advanced the Parisian 'Jacobin' myth (alluding to the monitor's place of residence). This Jacobin myth is founded on the Rousseauist principle of popular sovereignty, innate rights of liberty and equality for all men, on faith in the collegial leadership set up by the Convention and its Committees, on the determination to impose centralized state control at the expense of separatism and regional differences. All 'myths' begin by recounting a historical event (real or imaginary). Here, the event was the deposing and beheading of the king, the ultimate symbol of the abolition of the privileges enjoyed by nobility and clergy. Thus the Jacobin myth might be seen as a 'French republican' variation of Freud's myth of the murder of the Father and of a society of brothers in *Totem and Taboo*.

Would it be possible to generalize this proposition and to see all diagnostic group creation myths (at least in our culture) as variations on this Freudian myth? I can suggest here that in the case of the triple biblical myth of 'Paradise Lost', the 'Tower of Babel' and Pentecost God had to be dead before men could understand one another, despite the difference in languages.

The 'primal scene' constructed *ex post facto* by a diagnostic group to explain the origin of the law on which it is founded is thus a scene not of sexual relations but of collective murder. Moreover, this phantasy is consistent with the institutional difference stressed above: psycho-analytic treatment is initiated at a patient's request, the diagnostic group by a monitor's offer. In both cases the symbolic system is grounded: the pleasure-based relationship between bodies sets up the law of individual procreation as prime model for all laws governing sexuality and aggressivity; the murder of one individual who symbolizes the will to dominate lies at the origin of the rules of social and cultural life, providing this murder is followed by identification on the part of the murderers or their descendants, with the dead Father, now realized and turned into an internalized, impersonal law. From this point of view, it should come as no surprise that the twelfth and last session of the diagnostic group was devoted to a recognition of the law.

## Final remarks

In conclusion several remarks are called for.

(i)   The recognition and observance of the rules by the monitor correspond to the regulatory character of the superego. Their dogmatic definition, at the beginning of the course, in the form of a coherent and closed system presents the 'do not' character of the superego and hinders the diagnostic group process. It is quite enough to refer, at the outset, to the fundamental rule, now well enough known by practically all concerned, and to define the other rules as the problems related to them arise.

(ii)   The symbolic system of rules cannot be formulated perfectly by the monitor or understood by participants at the outset. Participants always phantasize about it and react to it emotionally; their phantasies and wishes have to be clarified and analysed during the course.

(iii)  The system described here is valid only for the set of conditions referred to. When a training group functions with other sorts of activities (psychodrama, case discussion, relaxation and other physical exercises, etc.), or in other forms (residential seminar combining several types of activities, 'slow open group' of unlimited duration, etc.) the symbolic system of rules is somewhat different. But the general features remain the same: the setting up of dynamic tensions between opposite poles, the introduction of breaks and links, the bivalence of what is said, the two-sided nature of the group experience, one a representation of the human condition and human life in little, the other the individual's unconscious projections.

(iv)   Any system concerning a human, not a physical, reality is subject to wear. This wear is slow for mythological systems, a bit faster for linguistic systems, and much faster for economic, political and educational systems. Psycho-analytic training is also subject to wear (see Anzieu, 1973). The wear in the effective operation of the rules is one form of the return of the repressed: sooner or later phantasies turn against the symbolic system of rules set up to apprehend them. In French psycho-analysis at the present time wear is accelerated by attempts, inspired by structuralism, to reduce treatment to speech and the unconscious to language. Because language is over-valued, subjects are put in the position of trying to 'short-circuit' it in order to make 'contact' with their wishes. The same wear is at work in the diagnostic group with the rule of free speech. This is used more and more by psychotherapists as a way of avoiding the internal dynamic inherent in the situation. Instead of trying to express what they feel here and now, they talk in order to keep themselves from feeling. When speech becomes disembodied it loses its impact as communication and its power to increase individual awareness. This is one of the reasons for the recent, sudden spread of group methods based on body expression and physical contact. They represent a reaction against what is seen as the excessive abstractness of methods based on linguistic communication. However physical contact is sought for itself, outside any basic rule and is therefore quite unsuitable as a training method.

(v) The wear of the rules should lead to their renewal and not to their elimination. We have discussed at great length the question of whether the statement of the rules should apply only to groups made up of people who did not previously know one another and whether it was not better to abstain from applying them in the case of a training group, made up of members of an institution who had worked together and were already bound by common rules. A double difficulty is to be avoided: that participants confuse training group rules with institutional rules, or that they use their participation in a group without rules to block or overthrow the rules of the institution. It is more comfortable raising questions about an institution than about oneself: this is what happens in certain cases of institutional analysis or anti-psychiatry. We will return to this mechanism of double defence: the institution serves as a defence against the group, the group serves as a defence against the institution; social conformism and a determination to change society whatever the price are two ways of avoiding personal change. Experience of individual psycho-analytic treatment, of psycho-analytic work in training and psychotherapeutic groups, and of institutional life has taught us not only about the interaction between individual and institutional change (changes of setting, rules, or situation condition internal changes; internal changes lead one to act with a view to revising – not abolishing – institutional rules and to reorganizing their operation), but, even more, the gap between them. In point of fact, there is always a gap – and an interaction – between the individual unconscious and the group (see Anzieu, 1972, p. 147). To be a person, in the full sense, is to be one who, while seeking affiliations, keeps a certain distance from groups, from institutions, from society as a whole.

To repeat, whether explicitly formulated or implicitly practised by the monitors, the rules are the symbolic guarantee that allows the subject to begin what Missenard (1972) has called a process of de-formation, while avoiding a breakdown. In the case of a training group within an institution, the rules need to be relaxed but not done away with; the monitor has to interpret carefully the reactions of the participants to the gap between the rules of the group and the rules of the institution; lastly, the psychodrama is a better type of activity than the diagnostic group for unfreezing habits, calling into question one's own behaviour, and leaving open the question of the meaning to be given to institutional rules. Let us now turn, therefore, to the method of psychodrama.

# Chapter 3
# Analytic psychodrama and physical exercises

## Specificity

The psychodrama, and the physical exercises that seem to me to be inseparable from it (we shall see why later), are essential tools for training in clinical psychology, as well as for the mobilization of the individual's instinctual resources and for the understanding of others.

Unlike the diagnostic group, the psychodrama and physical exercises are centred more on the individual's self-awareness and liberation than on the analysis of the group, communication with others being based primarily on the body, and only secondarily on language.

The aim of the analytic psychodrama is the search for the truth about oneself; the method it employs is the dramatic improvisation of situations, roles and conflicts; it achieves its impact by bringing into play – in the interaction between a number of protagonists – affects, identifications and phantasies.

## History

The psychodrama was invented about 1923 by the psychiatrist J.L. Moreno (1890-1974). Born on board a ship somewhere between the North Sea and the Danube, his birth of Spanish and Slav parents was registered at Bucharest. The wanderings of his Jewish parents brought him to Vienna while still a young child, thirty-five years after his famous predecessor, Sigmund Freud. At this time Vienna was a melting pot of the arts and sciences, of traditional religion and modern liberalism, of the Teutonic spirit and Roman civilization. From an early age, he was passionately interested in the theatre, staging symbolic scenarios with other children. Later, he organized children's theatre clubs. As an army doctor in a camp for displaced persons in the First World War, he became aware of people's ability to work out, in a spontaneous way, new forms of social life and organization. He was fascinated by psycho-analysis, despite his aversion to Freud. He dreamed of a dramatic religion that would revitalize not only men's dormant faith, but also a dull, lifeless theatre of convention. In the rather narrow-minded literary circles of his day he acquired an ambiguous reputation with his articles on God as actor, author and orator, and by his Dadaist-type outbursts during theatrical performances. He took an active part in the avant-garde movements that flourished in post-war Vienna. Vaguely influenced by Stanislavsky and haunted by the paradox of the actor, he opened a theatre of spontaneity, *Das Stegreiftheater*, exclusively devoted to improvisation. A theatrical director who did not himself act, and who did not allow his actors to create characters, but who conveyed to them the inner force required to unveil their truth to others, Moreno was inevitably led, by the logic inherent in his initial purpose, to pass from a theatre of improvisation to psychodrama. In the psychodrama the actor plays himself, for and to himself, in order to understand himself better and to be better understood by those with whom he lives or works; he allows himself to undergo change while being aware of who he is; in short, he tries to become himself.

Calling such psychodrama 'therapeutic' or 'psychotherapeutic' would limit its scope. For all men live with their secret dramas, which they do not themselves understand; they live on, and in spite of it. The intense attraction of the theatre resides in the public representation of this drama. Aristotle was the first to formulate it: tragedy brings about a catharsis of the latent, but dangerous, passions that secretly stir within the spectators (impossible love, incestuous feelings, homicidal or suicidal jealousy, anger, revolt, murder). By experiencing in phantasy – or, rather, symbolically, the unleashing of those passions and their tragic outcome, the spectator feels relieved and is able to overcome them. Moreno did not invent theatrical improvisation, any more than Freud invented the interpretation of dreams. Mankind had long known its methods and effects. But nobody before Moreno had clarified its delicate art, articulated its concepts, thus rendering the method scientifically transmissible and its effects of objective utility. The only progress from Aristotle to Moreno was to extend catharsis from spectator to actor, thus rendering it more powerful. All that is needed is for the actor to stop playing roles learned by heart and to improvise, submerging himself completely in the action he represents. Each human being hides within himself a slumbering child, an insane 'other' who is unaware of himself: that is his weak spot. He also carries within himself the possibility of being a speaker or an actor: Freud explored the first, Moreno the second. In those same 1920s, in France, the Surrealists described a third, intermediary possibility: all men are potential poets.

Moreno did not at first understand the importance of his discovery. Only after his immigration to the US, where social, demographic and economic circumstances were so different, did the psychodrama cease to be merely a therapy of marriage, divorce and jealousy.

In everyday life, with his superiors, his colleagues, his subordinates, his children and his neighbours, man needs to liberate his spontaneity, smothered by the disciplines of school, family, society and the unfortunate tendency of our civilization to produce and preserve ideas and feelings as though they were food. In this new form the psychodrama becomes an instrument for personal improvement: spontaneity allows the individual to assimilate the attitudes towards others fully (Moreno, following George Mead, calls them 'roles') required of him by his occupation, family, school, etc. Such spontaneity enables him to come up with solutions to the concrete problems posed by human interrelations, to go beyond his habitual way of seeing people and problems and to see them from the point of view of others. This enlarging of the scope of psychodrama took place between 1925 and 1930.

Shortly afterwards, Moreno developed a third form of psychodrama, the treatment of conflicts within (or between) groups, organizations, communities or sub-groups: the socio-drama. Useful for studying the origins and development of purely psychological inter- and intra-group conflicts, this technique has rightly been criticized; especially when it claims to apply to oppositions between races or social classes, it runs the risk of ignoring the decisive impact of economic, political and ideological circumstances.

Moreno described a number of procedures, among which are

the presentation of personal roles (I confronting my father, my rival); the presentation of collective roles (*the* mother, *the* boss); soliloquy (expressing under one's breath the thoughts and feelings usually hidden in a particular situation); the mirror (representing the subject's behaviour in front of him with a view to providing his reactions; the double (in the course of a scene with the subject a psychodramatist embodies one of the subject's internal characters that the subject himself has not sufficiently expressed in that scene); reversal of roles (starting a scene again or interrupting it, after asking the protagonists to exchange roles). This technique of role reversal is the one most often used and the most often effective because it best enables the individual to see himself as others see him and to understand others' reactions by taking their place.

## Psychodrama, relaxation and body exercises

Moreno's work in psychodrama begun in 1923 paved the way for the proliferation of group techniques in the US since about 1963. These then spread rapidly to Britain, France and other European countries. Psychodrama is at once a method of treatment and of training. It may be used on one subject, with a small group or a vast audience. Moreno himself used it on television. Depending upon the needs of participants and the interests of those running it, stress is put on bodily expression or verbalizations. Moreno always stressed – in contrast to psycho-analysis – the need to touch the actors and to encourage protagonists to develop physical contact between themselves, in order to release greater spontaneity and to involve them more deeply. The mimo-drama, the hypno-drama, the music-drama, the ballet-drama, etc., are variants of the psychodrama. The improvisation of a gesture, a rhythm, a nocturnal dream widened the choice of techniques, limited in the early days to a scenario proper. Improvisations have been tried in artificial sleep, under drugs, in conditions of sense deprivation or over-stimulation, as well as in the normal waking state. Phenomena involving collective expression – but without any therapeutic or educational purpose – such as happenings (incongrous improvisations in the street or during a serious official meeting), strip-tease (undressing before spectators), streaking (running nude in a public place), swinging (gatherings to exchange sexual partners) all trace their inspiration – rightly or wrongly – to Moreno. Such avant-garde theatrical phenomena as the Living Theater, the Bread and Puppet Theater, or Bob Wilson's mime plays and certain contemporary films – Jean Rouche's *Les Maîtres fous* and *Moi, un noir* or Rivette's *Out*, etc. – are directly inspired by the psychodrama. The model of the psychodrama has even been proposed as an explanation for the events of May 1968 in France.

For several reasons, we will not examine the techniques of body exercises independently of the psychodrama. To begin with, these techniques are derived from it and should be seen as offshoots.

But there is a second deeper reason: the principal lesson to be learned from the psychodrama is that a bodily activity – mime, the improvisation of a posture, an action, a rhythm, a series of gurgles, singsong, etc. – has the desired training or therapeutic effects only if it leads to verbalization. The psychodrama provides one of the best ways of steering a course between two obstacles: (1) speaking off the top of one's head without experiencing or communicating anything authentic and (2) acting and abreacting without worrying about understanding what one is doing. The psychodrama strikes a mean between the error, familiar to psycho-analysts or psychotherapists treating individuals in a group, of concentrating exclusively on individuals and ignoring group phenomena and the error, familiar to group monitors and followers of Ezriel, of attempting a psychotherapy or psycho-analysis *of* the group without any concern for the individuals composing it.

These remarks are confirmed by the experience of another method, that of relaxation, the invention of which preceded that of the psychodrama, but which did not become as well known: emphasizing the body mobilizes, often rapidly and strongly, phantasies and anxieties, thus opening the way for change, but also for breakdowns; only when the physical experience of a subject leads to its verbalizing (which, in turn, allows for adequate psycho-analytical interpretations) does it actually induce change, while avoiding the risks of a breakdown. Like the psychodrama, relaxation was originally an individual method whose application to group practice was validated subsequently. I do not deal with it in this work because, while I have had some limited, but instructive experience of it as a subject, I have had none running a relaxation group. A recent study, *La Relaxation: son approche psychanalytique*, by Michel Sapir *et al.* has shown that relaxation can play the same role as psychodrama in sensitivity seminars, providing there is an alternation between small and large groups.

Nor is it my purpose here to review the innumerable types of body exercises that have recently become available in groups. If they remain fragmented they are at best amusing and harmless, and at worst an opportunity for the satisfaction of perverse feelings. On the other hand, they may be excellent ways of warming up; they naturally lead beginners to psychodramatic improvisation. My experience with psychodrama groups in which some participants had experience in body exercise groups helped us grasp the difference; for such persons physical exercises remained 'exercises', whatever gratification they derived from them, whereas work in a psycho-analytically oriented psychodrama group, monitored by a psycho-analyst, unleashed processes the depth and intensity of which quite surprised them. The seriousness of the method is quite in keeping with the seriousness of what is at stake. Serraf (1974), who was the first to discover methods of using the body in groups, has listed those that develop participants' creativity. He also stresses the need after each exercise for verbalization and discussion of the experience. He criticizes giving in to the temptation of purely physical experiences: 'looking for non-verbal direct contact, unconscious communication, body dynamism, all the more exciting because it toys with prohibition, plays tricks on an obsessional superego, illegally recovers a forgotten freedom.'

In any basic questioning of oneself, the body comes into play: the truth is never disembodied; human speech is true only if it is backed by flesh. But training courses limited to bodily activities encourage an illusion described by Missenard (1974, 1976), the illusion that 'the body is the source only of joy, pleasure, well-being, without leaving any room for their inevitable counterpoint: castration, limits, the death instinct and death itself'.

## Small groups and bodily psychodrama

By integrating physical exercises into psychodrama, we are led to widen a limited form of psychodrama (the improvisation of a scenario) in which the theatrical model is important and in which a certain intellectual and affective maturity is required, and to envisage a 'generalized psychodrama', in which a very varied range of bodily activities may be offered participants, depending on the form and intensity of their psychopathology, and their commitment to the group. For example, to have psychotics listen to a musical passage and to ask them to express it physically (first standing, then lying down), then verbally (by formulating what they have felt and wanted to express through their body movements) (see Eiguer and Chanoît, 1974). Dautremont (1974) worked with a group of six psychotic adolescents of both sexes and two leaders in what he happily called 'bodily psychodramas': 'The rule is to release everything one feels with one's body, to let oneself go; this is a kind of physical free association. Participants are asked not to speak during the action, but are told that they will be asked to talk about their experience once the action is over.' One of the psychotherapists introduces a rhythm, a beat, marking the opening and closing of each scene; by varying it, he stresses what is happening, the changes that occur and the emotions aroused. Anna Pilon-Podhorski has (1976) made particular use of extra-verbal methods of analytic psychodrama in work with autistic children.

## The two theories of psychodrama

In addition to the two points emphasized above (the virtue of spontaneity for the realization of human possibilities), Moreno's psychodrama implies a theory of human existence that he incompletely developed under the heading of 'general sociometry'. Two aspects will be mentioned here:

(i)   Each personality is made up of a number of characters, which are sometimes unconnected, sometimes linked by certain limited coherences; with respect to these characters, the personality adopts attitudes that psycho-analysis describes as defence mechanisms (in particular, identification and projection);

(ii)  Each personality is a social atom: his behaviour is determined not only by the dynamic of the characters that compose it and which it has borrowed from persons who have played real, imaginary or symbolic roles in his life, but also by its position in a field of sympathy, antipathy and indifference and in communication networks that constitute the latent structures of the small human groups in which the personality develops and changes. In other words, the personality has no 'depth'; it is a fabric, an interlacing of relations.

Moreno's theory of the personality is complemented by his theory of effects. Psychodrama has four rather specific effects:

(i)   The effect on general affective maturation: in inverting the subject's real affective climate, psychodrama corrects negative effects and frees his unrealized possibilities;

(ii)  The effect on the specific emotional maturation when an aspect of the personality remains fixed or regresses to a childhood situation; the psychodrama resolves interior conflicts produced by this situation by recreating them first in an imaginary way (phantasy) and then in a symbolic way;

(iii) The effect on the control and adaptive functions: by acting themselves in scenes that express a range of attitudes and sentiments (permission and frustration, tenderness and threats, generosity, firmness, cruelty, etc.) psychodramatists (Moreno calls them auxiliary actors) serve as supportive examples that enable subjects to attain flexible self-control and naturalness;

(iv)  The effect on social maturation: by stimulating actions, then analysing them, the psychodrama puts protagonists into relationship with bosses, subordinates and equals, with key social figures (teachers, judges, policemen, bureaucrats) with co-operative, competitive, complementary attitudes with respect to others, and leads to a true recognition of the social rules on which the co-existence of men is based.

Psycho-analytic psychodrama differs from Morenian psychodrama in spirit, technique and theory. This is not the place to present their differences systematically. These have been developed in my book *Le psychodrame analytique chez l'enfant* (Anzieu, 1956). (See also Lebovici, Diatkine and Kestemberg (1958), Lemoine and Lemoine (1972), Basquin, Dubuisson, Samuel-Lajeunesse and Testemale-Monod (1972).) The rest of this chapter will deal exclusively with analytic psychodrama, and will outline the rules and illustrate the method. It is appropriate here to introduce a parallel between Morenian and psycho-analytic psychodrama concerning their working methods.

## Working methods

A session of psychodrama has three phases:

(i)   A preliminary phase of indispensable warming up: the ice must be broken, passive reserve and fear of having to be exposed, dissolved. Moreno does this by active methods: a lively exposé, encouragement, example, seduction-provocation. By contrast, when psycho-analysts practise psychodrama, they respect the rule of abstinence and devote this first phase to removing, by discussion and, possibly, interpretation, individual resistances to the search for a theme (i.e., to the working of the creative imagination) and to self-exposure.

(ii)  The action: psychodramatists respond to a small number of actors in a scene, the theme of which is to a greater or lesser degree of concern to them and has been more or less agreed in advance (cf. the *Commedia dell'arte*). The optimum number of participants for a psychodrama is six to eight, whereas it is eight to twelve for a diagnostic group, but only a few – two, three or four – act at the same time. The remarks of the psychodramatists should be sober, relevant, infectious: they should be aimed at encouraging subjects to act in a more involved, personal way, at releasing by externalization repressed or under-developed roles, at putting obstacles in the way of individual wishes and attitudes in order to confront the subject with the narcissistic wound and reality testing, and to lead him to behave in such a way that he takes others' wishes and attitudes into consideration while expressing his own. This is another important difference between Morenian and psycho-analytic psychodrama: Moreno is a director who doesn't act himself, who devises scenarios, who gets subjects and psychodramatists to act them, and who then provides an interpretation. In the psycho-analytic psychodrama, on the other hand, all the psychodramatists may act, their interventions often being 'acted out' interpretations – that is to say, given under the cover of acting – and always leave participants the freedom – and the responsibility – of choosing themes and roles.

(iii) For Moreno, commentary on what has happened is monop-olized by the person in charge: in psycho-analytic psychodrama it is a *collective* self-analysis, conducted, in a non-directive way, by the psychodramatists. Each participant – actors and spectators – tries to speak of what he has discovered during the session, about himself, about the group, about human interaction; here the psychodramatists take part in a more traditional form of interpretation.

## An experiment in collective analytic psychodrama at a university

The problem of how to give psychology students a clinical training at university is complex. Universities cannot really (nor do they want to) invest in the facilities and personnel necessary for such training. Generally speaking, student psychologists turn to organizations or associations – often expensive – for further training in, for example, psychodrama or diagnostic groups, *after* they leave university.

Also students preparing a certificate in clinical psychology for their Master's degree in psychology often think that this is the path of least resistance; they imagine that their wish – shared by two-thirds of psychology students – to become 'clinicians' has already been fulfilled and turn away from the arduous labour of self-questioning and from the rigorous rules of cast studies.

May 1968 swept away the resistances of universities, experimental, quantitative psychologists and traditionalist, organicist, psychiatrists on this point. Courses in clinical psychology were developed in several psychology departments in French universities. Such courses soon ran into methodological problems. Which methods are most suitable to the aims being pursued? Which are most effective in the case of university students?

Seminars in psycho-analytic theory and Freudian texts at once appeal to and disappoint students: they provide knowledge and, for the best students, a conceptual framework; but they are in no way a preparation for practice or for the introspective personal attitude required when handling relations with others. So-called 'Balint' groups seem to do just this; they have proved to be failures; students cannot speak of their (limited) professional experience as can practitioners with several years of experience. They speak of technical and conceptual difficulties, of their practical awkwardness, of their surprise at the seriousness of certain psychical disorders, of the prejudices of the doctors, teachers and psychologists with whom they work. They scarcely ever involve themselves personally in the group, or let others examine their emotional attitudes towards the case they have dealt with. So-called 'Balint' groups tend towards case studies centred on cases and a 'recycling' of knowledge. The teacher who runs them is asked questions depending upon his professional experience, but participants seldom question one another.

Diagnostic groups give better, but unequal results. Commitment is sometimes stronger and deeper, the concrete analysis of psychological experience probing and, when begun early in the academic year, they may help to strengthen the sense of group membership for the rest of that year. But too great a homogeneity (in age and in intellectual and socio-occupational interests) is a handicap.

In the light of our experience, the two methods that stand up best in the clinical training of advanced students in psychology are:

(i) the small group discussion of case material, together with an analysis and a synthesis of the case and, if possible, of the complete file;

(ii) the analytic psychodrama.

Among the many variants of the psychodrama – role-playing, Morenian psychodrama, bodily expression, education, analytic or collective psychodrama – is the analytic collective psychodrama.

In our experience, the collective analytic psychodrama gives subjects a concrete, effective sensitivity to unconscious processes. So the aim is clear. Students in clinical psychology are generally too young, insufficiently motivated, have too little emotional and sexual experience, on the one hand, and social and professional experience, on the other, to undertake a long, difficult psycho-analytic training that presupposes an individual commitment independent of all institutional requirements, and which is obligatory only for future psycho-analysts. Personal experience, however partial and limited in time, of unconscious processes seems to me, none the less, a condition *sine qua non* for clinical psychological practice. The analytic psychodrama provides just such an opportunity. The present tendency to reserve training by analytic psychodrama for practising psychologists only (not students) does not seem to me to be entirely justified.

The problem, then, is to know under what conditions this training can be extended to students. The following remarks are the fruit of seven years' experience with some twenty seminars in collective analytic psychodrama with students getting their master's degree in psychology at the University of Paris-X-Nanterre.

These students were finishing their university studies; they were preparing a 'C 4' certificate in clinical psychology and were only admitted to seminars if they had parallel experience in clinical or pathological work.

The psychodrama reinforces and complements the practical training as a transition between studies and professional practice. Students are able to choose a seminar in psychodrama from a wide range of techniques; it would make no sense to make it obligatory. All psycho-analytic experience requires voluntary subjects. About half of the students signed up for this '*certificat*' actually participated in psychodrama seminars.

At this stage in their studies, students in psychology demand practical initiation into analytic psychodrama, rather than systematic training. But systematic training is precisely what they need. For this reason a psychodrama training seminar for students is limited to a series of six to eight sessions on a weekly basis. Nevertheless, if a group wishes to continue beyond this series it can. Such extensions occurred on several occasions.

Sessions are part of the university programme of instruction: they are thus free, held in university buildings and run by a member of the teaching staff with psycho-analytic and psychodramatic training.

Not only are difficulties arising from the ambivalent dependency relations of students to professors easily analysable in discussions before or after performances, but these relations are soon transformed by the performances themselves. In fact, the instructor-organizer may be given a role, as can each participant. Seeing him act out this role, acting with him, and analysing his act along with those of the participants introduces a spontaneity and a simplicity within the group that seldom exists in normal teacher-student relationships. On the other hand, the fact that one of the organizers is not a teacher but a clinician, a psycho-analyst, by whom participants fear being judged, is a major difficulty for them. Here again discussion of the performances themselves and their interpretations gradually remove this difficulty, at least for participants who don't have serious inhibitions or structural neuroses. Sessions of analytic psychodrama give participants more than an initiation; they can experiment with and test their degree of 'normality' and of 'neuroticism'. Such experimentation is obviously indispensable if they are to know whether or not they have the psychological stability necessary for successful practice as clinicians, and to benefit subsequently from more extensive personal training, or, if more appropriate, either to change direction or to undergo analysis.

## The rules

The first fundamental rule of analytic collective psychodrama is that no spectators are allowed and that each participant must act at the appointed time. This rule requires – and conditions – the commitment of each participant. Several complementary rules follow from it:

Each person is free at any time to act or not: he acts when a role appeals to him, when the group asks him to do so, or when he has not acted for a long time; nobody can indefinitely refrain from acting.

The fundamental rule applies to the organizer as well as to the participants (which constitutes an important difference with Morenian psychodrama, in which the organizer is the director, not an actor).

Each session contains two or three plays; a participant may act several times during the same session or not act at all. It is not advisable constantly to choose scenarios that force all participants to take part; the training psychodrama requires, for each play, a differentiation between actors and spectators. Spectators are then expected to feed back their reactions to the actors.

The rule of group size limits it to between five and eight or nine persons. With fewer than five, it is impossible to differentiate actors and spectators, and the psychotherapeutic dimension of the sessions is overstressed. With more than nine, it is difficult to avoid confusing psychodramatic groups with diagnostic groups, and participants easily fall prey to the group illusion; instead of acting, participants get involved in endless discussions; they talk about themselves in a self-satisfied way in front of others, instead of questioning themselves and laying themselves bare during the play.

In this respect, too, collective analytic psychodrama groups are different from Morenian groups, which are characterized by the number of spectators (20 to 100), the preoccupation with theatrical effect and the catharsis of spectators through indirect participation in dramatic improvisation. The mass effects of the unconscious cannot be interpreted psycho-analytically in the same way as unconscious effects in a small group. Spectacular psychodramas fascinate and seduce spectators, and are incompatible with a work of interpretation.

The session lasts for an hour and a half. Participants commit themselves in advance for a fixed number of sessions (at least six). Naturally, they are free not to attend if they so decide. At the end they may continue their training in psychodrama either with the same group or by signing up with professional extra-university groups. University or extra-university organizations need to give students a choice of diversified activities, not to impose standardization training; as he or she progresses each student follows a path of his or her own through the diversified activities of one or more organizations.

The second fundamental rule specific to psychodrama is the combining of verbalization with imitative gestures. To play a role is at once to speak and to mime. As far as possible, actors avoid sitting down; they have to inhabit their bodies as instruments of expression. For example, if the theme of the scenario proposes to show people's reactions to an accident, an injury, or a physical infirmity, the organizer asks the actors to act out the accident, to play the part of the injured person. But the actors prefer defensively *not* to involve themselves, to begin the play by supposing that the accident was over or that the injured person is off-stage, out of sight; it is easier, but much less effective, to speak of an absent and imagined injured person than to experience having such a person present in the flesh. Many things change when, instead of remaining on the surface of a role (which happens in role playing), one experiences the role from the inside, in one's body. This constitutes the specific experience of psychodrama. Indeed, the participants catch on fast and enter fully into their roles, forgetting that they are acting in front of spectators. This brings with it a certain inner freedom, which enables a participant to externalize his identifications and to clear away some of the inhibitions that cut off unconscious from preconscious. The anxiety that such proof must be given, the wish to succeed in convincing the others, the joy of success – these constitute the affective tonality peculiar to psychodrama.

An analytic process can only exist if the situation induces transference and if this transference is expressed in verbal discourse by those experiencing the situation. To express certain deeply repressed wishes in analytic psychodrama, it may be useful to act out the parts of living being or objects. However, systematic repetition of these roles is, and has to be, interpreted as an escape from the recognition of unconscious processes, generally represented in the psychical apparatus as personifications: once secondary identifications are developed, psychical conflicts are stages as characters of an internal theatre. In analytic psychodrama, the organizer encourages the participants to choose personal roles, whether human or non-human, in contrast to the social or stereotyped roles evident in role-playing. Role-playing may, however, constitute a transition to analytic psychodrama proper; group members grasp the difference when the organizer clearly and firmly states the group's objectives and remains firm throughout the sessions.

The third fundamental rule is more difficult to define: if free speech is limitless (freedom in the choice of theme and roles, freedom in discussion before, during and after the plays), what limits are to be placed on the non-verbal, purely physical aspects of the action? Moreno puts his hands on the actors' shoulders or arms, while talking to them before the play about their roles, helping them to get into their roles as authentically as possible; this double contact, psychological and physical, helped to warm them up. Similarly, during the play he encouraged physical contact between protagonists in order to 'de-intellectualize' it as much as possible and to increase affective commitment. This, then, is an 'active' technique.

Psycho-analysts who have practised psychodrama have tended to apply the rule of abstinence in the same form as it functions in individual psycho-analytic work: one does not touch the patient, except to shake hands. This form of the rule goes back to Freud's abandonment of hand pressure exerted on the patient's forehead to aid mental concentration. Our early experiences with psychodrama soon led us to define the rule of imitative gesture ('one acts by pretending to carry out actions, one does not really do anything'). In fact during psychodrama sessions with maladjusted schoolchildren, tables and chairs were sometimes used for dangerous rickety constructions or as projectiles. On the other hand, where hyper-aggressive children were allowed free bodily expression they broke objects and struck organizers; the therapeutic effect of such actions is open to question. A pair of glasses broken on the writer's nose (fortunately with no harm done) decided us to adopt the rule of imitative gesture and to discourage the propensity to *passage à l'acte* in psychodrama.

Indeed it soon appeared necessary, in psychodrama involving teenage girls, for psychodramatists – especially male ones – not to touch participants. Touching was seen as an attempt at sexual seduction.

Every rule is bivalent, like the superego of which it is an expression: it operates as a regulator of the psychical economy and of interpersonal relations, but may also be repressive; if a rule is too repressive it paralyses its regulatory functions. This is what happened with the rule of imitative gesture. It induced taboos or horror of physical contact in certain organizers. In certain participants, it tended to restrict attention to a single theme; thus breaking down the *system* of rules.

Experience has since shown:

(i)   that body contact is natural during the performance – and it would be a mistake to prevent it – when it is a matter of social convention (kissing a parent or loved one) or when it is dictated by practical necessity (saving an injured person, giving one's hand to a child, etc.);

(ii)   that only sexual touching and physical aggression are prohibited; when they arise organizers stop the performance immediately.

(iii)   that this rule is self-evident for the majority of participants and that it is enough to formulate it explicitly when it is broken; to formulate it from the outset prompts participants to think that they are running real dangers and hinders their spontaneity;

(iv)   that the rule needs to be formulated – abstention from any gesture or act, whatever its nature, which does violence to someone else, and obligation to stop when the partner asks;

(v)   finally, that the psychodramatists, while not abstaining, must be discreet in their body contact with participants.

## The session

Each session is made up of three parts:

(i) finding a theme or analysing internal difficulties that prevent participants from finding one;
(ii) role distribution in the performance;
(iii) sharing impressions of spectators and actors concerning the performance and its meaning with respect to the group and the participants involved.

Finding a theme is part of the method of collective free association. As in the psycho-analytic situation or projective tests participants are encouraged to communicate their ideas as they occur. The organizer generally abstains from any proposition or suggestion. If the participants are unable to come up with any ideas, the organizer takes the initiative, if need be, by questioning each participant, analysing the difficulties and actively directing the discussion by formulating hypotheses.

Apart from their subjective difficulties (anxiety over exposing, questioning themselves, or being judged), students raise 'objective' difficulties: the superimposition of the student-teacher relation on the subject monitor relation; involvement with other academic work and with exams; non-respect of anonymity, since students of the same group know each other in advance (it is recommended that students of the same sub-group choose different psychodrama groups, but this recommendation proves of little use); the predominance of women in the groups (there are about three males in groups of eight or nine; the writer even found himself the only man in a group of women); earlier experience in psychodrama for certain participants, etc. The verbalization and recognition of these difficulties has always sufficed to free the group's creative imagination; if the blockage persists, then the crucial difficulty has not yet been uncovered; doing away with this resistance then becomes the objective of discussion, and it is sometimes useful for the organizer to encourage participants individually to facilitate the 'un-freezing', or for him to formulate hypotheses concerning the repressed themes.

Discussion after the action leads to an interpretation of what took place in the action (and possibly in the search for a theme) with respect to the development of the group in its present context. The organizer as a general rule gives no individual interpretations. The rule formulated by Ezriel for group psycho-analyses applies to training psychodrama groups: interpretation of underlying shared tension must pertain to the here and now.

Such an interpretation is not given by the organizer to the group. The work of interpretation is collective. The organizer is not likely to find the correct interpretation without the participants' free associations concerning the action that has been presented. Moreover, the emergence of the interpretation is instructive for trainees. One of their reasons for choosing such training methods is to experience the essential act of psycho-analysis: interpretation.

Interpretation centred on the group has indirect effects on individuals. Each person finds something of concern to him personally, something that brings him closer to some childhood situation, conflict, symptom or character trait. In addition to the satisfaction of having been able to play a role, the session of psychodrama gives the participants the satisfaction of having made such a connection. These two sources of satisfaction are a sort of introduction to psycho-analysis. They prove that the analytic process exists and that the participant is open to this process.

The same does not hold for psychotherapeutic groups where individual interpretations are required. But collective analytic training psychodrama may give participants their first experience of two types of interpretation that are particularly important in groups of therapeutic psychodrama: interpretations given indirectly, through the action itself, to the person concerned by the psychodramatist (this is 'acted out' interpretation), and correct interpretations which a lucid participant comes up with concerning another group member (this is the phenomenon of co-therapy). Although the individual interpretation is the exception in analytic collective training psychodrama, it is necessary for the organizer at one time or another to address each participant individually, to get his impressions, to initiate in him partial self-analysis, to see to it that such self-analysis is indeed working, to make each participant participate in the collective work of interpretation, to speak with him of personal difficulties that keep him from acting 'truthfully'. This individual relationship between the organizer and each participant constitutes one more specific, supplementary difference between diagnostic groups and groups of psychodrama. In short, collective, analytic psychodrama constitutes a personal, concrete initiation to the analytic process and to the work of interpretation.

## The theme of the prodigal son

The theme of the 'progidal son' appeared several times in different groups, until the associations of one participant pointed towards its interpretation. This theme (How do his parents receive him? Do they reject him aggressively or do they treat him overprotectively as a child?) appeared after a session in which inhibition was widespread and group members were very dissatisfied at not being able to act properly. The prodigal son symbolizes an attitude of defensive retreat on the part of the participants, an 'escape' from the psychodrama. The question 'How will the young man be received when he returns?' is a transposition of the implicit and anxiety-arousing question: 'If I expose myself in the group, how will I be received by the others? Will I be recognized for what I am?' What are the risks of running into aggressive and destructive incomprehension from a group member?

A psychodrama around this theme manifests a varied range of attitudes from the violent externalization of aggressivity to reparation for the injuries caused by such an act. Interpretation verbalizes these different positions towards aggressive threats.

## Themes of authority

Teacher-student, parent-child, employer-employee relationships are among the first mentioned after the group has overcome its initial anxiety over acting. The monitor is generally encouraged to take the role of an authority figure, which allows patients to externalize their ambivalence. Externalizing these stereotyped relationships is indispensable for the psychodramatic progress of the group. But interpretation must point out that acting stereotyped relationships puts the group prudently halfway between role-playing and the psychodrama proper.

Sometimes the organizer is given a role as anti-authority figure: he is a butt of jokes, a scapegoat, a weakling, a submissive object of ridicule. The derision poured upon him is a sign that the group wants to deprive the monitor of his position of authority. Making what is sacred grotesque is a well-known mechanism in tragedy and myth. The interpretation deals with reversal, whereas for the theme of the invalid child it dealt with symbolization. But, as a backlash, strong guilt feelings develop. If they are not analysed, they lead to paralysis in later sessions.

## 'Oedipal' themes

As in individual analysis, projection on to the analyst in psychodrama (e.g. phantasized identifications with a cruel, fearsome father) is a defence mechanism directed against the Oedipal situation. Participants act themes in which they externalize and challenge these phantasized identifications. In the first sessions they do so willingly and happily. Then they run out of steam, get depressed and bogged down; they cannot pass from a parent-child relationship to a man-woman relationship. Often interpretation is not able to remove this resistance: participants realize that psychosexual problems are the crux of psychodrama but, by choosing an introductory seminar, not a training seminar proper, they avoid dealing with these problems. If such resistance continues the monitor has no choice but to acquiesce. People cannot be forced into the analytic process against their will.

On the other hand, when a group asks to continue the psychodrama group beyond the six to eight sessions arranged for originally, the first session of the new series is spontaneously devoted to an Oedipal theme.

## An example of the sequence of themes in a psychodrama group

We will provide a brief resumé of themes successively acted by the psychodrama group that improvised the scene of the lover taken by surprise. This group was composed of nine female and one male student. The writer was the only monitor.

### First session

A girl tells her father and mother that she is pregnant. The acting caricatural: everyone laughs. It is a session to fend off anxiety and aggressivity.

## Second session

Two themes are acted out. In the first a (girl) thief is caught red-handed by the shop-walker of a large department store; she has stolen a pair of panties (allusions to short skirts; panties had not then been replaced by tights). There was a witness. The discussion stressed the desire to steal (the rule of the freedom to act out prohibited wishes) and the fear of having to denounce (the rule of commenting jointly on scenes acted arouses the fear of having to judge one's peers). The significance of the panties (which hide access to the secrets of sexuality?) is not analysed.

The second theme is a discussion by three girls of the advantages and dangers of drugs: one is an addict, one is opposed to drugs and one has begun taking them but is reluctant to continue. The manifest content has to do with the preoccupation of students faced with drug problems: how do addicts experience drugs? What can one say to them? One related problem is that of identification with the addict, seen as necessary for an understanding of his problems, but also as dangerous if carried too far. The latent content, left untreated, probably concerns the psychodrama: What sort of drug is it? What pleasures, what dangers does it offer? Can it help us to help others? Don't we need to be helped ourselves for our own problems?

## Third session

A husband drives his wife to the psychiatric hospital of Sainte-Anne in Paris; he tells her she is mad and wants her interned. For the first time the monitor (the present writer) is asked to act and given the role of the husband (the group, composed largely of female students, wants to be his wife; at the same time they express the fear that the psychodrama may awaken in each of them predispositions to madness). The action reverses the situation: it is the husband-monitor who is mad (rebellion against the authority-figure). The psychiatrist ends up by sending the couple to take psychological tests (Are psychiatry or psychology adequate defences against madness? Does madness exist only outside or can it exist within the group? Can the monitor doubt our sanity without our doubting his?).

## Fourth session

The first theme concerns a boy who dates two girls (allusion to the monitor who was running two groups simultaneously). The two girls meet by chance at the boy's house, discover what is going on, band together against him and together decide to ditch him.

The second theme is that of a lover surprised by the woman's husband. The role of the lover is given to the monitor. The only boy of the group, who plays the husband, shows no aggression towards his rival and tries unconvincingly to hold on to his wife. She chooses to leave with her lover, for he is older than she and she feels protected by him. But she tells him that this is temporary and that she will ditch him later (the participants agree to re-live their incestuous, Oedipal attachments in the psychodrama because they know that it is temporary; the phantasy of the group as the monitor's harem is brought up in the discussion).

## Fifth session

The theme of female homosexuality emerges for three explicit reasons: as a reaction to the heterosexual conflicts of the preceding session, because the group was composed almost exclusively of female participants and thirdly because of the wish to carry the transgression of what is prohibited as far as possible.

The first scene, entirely verbal, illustrated the jealousy between two women over a third. The second scene, which is more acted out, shows one woman trying to seduce another; the first appears more and more demanding in her gestures; the second, more and more embarrassed, rebuffs her. No interesting commentary is given. Two provocations aimed at provoking the monitor's reactions seem significant: (a) participants play at doing without men, i.e. because the monitor does not love them enough; (b) the first (aggressive) woman wanted to know if the monitor would tolerate a perverse *passage à l'acte* or whether he would stop her. Naturally, the monitor remained silent: the emergence of female homosexuality seemed to him to be a defence against the intensity of the heterosexual Oedipal wishes aroused in the preceding session.

## Sixth session

The session begins with a lively discussion in which the majority of participants object to the orientation of the preceding session. By way of reaction they decide to play a pimp and his prostitute. The role of pimp is played by the only boy of the group (thus restoring his virility to him).

Sessions of psychodrama alternated with large group meetings. Most members were satisfied with their experience in the large group; they worked out their dependence on the monitor; the only boy of the group displayed his virility by fighting a man in a café who insulted one of the girls of the group, and got a black eye. Then the psychodrama continued.

## Seventh session

The end of the psychodrama is approaching. The scene chosen is one in which a doctor tells a sick girl, in the presence of her mother, that she is fatally ill. The scene is acted with a seriousness that arouses intense feeling. The relation to the death of the group is obvious to all.

## Eighth session

The group synthesizes the diagnostic group and the psychodramas, acting the personality of each group member as it is perceived by the others. Three acts, using two participants each, then follow. In two of them, each actor plays the other. Such role swapping, although particularly difficult, is carried off with a fidelity that astonishes everyone, players, spectators, monitor.

## Ninth and last session

By tacit agreement nobody acts. Without any apparent transition, summing up begins. After a conversation between one participant and the monitor, each member in turn speaks of his transference on to the monitor, his relation to the other members, his interactions with them during the psychodrama and diagnostic group. For group members, the transference was positive. Group members recognized three stages in its past. At the beginning participants observed the attitudes and behaviour of the monitor. Then began a game of mutual seduction: the monitor won over the group which, in turn, won over the monitor. The diagnostic group that followed attenuated, but did not eliminate, this game. Finally, in the last sessions of the psychodrama, the group rediscovered the monitor, and monitor and group were reciprocally grateful. One of the individual effects of the course was mentioned: a female participant who for more than two years had not managed to have a child, although she wanted one, found she was pregnant. She gave me more details when she saw me later. Just after the end of the diagnostic group when she, like the others, felt very euphoric, she had sex with her husband and suddenly felt an inhibition give way within her (the removal of Oedipal wishes). Thus the first theme acted by this group of (mostly female) participants, the announcement of a forbidden but desired pregnancy, has been premonitory.

## Limits and scope of collective analytic psychodrama

The limits of this type of training need to be stressed. It should be repeated that this experience is limited: in time, by the fact that the participants know one another and study together, by the fact that the monitor is at the same time a teacher and that the number of male and female participants is unequal. Under these conditions it is difficult to know what the scope of the experience is. If it does not produce and handle the transference neurosis, its psychotherapeutic value is limited. What sort of training value does it have? To what extent does stimulating a sensitivity to the unconscious (its goal) not backfire in a more defensive reorganization and prevent such sensitivity altogether?

Training in analytic collective psychodrama consists essentially in playing with the unconscious. By acting, group members familiarize themselves with the functioning of primary process thinking, but this process is neither elucidated nor mastered.

Group members really act, but do not really commit themselves to self-analysis.

The following more positive observations may be made:

(i)   there is considerable interest in analytic psychodrama among those who have had experience of it;

(ii)  the teacher-student relationship is transformed faster than by other methods;

(iii) inhibitions concerning the wish to learn (the epistemophilic drive) are removed, at least partially and temporarily;

(iv) the desire to continue with personal training is reinforced;

(v)  phantasy activity is intense for participants, even if they don't act and even if the sessions seem empty caricatures.

These observations have been confirmed by other types of psychodrama experience. In fact, psychodrama may be used in many ways without losing its effectiveness. Side by side with the weekly psychodrama lasting one term, a semester or a year, our team of monitors experimented with other types that proved most fruitful: intensive (half-a-day sessions for a week or every fortnight) and mixed (alternating diagnostic groups and psychodrama groups during an intensive course lasting at least four days or a seminar lasting at least a week).

Generally speaking, the psychodrama enables courses, seminars, training or institutional groups to remove ordinary resistances by warming up and instilling in group members a sense of commitment, by freeing their creative spontaneity, by creating a group atmosphere that encourages greater familiarity with primary process thinking.

# Chapter 4

# Psycho-analytic work in large groups

## Definitions

In contrast to the small group, traditionally used in training courses and made up on average of between eight and twelve persons, the large group comprises from about twenty-five to sixty participants.

In our experience with large groups where prior acquaintance of members with one another is not a factor, and where there are not many sessions (about half-a-dozen), we have noticed more relations of indifference than of friendship or hate. At the end of the course one participant hardly knows more than half of the others. Nobody, not even the monitor(s), manages to get to know all the participants, but everyone knows that such knowledge is possible with enough effort and concentration.

The specificity of the large group is based on the existence of this theoretical possibility: a possibility conceivable but never, of course, realized. On the other hand, all or nearly all theoretical possibilities can be realized in the small group. Beyond the threshold of about eighty persons the theoretical possibilities are too numerous for participants even to imagine them; they thus give up a project of totalization (the project of experiencing the group as a totality of which one feels oneself to be an element is essential, however, for members of a small group) and are generally content to be a part of couples or clans, i.e. to reconstitute a couple or a small group within an ensemble felt to be too large and too disparate to achieve unity. For this reason I propose to call very large those larger than about eighty persons: let us add that the very large group remains for the moment the least understood of all. Our other threshold seems to be about three hundred persons; again there is a qualitative change; we move from the very large group to the crowd. Crowd phenomena were studied before those of small groups and are well known: contagious emotions, weakening of reality testing, alternation between apathy and the paroxysmal expression of drives, dependence on a *leader*. These phenomena, present as background in very large groups, come to the fore in crowds.

The study of large groups is interesting for three reasons. For basic research: unconscious psychical processes, less frequent or less visible in small groups, are strongly marked in large groups; their role and function thus become more easily decipherable and the correspondence between relational situations and modes of psychical function can thus be better and better known. For applied research: in social reality, in institutional life, large groups are more common tham small groups; instead of being reduced to a blind empiricism, to formal defensive rules, or to manipulation by appointed or spontaneous leaders, it would be helpful to acquire a better understanding of the group unconscious. Finally for the training of psycho-analysts and group practitioners: in the large group regression is generally carried farther than in individual analysis or the small group, and the experience is very useful to those apt to run into similar states and processes in training practice or in psychotherapy.

## A particular case: the alternating large group

Everyone has had experience with natural large groups (learned societies, corporate bodies, cultural, economic, socio-political organizations, students' or teachers' meetings).

In this book we shall deal only with artificial live-in large groups lasting one week. We work with 'alternating groups', i.e. seminars that alternate between large and small groups; small groups function alternately as diagnostic groups and psychodrama groups (even ones giving exercises in bodily expression). Each day all the participants of the various small groups as well as all the monitors meet in a large group. Such alternating large groups meet for six sessions of an hour or an hour and a half each.

## Instructions

As in the diagnostic group, neither themes nor working methods are suggested in advance by the organizer of the sessions; there is no prior organization. The fundamental rule given to participants is an invitation to experience a new type of group, the large group, and then to try to verbalize for the benefit of everyone present what has been thought or felt 'here and now'. These instructions come from one or several monitors chosen in advance by the other monitors: one is appointed to signal the beginning and the end of each session. As the two activities of the small groups are non-directive discussion (diagnostic groups) and the psychodrama, it seems useful to stress that participants in large groups may also adopt these two types of activity: the free exchange of ideas and the improvisation of roles or scenarios. Indeed, the large group is seen as more restrictive if it is suggested that its working methods are only those of the large diagnostic group.

A second recommendation applies to the spatial character which, of secondary importance in diagnostic groups and psychodrama, becomes of central importance in large groups. Hence, if one wants to bring out the role of phantasized space in the conversations of group members, it is preferable to structure this space as little as possible, by, for example, not arranging chairs (or tables) in an obvious geometrical form (rectangle, circle, ellipse, regular rows) and to leave participants free to organize the space within the room as they wish.

## Monitors and their function

Psycho-analytic work in large groups is more difficult if there is only one interpreting monitor. As we shall see later, the multiplicity of individual transferences is beyond the grasp of one person and, if there is collective transference, it is negative from the outset. Experience shows that there is nothing more difficult for an interpreter than multiple negative transference; even the correct interpretation of collective aggressivity is generally without effect when such an interpretation comes from the person at whom this aggressivity is directed. If the monitor's team members are observers in the large group, far from helping the monitor in working through his counter-transference and in the ripening of his comments they are led to criticize him systematically for both what he says and what he does not say. Jealous of his position and troubled by the regressive situation of the large group, they also establish a negative group transference on the monitor, symmetrical to that of the participants.

When a large group is run by a couple of monitors, a man and a woman, it works better. But experience has led us to adopt the rule of the differentiation of levels (see chapter 1): there is a specific unconscious process for each level of regression and it requires a different sort of psycho-analytic work. In individual analysis, the psycho-analyst functions alone with his patient. In training group or therapeutic situations, psycho-analytic work requires either a couple of monitors, preferably a man and a woman, or, if there is only one monitor, the presence of an observer. In both cases, the monitor can discuss the counter-transference with a colleague and thus be more aware of the participants' transference, identifications and projections. Large groups require several monitors. We have found that three or four produce the best results.

There are four reasons for having several monitors rather than a single one. A practical reason: in order to organize the various small diagnostic and psychodramatic groups within one large seminar, several monitors working closely together and forming a closely knit team are needed. A theoretical reason, concerning, as we shall see, the characteristics of split transference in large groups. A clinical reason: the nature and intensity of the anxiety aroused by the situation of the large group are, as we shall also see, more tolerable and therefore more understandable to several interpreters. Finally, a technical reason: to begin a process of unconscious fermentation, there must be a dissymmetry between subject(s) and interpreter(s); in large groups dissymmetry is introduced by the presence of a small group of monitors who know one another well, are used to working together and expect to do so in the future, whereas participants know virtually nobody, feel numerous and not bound together and know that once the course ends, they will never see one another again: without this situation, which allows participants to perceive the monitors, in a defensive way, as a unit, the fear of fragmentation would be so severe that their unconscious fermentation would be arrested.

Monitors of large groups may be observers of one of the small groups of the seminar; conversely, monitors of these small groups are present as observers at the large group meetings. Monitors may also run the small groups and the large groups at the same time.

R. Kaës has described some of the features of the interpretative approach to large groups:

(i)    the elaboration of the interpretation is a group activity; the full team of monitors of the seminar as a whole and a small team of monitors of the large group prepare the way for interpretation during their respective daily meetings;

(ii)   who gives the interpretation is left open; it may be decided that a given monitor will give it or it may be given by the one who feels best qualified to do so in a particular context; it may be used for a discussion between monitors before the large group;

(iii)  because the interpretation is given by several persons, no one monitor may claim special access to the truth; he communicates a viewpoint that reflects both his personal experience and certain unconscious currents in the large group; another monitor, influenced by other aspects of the unconscious life of the large group, may have another view-point; the number of transferences requires a diversification of interpretation.

Two more characteristics should be added to those listed above. The interpretation, which more or less explicitly refers to the corpus of psycho-analytic knowledge, is for the monitor one mode of intervention among others, even more so than individual analysis or in the small group; it is necessary, if timed correctly, but loses its effects if it becomes mechanical. Monitors who endlessly repeat interpretations of a supposedly shared phantasy (though the tangling and confusion of phantasies is an essential characteristic of large groups), or who offer reductive interpretations ('you are like children who . . .') are incapable of initiating psycho-analytic work. A gesture, a movement, a facial expression, the voicing of a personal feeling, a remark addressed to the whole group, the use of fable, a retort – all constitute other equally necessary and sometimes more effective ways of making participants understand what is happening in and among them.

Psycho-analytic work in a large group requires a team of psycho-analysts and provides an opportunity tor psycho-analysts trained in individual therapy to work on interpretations as a group of psycho-analysts; this method of working is in turn indispensable for all social psycho-analysis, particularly for psycho-analytic work in teaching or medical institutions.

## Principal variables of the large group

### 1 The danger of losing one's personal identity

As I have said, participants do not know one another well in a large group. They feel drowned in the collective anonymity; there are too many of them to create the inter-individual relationships that allow them to feel they exist; they feel that the monitors are indifferent to them and that the other participants are potentially aggressive; they feel doomed to an ephemeral collective existence. By contrast, the monitors appear to them to be a closely knit team, i.e. a group having all the characteristics they lack: it is small and lasting, rich in mutual friendship, and guarantees each member a personal experience. Thus participants experience a situation in which their own unity, both as a group and as individuals, is beyond their grasp: unity appears to be an attribute of the monitors, diversity, even fragmentation, an attribute of the participants.

More exactly, each participant in an alternating large group soon recognizes the monitor and most of the members of his small group; he has trouble knowing who is in the other small groups. The aim of getting to know one another is explicitly stated by the members of a small group, and implicitly suggested by the monitor of a small group when he encourages the participants to use first names or name cards. But in a large group this is not expected by either participants or monitors. Indeed, monitors, like participants, don't know the names of all the participants of a large group even at the end of the seminar, whereas they soon know all the first names of members of a small group.

The difficulty of knowing others in a large group involves the danger of losing one's ego identity. Our team of psycho-analysts took a step towards the understanding of large groups when it occurred to us that everybody, monitors included, had what Melanie Klein has called psychotic anxiety. Reference to Klein was of exceptional help in enabling us to identify as depressive or persecutory anxiety, collective, affective currents running throughout the group: we were thus able to avoid being disarmed by them, to organize the large group situation in purely psycho-analytic fashion without the psychological crutches that I shall list later (i.e. to tolerate the profound regression that the situation instilled), and to recognize in the small group, where they are more subtle, the anxieties and defence mechanisms related to the psychotic core of the personality.

The experience of a purely psycho-analytic alternating large group and our reflexions on this experience led us to study the unconscious psychological effect of number. Participants regress to the situation of the infant who tries to constitute the object outside himself, in the psycho-analytic sense of the love-object, to organize the world of objects, in the ordinary sense of the term, and who is faced with his own projections, which come back to him like a boomerang. Any group situation tends to provoke this regression. The difference is that in the small group this situation is relived with material projection (the group is a mother-substitute, the monitor is supposed to keep track of each member; the others are mirrors that reflect something of each member to the others), whereas in the large group participants experience the loss of maternal protection (the group has no unity; the monitors stick together, excluding the participants; they are a mirror that reflects nothing). Hence we can conclude that the small group, like the family, 'neuroticizes' the primary psychotic mechanisms; and the large group, like maternal inadequacy, 'psychoticizes' them, confronts them with pure, archaic mechanisms (the splitting of the object, the projection of destructive drives, the search for bonds); the large group undergoes a temporary experience of depersonalization.

The most common form in which, little by little, participants and monitors verbalize this experience is that of the unconscious phantasy of breaking apart. In view of its importance, we will deal with it in detail later. Suffice it to say here that it is an archaic anxiety that the personality will fragment – will be torn apart and devoured – and is thus more than neurotic castration anxiety. The fragmentation phantasy is strengthened by the presence of a rather large number of anonymous individuals and by the disparity between their comments and their transferences. The phantasy of being devoured is strengthened by the basic rule that one must verbalize what is felt: the symbolic equation 'speaking =

devouring' underlies the silence of a great many participants; they fear that opening their mouths will be interpreted by the others as wanting to bite and that the others will bite in retaliation.

Those who dare to speak talk to themselves out loud or to nobody in particular. A collective monologue replaces a dialogue. Those who speak to somebody – generally a participant who has just spoken before them or to the group of monitors – do so generally to criticize and attack them. Looking at someone is phantasized in the same way: to be seen is to be devoured by fifty pairs of eyes. On the other hand a returned glance is understood as proof that one exists in the eyes of someone else.

What has just been said illustrates the phenomenon of projection. We shall return later to the phenomenon of splitting. A few comments here on the search for bonds. If participants are allowed freely to sit where they wish, one can observe the tendency of most of them to aggregate. Turquet (1974) has also noted that neighbours contact one another (visually, verbally, by gesture); in other words, Turquet believes, they try to find a common 'skin'. This is a fine example of Bowlby's theory that, in addition to aggressive and sexual drives, there is another drive equally primal: the attachment drive. It is characterized by a desire for heat, gentle skin contact, the need to hang on, to be held and carried. Frustrating this attachment drive is a major characteristic of the large group: participants complain that it is 'cold' physically and psychologically. They say that there is no 'contact' with monitors and other participants, that the others are harsh, that the group is not supportive and that they are left aside. The small group operates above all on the dualism of the sexual and aggressive drives. The dual drives functioning in a large group – the attachment and the self-destructive drives – are quite different.

In large groups of an exclusive kind (e.g. meetings of scientific associations, directive classes in school), one finds the same anxieties, but the institutional defences serve to reduce the danger of identity loss; participants identify themselves before speaking, the roll is called, name tags are distributed, lists of participants are handed out. More so than small group situations, large group situations threaten the integrity and relative autonomy of the ego. This explains the phenomenon, which Freud discovered, of the common substitution in a group of the group ego ideal for the individual ego ideal. This also explains the stress Lewin and his followers place on group dynamics, although to us this emphasis seems defensive. For them, a *group ego* is characterized by a sense of membership and belonging, obedience to common norms, a network of mutual friendships, stress on rational thought, communication, comradeship and decision-making within the group. The group is a subjective projected topos, as I have noted (Anzieu, 1972). In the large group, participants project their egos on to the team of monitors as a perfectly unified group, i.e., with an 'unbreakable' identity: ego and ideal ego at the same time.

As the number of participants grows, the individual ego regresses and has more and more trouble controlling the instinctual representatives (representations and affects). In the small group, where each member is perceived in a distinctive manner by each of the others, the ego tries to function in narcissistic identification with others, as Missenard (1972, 1976) has shown. In large groups, there is no more than a bodily pre-ego; the 'ego-skin', as I have called it (Anzieu, 1974b), is indissociable from the image of the inside of the mother's body projected on to the large group. This weakening of the ego could explain the relative frequency of 'acting out' in the large group situation (windows are opened and closed, certain participants arrive late and leave early, drink from bottles, converse in low voices, etc.). Springmann (1976) has shown that fragmentation is a defence specific to large groups. Beyond the large group, in vast groups and crowds, it is possible to maintain one's individual ego, the image of the nursing or devouring mother is omnipresent; the ego functions are projected on to the leader.

Loss of maternal protection and threats to personal identity constitute the first register, if not of interpretation, at least of the monitor's psycho-analytic intervention. We shall examine shortly what mode of psycho-analytic intervention is required.

## 2  Small group mediation

Each person, whether participant or monitor, attends daily both the alternating large group and a small group (a diagnostic group or a psychodrama group). From this alternation comes a second register, this time of interpretation proper: interpretation of the unconscious representations and affects cathected in relations between the groups. In fact, members of the various small groups of a seminar try to discover the differences and similarities of their respective groups: during large group meetings or spontaneous inter-individual contact, they try to know whether they function 'normally' – i.e. like the others – or not. This rivalry, like all fraternal rivalry, functions with respect to a third party, which in this case is the group of monitors experienced as parental surrogates and from which participants expect preferential treatment or rejection. A second level of interpretation therefore deals with 'group' transference which, in the large group, is directed at the team of monitors and which comes from participants who themselves belong to small groups.

For example, in a seminar, members of a small group run by a man and a woman speak up more during the first large group meetings; then members of another small group run by two men speak up. In both cases, the most active small group during the large group meetings is the one whose collective representatives coincide best with the collective representatives of the large group. In fact, the team of monitors was at first believed to be directed by a man and a woman (hence the members of the small group run by a man and a woman felt favoured), then at the end, by one monitor who was one of the two running the other small group (hence members of this group felt favoured). Group relations within the large group magnify collective projections on to the team of monitors. These projections appear in common themes of alternating large groups: unity or breaking apart of this team (generally called 'the staff'), its cohesion or disagreements its authoritarianism or its laxity, its know-how or ignorance, its honesty or its manipulative mendaciousness, its heterosexuality or its homosexuality, its genitality or its perverse polymorphism, the monitors' supposed desire for one another, their supposed pleasure at being together, their determination to hide these desires and pleasures from the participants, the corresponding absence of any desire for participants, their wish to keep participants in the group without letting them out, etc. All this constitutes the material of the second register of interpretation in the framework of the triangular relationships of small groups among themselves and with the team of interpreters.

## 3 Space

Large group meetings have their own spatial characteristics, different from those of individual analysis. They are also different from those of the diagnostic group or psychodrama (the group as the female body acts out with the monitor as phallus a scene sometimes of seduction, sometimes of castration; at times the group acts out a primal scene in which the parental couple is the monitor and the observer or two group members: the space of the small group is that of primal phantasies).

The rule of free spatial distribution is too recent to enable us to make an exhaustive list of the uses large groups make of space. What we can say is that participants try to sit side by side: we have already mentioned their tendency to stick together, i.e. to reconstruct an ego-skin. Another common spatial arrangement (favoured perhaps more by monitors than by participants) is putting the chairs in an oval, a rectangle or three concentric circles, thus closing off the space so delimited. This central space is so large that participants and monitors need to reduce it by placing tables in front or in the middle. Whether marked by a void or table, this central space is experienced by the participants as the phantasized place of the team of monitors (whether or not they actually occupy it). Though the monitors in large group meetings are in fact dispersed around the central space, they are phantasized by the participants as a body in the middle of this space (its heart, or seed). The correlative problem of orifices also involves important phantasies, which are supported by the real need to open doors and windows at certain times.

The space of the large group is thus experienced first as the chaos resulting from the loss of maternal protection; this chaos, it is felt, must be filled in by sticking together. Then it is experienced as the surface or the interior of the mother's body – a surface and interior to be explored. Certain large group sessions resemble the mythical voyages described by anthropologists in curing or birth rites (see Lévi-Strauss, 1958, Chapter 10, in which he speaks of rites to help women having difficulty in childbirth). This is related to the two unconscious wishes behind their presence in the group: we came to be cured, we came to be born. These two wishes are in fact one: acquiring autonomy from the phantasized mother's body. Participants have a paradoxical attitude towards this wish: they jealously defend their ego identity, i.e. their personal autonomy, with respect to the large group, a substitute for an indifferent mother; and they feel comfortable in the small group, as in the womb, and don't want to leave it. The phantasized space of the large group is experienced as the inside of the mother's body, with the team of monitors as the internal phallus to which the participants as mouths try to hold on as they would to a breast, in relation to which they are both inside and outside. Annie Anzieu's (1974) descriptions of the reciprocal 'encasement' of analyst and patient in individual analysis may be transposed to large groups.

From our work with alternating large groups we can make a few other observations.

In large groups the emergence of the symbolization process seems to correspond to the appropriation of the mother's phantasized body and to the sublimation of the anxiety over losing it. For example, one of our seminars, led by a team of monitors well known as psycho-analysts, was turned into a religious institution at the service of our Holy Mother the Church . . . of psycho-analysis. These symbolization processes come out in alternating large groups because they are alternating. The metonymic relationship between the large group and the seminar induces a mother-child differentiation in terms of container-contained.

The rivalry of children (children-penis, children-excrement) in the mother's womb, a rivalry destructive either for them or for her, is intense in large groups; it may be at work either between small groups, as we have said, or towards participants who, by taking an active part in large group meetings, become leaders and are therefore violently and sometimes destructively criticized if the monitors do not intervene in the right way.

Phantasies about parents in conjunction and the primal scene are usually projected on to the monitors and their 'secret' meetings, i.e., on to their phantasized, segregated space. The space inside is thus only for the monitors; the space outside is for the participants. Sometimes a couple of participants display their feelings for one another during the large meeting (see Bion, 1961, on couples). This is a reflexion of the monitors' supposed segregated sexual activities and demand to do as they do. While parents enjoy adult pleasures, children are left aside, unhappy, impotent and furious: this effect is grounded in the dissymmetry between the closely knit group of monitors and the scattered large group of participants. Arranging seats in rows, as a panel, around a table, in a star shape, in Phillips 66 – are defence mechanisms against phantasies of the mother's breast, usual in large institutional groups.

When the group is in an oval, certain participants sit behind the line, thus placing themselves as an appendage of the mother's body or as her excrement. The phantasized space of the large group here represents the primal cloaca with its fluid and orifices.

It is possible to extend the analysis of the phantasized space by introducing bodily expression exercises and relaxation in the seminar. Sessions standing or lying down are also valuable when compared with observations of natural large groups (assemblies, dormitories, theatres, etc.) where people are put in these positions.

Kaës (1974b) in his psycho-analytically orientated article, 'Le Groupe large, l'espace et le corps', has more systematically analysed the phantasized space in large groups.

The following complementary remarks on the functioning of orifices in this phantasized space we owe to Joseph Villier, who has kindly allowed us to print them here.

In 'group space' we ought perhaps to consider the holes, the empty spaces, windows, cracks, or other openings with the idea that we have here a series of open structures with several perhaps essential functions.

For example the group illusion may be experienced as an attempt to eliminate all holes in the group, which tends to close in on itself.

Or we may wonder whether the non-participating observer is not cathected by group members as the person who remains in touch with the outside, who is between inside and outside; he is less 'inside' than the monitor.

The 'free evenings' are perhaps openings to the outside that monitors create out of a fear of being smothered, asphyxiated or of having indigestion. (God knows, enough *is* eaten in the seminars.) Cultural activities in this type of seminar are not, it seems to me, merely cultural.

The secretary (at certain times for certain participants) also seems to fulfil this function. She too must find an opening to her office space where mini-groups meet and she insists upon being integrated into the team of monitors – or she becomes depressed.

We could no doubt find other examples for either large or small groups, each having its 'holes' at certain times. Perhaps, too, certain parts of the large group (small groups or partial groups, based on acquaintance, friendship, for example, in the small groups, etc.) function as holes.

These functions are not unlike those openings for food, air, elimination and the seminar as a whole may be represented as a structured organization of openings, linked by canals or compact masses. There are cracks, openings, holes, ducts that the staff of monitors works with consciously and those it uses as defences (which may also be true of those the staff works with). For example, the situation of the group illusion, inasmuch as it plugs holes, leads predictably to the monitor's interpretation, which thus 'makes a hole' and enables the group to revive.

In one of our seminars groups spontaneously organized the evening before by certain participants appeared and centred discussion on the body. Was their appearance a hint that the staff organization was too close, didn't let the group breathe, or, on the contrary, were there too many empty spaces, a rush of too much cold air, so to speak, with the reaction that participants tried to get together to warm up?

I well know that all this is perhaps no more than images and ways of imagining things, however I have in mind Freud's 'Project for a Scientific Psychology' (1895) in which the idea of channelled energy with regulation systems brings us back to the notion of empty spaces, of channels through which energy flows. I wonder if we might not have here a way of approaching the circulation of the libido and the possibility of distinguishing between ego-libido and object-libido.

## The duration

The time of alternating large groups is experienced at first as dead time. When compared to the small groups, where they find a certain warmth and life, the plenary meeting of the large group represents a pause for the participants, an empty time, a 'deadly' boring exercise. Dead time between highly cathected activities represents the time of death: hence the general passivity and ephemeral attempts at leadership on the part of certain participants; hence the feeling of monotony, of heaviness and of overwhelming immobility; hence also the fact that large groups do not progress as fast as small groups and their sessions are

dominated more by the repetition compulsion and self-destructive
drive. We have noted, however, that these characteristics fade
when monitors have a better grasp of the theory and technique of
the large group.

One readily realizes that the time experienced by the large
group is closed in, repetitive, cyclical, the time of waiting for the
absent mother. We had far more trouble understanding what the
introduction by the participants of this time into the context of the
small group seminars meant. Introducing large group time was felt
by monitors as an enormous resistance and sometimes criticized
openly as such – without any liberating effect. For to note the
existence of a resistance without explaining its mechanism to
participants doesn't change it, and instead irritates participants
and drives them away from psycho-analytic work. Bernard Gibello
suggested linking it to paradoxical communication, the nature and
pathogenic mechanisms of which have been uncovered by the
Palo-Alto school in California. I shall devote more attention to
this subjection in chapter 11, 'Paradoxical Resistance', but include
there a brief summary.

Participants of training seminars in psychology generally know
psycho-analysis well: they are psychiatrists, psychologists, psycho-
analysts, nearly always teachers. In fact, they come to see a team
of psycho-analytically oriented monitors function. In the small
group they manage to commit themselves sufficiently as there are
only two monitors (one for the diagnostic group and one for the
psychodrama), but in the large group where the entire team of
organizers is present, they are on their guard, which prevents
progress or at least severely inhibits any interpretation. Thus the
team of monitors that the participants have come to see at work
works in a vacuum. The whole situation is thus a double trap. A
trap for the monitors: if they keep quiet and wait, nothing
happens; if they interpret supposed underlying phantasies they
miss the point, and teach participants nothing they do not already
know. A trap for participants: by rendering the monitors
powerless, they draw them into their own failure; as a drowning
man pulls down with him the person who tries to save him. When a
situation is blocked by such a paradox, aggressive tension and
feelings of impotence and failure mount, and explanations that
miss the point only reinforce the paradoxical character of the
situation. Psycho-analysis works, as we shall see later, by
unblocking what is paradoxical: the time of indefinite waiting, of

the suspended threat of death is transformed into evolving, progressive time.

## The transference

There are two characteristics of large group transference that always appear in the early stages and frequently recur later: the frozen silence of most of the participants and the fragmentation of the individual transferences. The silence is due to the number of participants (there are too many of them for them all to speak) and to unconscious motives: the anxiety of being devoured, which, as we have said, is more acute in small groups, propagates the symbolic equation 'speaking = devouring'. Some speak or occasionally act: by doing so they express an *individual* transference on to the monitors or on to the seminar-object. Then others intervene, usually reacting to what has been said or acted out, and so express an individual lateral transference. The multiplicity of these individual, central and lateral transferences, the fact that they are malleable and the relative lack of resonance among the mass of participants and monitors, amplifies this silence and the corresponding fragmentation anxiety. Hence the need for several interpreters whose various interpretations constitute to a certain extent the unifying resonance.

Sometimes an individual transference manages to catch the group's attention and trigger off a collective transference. In our experience, this only happens when the individual concerned makes his transference public.

The brutality of these transferences – in form and content – is not without impact on most of the participants and even monitors. These are lively, unifying moments, when the large group emerges from its inertia, its routine and its fragmentation. They are also tense, even threatening moments, when monitors are called upon to drop their reserved manner, that is to say, their apparent indifference, and while respecting the benevolent neutrality of their function, have to speak in a personal, caring way. Interpretation may be confined to considering the reactions of members of the large group towards one participant or a couple of participants, with a view to finding out what group reactions are being reflected back to the monitors.

A truly collective transference, that is to say, one shared by a great many members, may also appear in a large group. Experience shows that a small group belonging to a seminar lasting at least a week achieved far greater intensity and more valuable results than a diagnostic group or psychodrama group condensed into a few days or spaced out in weekly sessions over a year or more. The theoretical explanation for this was discovered by Béjarano (1971, 1976): the seminar situation fosters the split transference; positive transference tends to be concentrated in small groups, negative transference in the large group. The fixation on the large group of anxieties concerning fragmentation, devouring and destruction, as well as persecutive and depressive anxieties keeps participants at an archaic level of regression. On the other hand, it frees evolutive libidinal processes and enables them to find their place more easily in the small diagnostic group and the psychodrama group. Furthermore, in small groups, one encounters questions of pregenital and genital sexuality, the relation to authority, to law and to the forbidden, guilt feelings and their eroticization, the diversity and mobility of libidinal choices. When the transference is split participants have the impression that their small group is coming along splendidly and that it is the large group that is not working well. In fact, the fluidity of the transference and the interlacing of the positive and negative transference often defy the monitor's powers of analysis in non-alternating small groups. The seminar situation, which alternates large and small groups, simplifies the transference process and renders it more effective in small groups. It also has another advantage: small groups, whether non-alternating or alternating, tend at certain times to produce the group illusion; the situation of the plenary meeting, by forcing members of different small groups to come face to face with one another in this way, encourages them to go beyond this illusion. We have never seen the group illusion produced in the large group, but when small groups do not manage to go beyond the group illusion, it may be discussed and dealt with in the large group. Finally, as we mentioned earlier, the splitting of the transference between small and large groups tends to fade when monitors feel nearly as sure of themselves in the second as in the first.

Thus the collective transference generally appears as negative transference in non-directive large groups. When such negative collective transference first appears it is generally experienced as an expression of self-destruction. Then, there comes a time when it assumes the form of open aggressiveness against the monitors or against one of them. This aggressiveness may also be displaced laterally on to one participant (the eldest, the most defensive, the first to speak or to try to direct the discussion). Such collective aggressive transference, well-known and relatively easy to handle in small groups, assumes a scope and intensity in large groups that make it extremely difficult for monitors to deal with and which may lead to the breakdown of the participant chosen as victim if interpretation is not timed properly. If there is only one monitor for the large group, he is particularly exposed to collective negative transference: this is one of the reasons why large groups need to be run by several monitors.

Once the large group can go beyond negative collective transference, it is open to positive archaic collective transference, the mythic and joyous exploration of the inside of the mother's body.

A. Béjarano (1974) has published a detailed study of the transference and resistance in an alternating large group.

## The counter-transference

The situation of the large group, with the regressive characteristics referred to above, is troubling to all those in it. The resistance most commonly adopted by participants is passive defence: non-involvement, lack of interest, purely physical presence while the mind wanders or vegetates, an ironic attitude towards those who try to do something. The monitor's resistance may be just as great, but takes a different form; changing the situation so that participants don't act regressively. The case of Bethel's National Training Laboratories is a telling example. Hardly had the T group been invented before the subjects' new-found freedom in small groups was withdrawn − or avoided − in the large group. When T groups were introduced in France in 1956 by American experts, the principal problem during preparatory sessions was not whether to introduce directed activities along with the T group, but rather what these activities should be. Of course, there were lectures and practical demonstrations on the psychology of communications, on team work, leadership and friendship networks. Thus participants, on the one hand, were supposed to discover all these things by themselves and about themselves in small groups (Roger's theory of learning formed part of the seminars' official philosophy), but, on the other hand, it seemed necessary to instruct them during large group meetings lest they forget what they had learned – or did not find what they were supposed to. Thus it was shown that the clinical method could usefully be applied to group situations – a revolutionary idea at the time, encouraging group members to be free subjects. But this was counterbalanced by so-called laboratory experiments in which subjects were manipulated like guinea pigs. The discussion during preparatory meetings of this seminar was essentially a struggle between clinicians and experimentalists for the possession of the group-object, with the attention accorded certain persons and activities being continually brought into question: the programmes and handling of the first French seminars were, like neurotic symptoms, compromise solutions. The theoretical references that governed the monitors' handling of the situation displayed the same defensive character: though each member could project on to the group situation his own psychical organization, monitors interpreted what went on in terms of political philosophy. Following Kurt Lewin's example, situations were 'authoritarian', 'democratic' and 'laissez-faire' (i.e., anarchic), depending on the way they were run. The group situation was seen as a microcosm of society at large and not as a projective surface for certain social representations which in fact it is. Thus we can see how the *socius* may be used as a defence against the *psyche*.

A. Bethel ran a large group in France (on the model of American liberal, federal, free-enterprise society – hence its failure in France): participants were divided into subgroups arbitrarily given socio-economic or socio-cultural roles (workshops, classes, committees, pressure groups, etc.) and encouraged to interact on a common problem defined in advance. For example, representatives were chosen to negotiate before the whole group solutions to a given problem, which was institutional, organizational, economic, political – never psychological. The large group was thus devoted to a sort of large-scale business game based on a part technocratic, part sociodramatic model. Participants found themselves assigned an apparently coherent double task: to experience and to analyse relations between individuals in the small group, and the relation between small groups in the large group. But the coherence was only apparent, as sub-groups were made up of different participants from those in the basic T groups; the theme of the large group was artificial and did not correspond to the real problems; finally, the phantasized relation of the individual to the group was not taken into consideration.

One more anecdote. From the time Bethel began its seminars in 1956, it was decided that each day part of the plenary meeting was to be devoted to a joint appraisal of the seminar by participants, in addition to lectures and demonstrations. Such appraisals were called regulatory sessions, for another element of the official philosophy of French and American seminar organizers was the introduction of the concept of feedback, a self-regulatory system. The first regulatory session was devoted to superficial criticisms of seminar materials (tables, lighting, time-tables, speaker systems, etc.); the second session to much livelier criticisms of the seminar; the third abandoned criticism. Criticism died because monitors had not interpreted the splitting of transference in the seminar, nor the concentration of negative transference on to the large-group meeting; thus, visibly relieved, the monitors had no choice but officially to do away with it. The matter of why regulatory sessions did not regulate anything was left in the air, and the same experience was repeated during succeeding seminars without the slightest theoretical or technical progress.

The story of the team of monitors of alternating groups to which I have belonged since 1962 is one of a succession of resistances to regression and to the transference provoked by this situation; it is also the story of the difficult collective working through that removed these resistances one by one. Lectures, debates, practical demonstrations, the exchanging of notes gradually came to be seen as leftovers inherited from Bethel-type seminars. The counter-transference underlying these practices turned out to be made up of our desire to feed participants so they wouldn't go away hungry, having got nothing from the experience and dissatisfied with us. If such was indeed the counter-transference, then the transference showed dependence and oral avidity and aggressivity. And if such was the transference, was it not appropriate to apply psycho-analytic lucidity rather than cater to its demands?

We were not able to draw the correct conclusions at once. Lectures, exercises and notes were eliminated from large-group meetings, but participants were not given total freedom. They joked that seminars were held in a government building belonging to the Justice Ministry and housing the headquarters of the borstal service. Certain large-group meetings were non-directive; others were programmed in such a way as to retain a symbolic character – a film dealing with a group problem was shown, ethologists or anthropologists were invited to symposiums to compare the groups in which they were taking part with groups of animals or those to be observed in so called primitive societies. Moreover, 'free' plenary sessions were not entirely free. Participants were asked to discuss matters openly, but to stick to some very general theme that constituted the subject of the seminar. If participants were too passive, discontented or wandered too far from the subject – as they inevitably are and do in a large group – a more 'structured' approach was adopted: organizing a panel or a Phillips 66 with volunteers or delegates from the small groups. The cycle of plenary meetings began and ended with a speech by one of the monitors in which he expanded on a number of mythological references in the form of a fable – another attempt at achieving symbolic resonance. The counter-transferential need to keep primary processes controlled by secondary processes at last became conscious, and we were thus able to see the large group from a purely psycho-analytic point of view, without resorting to psycho-sociological techniques and theories.

Thereafter, handling the resistance of the monitors took its place among the formulated goals of the group. One of the goals proposed was to conceive of the large group as a totality of which small group activities were fragments: a counter-transference defence against fragmentation anxiety. Another objective, inspired by the Tavistock Institute of London, was to enable the group to foster a connection in participants' minds between the here and now (the experience acquired in the seminar) and the elsewhere (the possibility in the future of using this experience in their everyday lives). Emphasis on this goal – which is obvious but which must be up to participants to work out for themselves – comes from the counter-transferential wish to harmonize inside with outside, that is, to let participants side-step the problem of splitting inside and outside and having to reconstitute on intermediary 'level' or surface.

When it is not present at the outset, the monitors' counter-transference is put in its 'proper' place in the large group, i.e. is expressed through the monitors' attitudes and their way of handling the group. It may therefore be elaborated and analysed during the monitors' meetings.

The monitors' – and participants' – most common defence is silence, not voluntary tactical silence, but paralysing, frozen silence, the sign of the anxiety of devouring and being devoured. Awareness of the fragmentation phantasy – if participants speak, they attack us; if we speak to them, we may destroy them – is a way of dealing with it. Self-analysis, in monitors' meetings, of difficulties in the large group is another. The first time we tried this we found two sources of difficulty in analysing monitors' defences: the transition from the small to the large group reminded most of us of the childhood anxiety felt when going to school for the first time (loss of family protection, confronting a large number of peers) and to some, childhood traumas (accidents, operations, hospitalizations, in short, circumstances in which separation from family was accompanied by physical injury). In this way we were able to shed light on two sides of our counter-transferences: fear of the large group as repetition of the anxiety of going to school for the first time (Béjarano lays great stress on this aspect), the wish to face the large group in order to relive the early 'breaking apart' by mastering it, i.e. the wish for post-traumatic reparation in a heroic-masochistic identification with legendary figures who were wounded in their victorious battles against monsters.

Monitors rally the defence mechanisms described by Melanie Klein against persecutory and depressive anxieties: it took us two or three years after recognizing these anxieties before we realized the extent to which we were in the grip of defence mechanisms against them. The obsessional defences: for example, a report on some aspect of psycho-analysis (or sociology) disguised as an interpretation and cut off from the dominant affects present in the large-group meeting. The hypomanic defences: longwindedness, jokes, funny stories, puns, usually echoing a similar climate among the participants. The hysterical defence: provocation, seduction, trying to get a reaction from rather than interpreting the seminar (see Kaës, 1970a); this defence is similar to the provocative public declarations made by some participants, mentioned above.

Because of the regressions, transferences and counter-transferences specific to large groups, the work of interpretation is more complex than it is in individual analysis or in the small group. To get rid of the defences outlined above, to be aware of the extent, the violence and the intensity of the transference, to prepare the team of monitors to behave and speak in the appropriate manner, to adopt the appropriate style, requires psycho-analytic work on oneself as well as teamwork.

## Psycho-analytic work

*If the truth is not formulated in the seminar, it is experienced as the realization of an illusion*

The sense of pleasure in the small group and the sense of death in the large group are accompanied by an important, but incomplete intuition of the way the psychical apparatus functions. We have in mind here Bion's third drive, the wish to understand, which he places beside the libido and the death drive. The shared experience of interpretation (shared by monitors and participants) gives rise to a particular kind of pleasure, understanding. Because of the functioning of the transference, discussed above, the small group may prefer libidinal pleasure to the pleasure of understanding, whereas the large group has no choice but to choose the pleasure of understanding over the fear or temptation of self-destruction.

Wherever there is transference and interpreters are present, psycho-analytic work is both possible and necessary. It is possible because once discovered and verbalized by interpreters, the truth of the situation is recognized by most participants. It is necessary because the pleasure derived from the positive transference, if it is the seminar's final act, is no more than a red herring: participants tend all too frequently to believe that they can take this pleasure with them into their outside life. However, they must pay the price, unknown to themselves, of splitting and of a projection of the death drives into the large group, and run the risk (at home or at work) of depression, if they do not recognize the gap between social reality and the belief that they carry away with them from the course. Let us take one seminar as an example. It is Saturday noon. The small groups had just finished. The general atmosphere was one of euphoria. In the large group meeting in the afternoon, a number of participants tried to extend their satisfaction and to 'thank' the monitors. Once a few interpretations were given of the collective transference on to the group monitors, the atmosphere changed completely: it was enough, at the end of the seminar, that this atmosphere should be designated as such, that the function of interpretation be fully recognized for what it was. The last word of a seminar not only brings it to an end, but also emphasises that an attempt has been made to tell the truth.

### Interpretation in the large group requires inter-transferential analysis in the team of monitors

The exercise of interpretation in the alternating large group requires interpretation. René Kaës (1976b) has called this 'inter-transferential analysis'. Only what has entered the unconscious phantasies of the monitors, only what has been part of their anxieties, conflicts, tensions and what they manage to verbalize among themselves, may be recognized as transference in the large group, understood in its double dimension as phantasy and defence, may be clearly communicated to and effective on participants (qualities without which an interpretation never has any real impact). At the beginning of a seminar the monitors' need to understand and to get together is a defence mechanism. In large group meetings the anxiety that one does not understand any more, the fear that the seminar will fail, or the feeling that everything is going wrong all mean that the unconscious is welling up. Arguments between monitors, withdrawal on the part of one who takes a marginal or opposed position, a strong sense of depression in one or hypomania in another are sometimes a necessary stage, for they are provoked by the appearance of phantasies predominating in several participants and which are acutely echoed by the phantasies of a particular monitor, whereas the other monitors, having a different psychical economy, resist giving way to them. For example, myself and other monitors on the team had noticed that one particular monitor was more easily carried away by the projection of a cruel father, another by a conquering, parricidal son, others by disputed authority, or by a dominating woman or by a conciliatory, gentle mother, or by the counter-aggressive defence through homosexual attachment, or masochistic suffering. This collective self-analysis of the counter-transference within the team of monitors requires that they verbalize personal material analogous to that needed for individual analysis: night dreams, memories of childhood, daydreams, puns or witticisms relating to the situation, the restitution of significant elements in private conversations or readings, etc.

However, one should resort to inter-transferential analysis only as a tool or when the circulation of phantasies in the seminar poses problems. When inter-transferential analysis is practised systematically, the pleasure thus derived may obscure the main goal (fostering the right interpretation and communicating it effectively to participants) behind a secondary goal (restoring the idealization of the team of monitors, threatened affectively by the seminar situation). The group illusion is a temptation for all groups, groups of monitors and psycho-analysts included. Reducing the libidinal desires of participants towards monitors and the transformation of this object libido into narcissistic libido, cathecting the team of monitors as ideal object, is a schizoid defence analogous to the affective indifference of certain mothers of future schizophrenics towards their children.

A complementary and obverse illusion is sometimes expressed by certain monitors who want the meetings of the team of monitors to be seen and heard by all participants: this is a glass-house Utopia. Apart from the fact that the sought-for transparency of psycho-analytic work runs counter to the opacity of the unconscious, there is always something perverse in wanting, for example, to practise sexual education or castrating in wanting to exhibit the team's functioning before a group of people who function poorly. There is a proper place for everything: the monitors' inter-transferential analysis in closed meetings and the analysis of collective transferences in large-group meetings. The fact that the latter often takes the form of a dialogue between monitors and the group gives it all the more impact.

Members of the large group pay particular attention not only to interpretations, but to all remarks and gestures made by the monitors; the monitors' behaviour in such a regressive situation is an overvalued identification model. Imitating the monitors does not function at the same level as it does in the small group where certain participants willingly play the role of monitor's or observer's assistant, a defensive role easy to analyse. Sometimes this gives rise in insufficiently trained monitors either to paralysing, sphinx-like silence or to a propensity towards wild and purely cerebral interpretations. However, in small groups, this process is limited; as Missenard (1972) has shown, in small groups specular identification of participants with one another are of critical importance in preserving the unity of the ego while encouraging personal change. Since these identifications come into play only very slightly, if at all, in the large group, the maintenance of personal identity, which is of vital importance and excludes any wish to change, depends therefore, on projective identification with the monitors. The monitors cannot refuse this projective identification without definitively sterilizing the large group or even provoking breakdowns. At the same time, the monitors set the example for the choice of a psycho-analytic response which, without being necessarily an interpretation, is appropriate to the process or state that is triggered off in the participants by the situation. If the state is like an infant's distress when deprived of maternal help, the appropriate response (as we know from Winnicott) is not an interpretation, which merely accentuates this distress, but holding and handling the 'body' of the large group. If the process is one of negative collective transference, the psycho-analytic response, before reaching the interpretation, consists of showing, by a certain way of speaking and behaving and without being insensitive, that this aggressivity has neither destroyed the psycho-analyst, nor incited him to vengeful cruelty. As Bion has shown, the task of the psycho-analyst is to restore the alpha function of symbolization in place of the beta function of fragmentation and projection: inter-transferential analysis makes the interpreting team a group-container (Kaës, 1976c). If the collective resistance of the 'trainees' – psychologists and training staff who have come to see 'super-monitors' at work – falls into the trap of a 'double bind' and fetters the monitors, the psycho-analytic attitude, which must here take into account the work of the Palo-Alto school, deculpabilizes the normal feelings of those forced into a dilemma and frees the wish to understand of the shame that negates it: it is then possible to dismantle the mechanism of the 'double bind' and to render visible its link with the wish for self-destruction (see chapter 1).

Three examples of personal psycho-analytic work in an alternating large group are provided here. At the second plenary meeting, the participants complained of the overwhelming weight of the situation, of the indifference of the monitors, who not only didn't help them but did not seem to feel what they themselves felt. Several times participants asked the monitors to do something. I identified these requests and complaints with the insatiable oral avidity of the baby at the breast afraid of losing the love-object and who prefers biting it to losing it. At the same time I felt torn between the wish to intervene, but fearing to appear to be yielding to their demand, and the wish not to intervene with the consequent risk of getting bogged down in the situation. So I decided to say openly what I felt personally and physically: personally, in order to show that monitors are not robots and that they, like the participants, have feelings; physically, because up until that time the rule of free speech had encouraged superficial or intellectualized conversations. I said that my body felt split in half; the right half was intact, the left half was eaten away by the reiterated, greedy demands on the monitors. What I said provoked little manifest reaction at the time but proved effective from the following day on: the large group began to feel less like hospital patients; the interpretation of the splitting of drives and of the object, prepared for by my metaphor of the split body, could be formulated and understood; lastly, the collective discourse was no longer cut off from individual experience and the suggestion from a few participants to do bodily exercises came as soon as it was possible to speak of one's own body. Another comment: it is not advisable for monitors to appear systematically unemotional, insensible to the difficulties of the situations and to uncertainty. Not only because this is not true, but also because one of the few resorts possible in a highly frustrating situation is to turn to the person who frustrates and try to 'touch' him, as in fencing: if monitors do their best to show that they cannot be reached by anything the participants may do, they reduce the participants to total powerlessness and block any possibility for development in the large group.

The second example concerns the last meeting of this same large group. The four monitors of the large group (of which I was one) had got into the habit during their daily meetings of trying to anticipate – in the light of the large-group meeting of the previous day and of the scenes acted out during the day in the small psychodrama groups – the course the next large group meeting would take. We four monitors tried to foresee, not what interpretations would be appropriate, but rather what attitudes would be most suitable. Each of us, by giving his suggestions, began a sort of rehearsal, the tone, style or content of which the others criticized or agreed with until, bit by bit, we agreed on the form and theme of our intervention; a certain tone and attitude as thus internalized by the four team members, each with his individual variations, before the beginning of the large-group session. Thus, before the second plenary meeting, we agreed to try to speak of our physical sensations; otherwise I would not have ventured to speak up as I did. Before the final meeting we thought it useful to let each participant decide, for himself rather than publicly, what he had got out of the seminar and at the same time to help him make the transition from the rather particular group that he had just experienced to the familial and professional reality to which he would soon return. To do this, we agreed not to provide interpretative explanations, but rather to refer to what we were feeling at the end of the large-group seminar, but without making this explicit. We tried to speak for ourselves rather than for the whole group, and to alternate our respective comments; in short, we aimed at a sort of 'Winnicottian' atmosphere, which seemed the most suitable to our two objectives: serious reflexion and the organization of a transitional space (see Winnicott, 1953, 1967). This is what we did. Because we were able to agree on where to pitch what we said, we were able, at least partially, to communicate this atmosphere to the large group.

A final example illustrates how psycho-dramatic improvisation may be used in large groups. The example is taken from a seminar held at the end of the Algerian war, after the failure of a military putsch set off in Algeria by officers supporting a French Algeria and before the opening of negotiations with the Algerian nationalists. The large group seminar was organized in Paris by a large French military academy and held in an isolated building about twenty kilometers from the main academy buildings. It was for about thirty officers who had just been appointed instructors at this school, with a view to preparing them for their future educational work. With the exception of a few rare civilian teachers, instruction in these schools was in the hands of military career men assigned to academies for two years, although generally they had no previous experience in teaching. This was why the general staff had decided to introduce psycho-sociological seminars in all the major military academies. As a psycho-sociologist, I had already run a number of these. These assignments had been unenthusiastically accepted by most of the officers who, coming from Algeria, would have preferred to go on fighting rather than return to France and go back to school, albeit to teach future officers. We may add that several of the youngest had participated in the putsch – one was released from prison to come to the course – and regarded their new assignment as a disciplinary measure.

It was a difficult seminar. It was run by a colleague and myself. Sessions of the diagnostic group (participants were freely divided into two small groups) alternated with plenary meetings which, as was customary at the time, included debates and practical demonstrations. The small group made up of the oldest participants went along with what we were doing, but the group of young officers, most of them putschists, had refused the instructions and gradually adopted a position of non-co-operation and defiance. What little they talked about revolved around what they considered of the utmost importance: disobeying orders (attacking rebel bases in Tunisian territory; torturing prisoners to obtain information). The atmosphere was tense; during the breaks my colleague and I overheard sarcastic comments directed at us. The cultural isolation made things worse. The participants ate and slept in, with a minimum number of lower ranks. The only other inhabitants were five kilometers away in a village in which our hotel was situated. A military vehicle collected us both and took us over a particularly bad road on which the driver deliberately passed close to a sheer cliff while bouncing us around like peas in a pod. During the daytime we were the only civilians in the small isolated camp. Though we had tried to get the participants to take an active part in plenary meetings through stimulating practical examples, diligently going to colour ceremonies and playing volleyball between sessions, we did not manage to break the ice. One senior officer, shocked by the turn of events, said there was talk of doing away with us and advised us to leave immediately.

The seminar dragged on in this way for four days. On the evening of the fourth and next to last day, my colleague and myself were upset. We were anxious not about the threat of murder, which we did not take entirely seriously (we were in France, not Algeria), but about our failure in running the group. We were also upset at the idea of the way these young officers might behave as teachers. We decided to stay to the end, to try a plenary meeting the following morning, to announce that we were going to have a psychodrama for the two of us and, using this means, to communicate the way we judged the situation. We thus improvised on the theme we had agreed upon but which we did not announce to the participants (we asked them only not to interrupt before the play was over). This theme was the parallel between the

image which, before the group began, we had of a French officer –
disciplined, honest, active, human – and the image that the
participants had gradually given us: devious, undisciplined,
passive, ironic, threatening. To which we added that although the
breach between soldiers and civilians was widening (the opposition
was growing in the country, particularly among intellectuals, as the
war went on), we, as civilians and intellectuals, had accepted
intensive contact with military men for a week and without taking
this breach into account. Also we wanted to help them train new
officers and we recognized regretfully how much they had opened
the breach, when compared to us.

For the first time they listened attentively and silently for forty
minutes. We asked them for their reactions. The youngest
lieutenant was livid with rage: 'We have heard enough, I expect
orders from my superiors to put a stop to this.' The captain, who
happened to be the oldest and who ranked the highest,
immediately began speaking and spoke at length. Very upset, he
explained the misunderstanding that had paralysed the group:
there was a rumour that we were two officers from the information
service disguised as civilians, with instructions to listen to
participants and report to the high command on the loyalty of each
one of them – in short, that we were spies who were putting the
careers, and perhaps the freedom, of the participating officers in
jeopardy. After these declarations, tongues were untied. We
learned that the programme of the seminar posted at the entrance
had been bordered with black drawing-pins, as a warning, and that
the officers had gone to Paris to see whether the psycho-
sociological organization really existed at the address given and
whether it was a civilian or military building, etc. At the same
time, the immense anxiety of these officers, the drama, for them,
of the inevitable withdrawal of France from Algeria, their feeling
of failure, their uncertainty about the future – all this came out:
they became human.

Once things were aired, the atmosphere changed entirely and
the participants began to make up for lost time during the last day.
They were at last able to speak in their diagnostic group of their
anxiety and to confront their real problem: go underground and
rebel (for ten years they had struggled against a rebellion they
disapproved of) or preserve above everything else the unity of the
French army and keep it ready for other missions. Here we did not
need to be monitors and to interpret. Our mute presence was

enough to guarantee the freedom of opinions and the necessity to speak truthfully. I can still remember the emotion with which I listened to them: in my experience as a monitor I have never witnessed so tense, so dramatic, so dense, so passionate a debate; or one in which the consequences were so serious. It is hardly necessary to add that they all chose the unity of the army. This result was the theme of the morning's conversation when, once the persecutory anxiety was removed, it was possible to speak freely.

## The psychology of large-group monitors

The capacity to tolerate not only persecutory anxiety but also fragmentation anxiety and destruction anxiety, the ability to regress to archaic body images while maintaining intact certain ego-functions (for example, reality testing, communication with others, a sense of humour) are some of the principal psychological qualities required of a large group of monitors. Inter-transferential work within the group of monitors during the course of the seminars has allowed us to note the difference in psychical economy underpinning the differences in attitude towards the large group and led us to the following hypothesis. The specific uneasiness of the monitor faced with this situation seems to be related to how early his childhood traumas occurred. These traumas may be related to the loss of the good breast, to being devoured by the bad breast, to separation anxiety. The monitor, who, as a child, experienced such trauma *early* feels horrified at the idea of having to run a large group. Those who went through this period of their childhood without major problems are interested above all in small groups. On the other hand, if these experiences are accompanied by traumas during the second year, when the child has already passed the mirror stage and begun to talk, it is possible for him to start repairing the damage by over-cathecting language, giving him a predisposition in adult life to monitor a large group; the monitor is then strongly motivated to master the traumatic episode by repeating it. In fact, such motivations are characteristic of pioneers in psycho-analytic work in large groups: they face the situation, but their 'traumatic' way of experiencing it does not always make things easy for the other monitors (for whom such colleagues increase the dangers) and gives participants a questionable model of heroic-masochistic identification. This is less often the case, now that the theories and techniques of large groups have progressed. The anxiety aroused by a strongly regressive situation, when no longer accompanied by an anxiety of the unknown and a fear of ignorance and powerlessness, is normally quite bearable to small groups of psycho-analysts. Thus large groups may be run in a rational way and avoid the extremes of apathy and tragedy. It would seem advisable to achieve a 'balance' between the various monitors' defence mechanisms against archaic anxieties.

We know of no method of selection for evaluating the personality of a monitor-to-be. Psycho-analytic training seems to me to be indispensable, but all psycho-analysts are not able or motivated enough to run small or large groups. As in psycho-analytic training, persons with narcissistic psychical organizations tending to the perverse or psychopathic or, with psychotic or pre-psychotic structures (schizophrenic, melancholic or paranoid) and obsessionals are advised against becoming monitors. As for psycho-analytic training, monitor training is a training-selection: in the training, candidates prove their aptitudes. In this light, one stage in this training-selection is participation as a participant observer in groups of monitors during a seminar.

# Chapter 5
# Group phantasies

## Introduction

Human groups are the consequence of topographical, subjective
projections; if the individual did not project on to the group, the
result would be a mere aggregate of individuals, not a group. This
is the guiding theme of the chapters that follow. A direct result of
psycho-analytic work with groups, this theme is complementary to
the psycho-analytic concept of a group as the object of cathexis.
However, the earlier psycho-analytic concept had little practical or
theoretical value without further work; when complemented by
our theory of groups as topographical, subjective projections, the
psycho-analysis of groups becomes operative. The individual
psychical apparatus protects itself and uses external stimulation as
well as internal drives to organize zones within mental space.
These zones correspond to what Freud identified as the id, the ego
ideal, the superego, the ideal ego and the ego (the ego being
subdivided into a system of conscious perception and unconscious
mechanisms of defence). Each of these agencies tends to bring
together the others in dealings with the outside world and with the
body; it is not a centre governing the functioning of the apparatus,
as anthropomorphic views would have it. Thus the unconscious id
'envelops' the biological body, the ego 'envelops' the unconscious
processes, the system of conscious perception 'envelops' the ego.
In this limited series of networks the 'centre' may be defined with
respect to such-and-such an envelope: they are 'inside', 'outside'
(as are the ideal or repressive agencies) or on the 'fringes' (as is the
hidden self).

The only way a group can protect itself and make use of external
stimulation, and the wishes and drives with which it is cathected by

its members, is to fabricate an overarching group psychical apparatus on top of those of the individuals composing it. René Kaës has studied the isomorphic and homomorphic relations between a group apparatus, on the one hand, and the individual psychical apparatus, on the other. Kaës identified an intra-systemic conflict, within the group apparatus, between the tendency to identify group and individual (isomorphic relation) and the tendency to differentiate the individual psyches (homomorphic relation). My contribution to group theory is to add the concept of an 'envelope': to exist at all the group needs an overarching agency that envelops it. Thus the group is organized around the same agencies as the individuals composing it. The unconscious and conscious functioning of the group will differ depending upon the agency that serves as envelope to the group psychical apparatus; the enveloping agency also affects the behaviour of the group, its goals and attitudes towards external reality.

The fundamental insight that the ego ideal (one of these agencies) could guarantee the unity and cohesion of a gathering was Sigmund Freud's. He also showed the importance of the imago in crowds and societies. Kurt Lewin, the inventor of group dynamics – but not a psycho-analyst – sought to get group members to substitute a collective group ego for their individual egos, and believed this essential for democratic groups. My work with groups led me to discover that the group envelope could be a commonly held ideal ego, as in the phenomenon of the group illusion. From this beginning I was able to systematize my discoveries. A group may obviously be organized around or against the superego. A group may also use the id as envelope: according to the nature of the dominant wish or the stage of its development, different collective phenomena appear. In the following pages I shall deal with examples of phantasies of the group as breast-mouth or womb-toilet, phantasies of breaking-apart, phantasies of the group as machine, phantasies of paradoxical resistance. These phantasies are expressions of libidinal, aggressive or self-destructive wishes, and are more or less regressive. In fact, group phantasies are produced by a circulation of individual phantasies among group members; for the group is the result of economic and topographical organizations, which it represents and disguises. But in turn it produces particular effects on the thoughts, affects and behaviour of group members.

I have concentrated on group phantasies because of their intermediate metapsychological status. The study of group phantasies is an excellent way of approaching the economic and topographical structure of the psychic group apparatus. At the same time, this study contributes empirical reference points useful in understanding what is going on or what is not going on in a group and useful to the monitor. This leads me to distinguish between structure and organization. A particular agency (e.g. ego, superego, id, etc.) common to group members structures the group psychical apparatus; this structure in turn provides the organization for certain phantasies. In the concluding chapter, I shall try to show that group phantasies may be organized around an individual phantasy, a primal phantasy or an imago.

Two problems underlying the following chapters are the articulation and interaction of group phantasies with the individual unconscious, on the one hand, and the social unconscious, on the other. Those who have had experience with groups as psycho-therapists, organizers, observers, monitors or participants know how varied and often unforeseeable are group destinies on account of the often decisive role of certain individual personalities. The theory here proposed explains this empirical fact: the personalities of group members construct a group *first* around a common agency (e.g. id, ego, superego, etc.); then they do so around an organizing unconscious phantasy or imago. This agency and this organization may or may not be appropriate for realizing the goals ascribed to or assumed by the group. Other factors affecting the group's destiny include the composition of the group, its educational level and the degree of contact between members, as well as the attitudes of other groups and the overall social context. In the final chapter I shall provide several hypotheses concerning, on the one hand, the influence of unconscious social models on group functioning and, on the other, the multiplication of spontaneous groups in crisis situations affecting the collective mentality.

## 1 Realities of group phantasies

Every group is a pooling, a sharing: this is a commonplace often repeated in different forms by those working with groups; it verges on the tautological. The difficulties begin when one asks: a sharing of what?

Popular imagery proposes an idealized answer: the group is the pooling of the energies, enthusiasms and capacities of individuals who freely assent to the discipline of the group. Early sociology, with Durkheim and the *Année Sociologique* school, adopted the hypothesis of a collective consciousness and its articulation on the three mental realms described by classical psychology: the group is the sharing of representations, feelings and volitions. In nineteenth-century France, Fourier believed that groups produce collective feelings; if this process is disorderly, tumultuous, anarchic, the group can be maintained only by expensive and annoying external controls: the Phalanstery produces harmonious feelings in their total diversity and natural complementarity. For Tarde, the group involves the imitation by a sort of quasi-hypnotic suggestion of those who invent it. Freud develops this idea later: the group involves the identification of the members with its leader.

From about 1930, a science of groups, distinct from individual psychology and sociology, made its appearance. For Moreno, the group was the community of likes and dislikes distributed according to the schemas of sociometry. For Mayo, the group involved a common mentality, with its own norms and logic; the autonomous group, characterized by a strong sense of belonging, frees individual capacities and allows them to be more easily realized by both participants and the organizations employing them. For Lewin, the group represents interdependence not only between individuals, but also between variables functioning in the group; the democratic group allows members to participate more actively in determining and pursuing its goals, to pool their individual psychological resources and to continue to resolve tensions. For Bales, the group is communication between its members; the group members who discuss face to face progress only by pooling the perceptions of each member concerning the others.

All these conceptions are based on observable group facts, whether the group is considered from the point of view of monitors, participants or as a whole. These facts are themselves caused by psychical processes that take place within and between individual members, that is to say, at the molecular level. Moreno's sociometry, Lewin's group dynamics and Bales' interactionism reproduces the behaviourist attitudes that Watson gave individual psychology: here the reactions of living organisms to certain stimuli were studied; what happened in the organism between the excitation and the response did not interest the behaviourist, who left such questions to physiologists; psychology dealt with the relation between stimulus and response. Similarly, group psychology describes the relation between inter-individual affinities and group morale; if dislikes reach a cetain point, particularly if they are directed towards group monitors, morale will be low; if likes are numerous, towards most participants as well as monitors, morale will be high. But why should one individual like, dislike or be indifferent to another? How do these affective impressions reinforce and modify one another? Sociometry does not tell us. Lewin notes that when the group feels free and united, its decision may be stronger than individual preferences inciting members to act in the opposite way; in other words, the stimulus is the sense of belonging to the group; the response, the modification of individual habits. Thus American housewives during the last world war were disgusted by certain cuts of meat, which they didn't buy (kidneys, hearts, sweetbreads); when they met in small groups they discovered economical and dietary reasons for eating these cuts and recipes that turned them into pleasant dishes; many of the housewives then went ahead and bought some. But why were these cuts thought disgusting? Discussion showed that it was because of their smell and consistency. But what was peculiar about this smell and this consistency? What did they evoke in the minds of these housewives? What affective chord did they touch? What emotion did they arouse to produce so powerful and widespread a refusal to buy them? And how did the discussion overcome their disgust without explicitly dealing with these affective aspects?

We can guess what the answer was. Lewin's article prudishly alluded to it and then lost sight of it: kidneys evoke the smell of urine, sweetbreads the consistency of testicles, hearts blood pumping, through the veins or being shed, the fear of wounds, operations, mutilations, while its rubbery consistency aroused unconscious memories of the breast or bottle. The psychological roots of these 'lower' animal parts, the name of which makes one think of the 'lower' parts of the body, the zone of pleasure, of mystery and filth, are those of weaning and castration and of the danger of 'low' desires, linked to the erogenous zones. Indirectly, this is what was discussed in these small groups of housewives; these questions, never raised and kept secret, were broached together; group members discovered that they thought the same things about these cuts of meat. Their group could discuss jointly the political, economic, calorific and gastronomic reasons for eating these cuts only because they first looked collectively at the phantasies, anxieties and emotions associated with each of these pieces. These phantasies, anxieties and emotions varied according to the individual's past, but were consonant with those of another group member.

The feeling of group membership, whose strength, according to Lewin, incited housewives to buy these cuts and thus to overcome their 'prejudices', does not, as Lewin implies, come from the fact that each housewife was able to participate actively in the meeting usually run by a psychologist and to discover in the group her real interest and what this had in common with the interests of the others. The group situation itself allowed housewives to examine a problem objectively (the purchase and preparation of meat) which individually they were incapable of discussing with the same objectivity, if ever it occurred to them to speak about it at all. This is a rational view of things. Often, meetings in which all members participate actively and in which the common interest is clear lead to firm, unanimous, valuable conclusions, followed by action.

Housewives could speak openly because the group was non-directive and did not last too long: this is a condition, not a cause, for there are many non-directive meetings where people never manage to say what is on their minds, especially if they know this is what is expected of them. A meeting only works if a few members speak of what they really care about and if this is echoed in all or nearly all the others. By 'working' I mean changing certain of the participants' habits, attitudes or ideas. In the meetings of the American housewives, the group worked because the theme, the personality of the women, Red Cross volunteers, and the personality of the organizer all coincided.

## The group, group echoes and group phantasies

The group is a place where images are transformed in interaction. When human beings are together to work, to play, to defend themselves, to steal, to kill, to believe, to change the world, to be taught or cared for, feelings, desires, fears and anxieties excite or paralyse them. They may experience a common emotion, which may give them an impression of unity: conflicting emotions may tear the group apart; several members may withdraw and defend themselves against group emotions that they feel to be threatening, whereas the others, frantically, joyfully, let themselves go; or most members may withdraw when faced with invasive emotion, in which case the group is dull, apathetic and wordy.

An administrative meeting is blocked by a question of procedure, gets bogged down on a point of secondary importance, splits hairs, makes mountains out of molehills or fails to see certain difficulties, gives way to private quarrels, ignores the programme in hand and goes off in several directions at once, takes up problems that are not its own, avoids its responsibilities, takes too much notice of rumours, suppositions, Machiavellian intentions attributed to superiors, neglects essential information that it does possess, gives tasks to those least able to succeed, criticizes and destroys everything proposed and stops any worthwhile conclusions which, upon leaving the seminar, members promptly forget.

Teams in laboratories, workshops, or athletics drag their heels, cheat; or they pat themselves on the back, dream of exploits; or they isolate themselves, are self-satisfied, take no interest in others, nurture their differences; or they seal themselves off, become inaccessible, pursue secret hidden goals, become tainted with unorthodox ideas and practices; or the team breaks up into cliques or self-centred individuals, exhausts itself in internal struggles, accentuates likes and dislikes; or it gathers around a hero, a teacher, an important person, who like a magnet attracts those worried, complaining beings who are easily lured in their search for truth, faith or pride and who expect the world of others; or the group uses the best of its members, spurns those it had previously chosen, consuming ideas, energies, devotion; its members are prisoners on whom it exudes its venom, fruit that it squeezes, then throws away.

If a group behaves in this way, it is because certain emotions lie behind its behaviour and because these emotions are aroused by the sudden appearance in the group, of precise, powerful, but unperceived images. Brothers in the same monastery, militants in the same cell, volunteers for polar expeditions, crews of submarines or atomic bombers, boarding students, castaways from some *Medusa*, oil men drilling in the desert, all constitute groups:

they have the same interest, the same needs, they face the same situation together, either because they have chosen to undergo it, or because they have deliberately chosen to measure themselves against it, and can succeed only if they remain closely identified with it. Logically, therefore, everything tends to make them co-operative, willing, disciplined, united. The reality is far removed from this logic; do not all men, intellectuals and non-intellectuals alike, dream nostalgically of a group life in which people get along well in mutual understanding and are capable, as a strong, but flexible whole, of devoting themselves to a common objective? Are they not indignant at the tensions, misunderstandings, dramas, ostracisms and antagonisms in all real groups? The reality is so far removed from its ideal image that groups shun any objective investigation that might establish the facts as they are and look for causes.

What psychologist has been able to gain access to a religious community or a political party to study its real functioning, to observe the birth and development of conflicts, to try to link this functioning and development to the morphological, structural, or psychodynamic variables of individuals or of the group? Is it feared that such a psychologist might see that believers and militants, preaching charity and justice, who have come together to help one another practise what they preach, are torn apart by inexpiable, unjust hatreds? Yet this is a common theme of novels and poetry; it would be an important step forward for the science of human relations if it could be demonstrated that confinement, that is to say, deprivation of contact with the rest of society and the obligation to live side by side with the same small number of persons for an extended period of time, exacerbates hostile drives between these persons, and if it could be shown from what degree of deprivation, what duration, what size of group, etc., this reaction occurs or disappears. When society refuses to give science what it needs to work and when intellectuals cannot find the courage needed to back unpopular hypotheses – whereas the history of science shows this has always been the case – literary figures, under cover of artistic transposition, take over these obscure truths. Thus Sartre, in *Huis Clos*, deals with the mutual hate of three persons forced to live together without being able to turn off the light, or to isolate themselves from one another: 'Hell is other people.' Thus Jean Cau, in *La Pitié de Dieu*, describes prisoners sentenced for life who share the same cell and end up by killing one of their number. From Gide to Mauriac, a whole generation of novelists has seized upon the theme of the bitterness and resentment so often to be found in the modern family, whose members, now so much reduced in number, live in close emotional proximity. The Scandinavians were so surprised and ashamed of two Scandinavians – the first explorers to have crossed Greenland on foot, who, after eight days of sleeping in the same sleeping bag, and doomed to die if they separated, came to hate each other, refusing to speak except when in grave danger, refusing to see one another again after their triumphal return – that they attributed this behaviour to the polar climate rather than to human nature.

The violence of emotions – the power of the images that triggers off or sustains these emotions – are group phenomena at once patently obvious and masked: but those that are most obvious to an observer or even to a naive participant are the most masked for the people involved, especially those in charge. Psycho-analysis has discovered the intense narcissistic cathexis which, in the case of illness, physical wounds, physical or mental inferiority, weak spots in an individual's emotional economy, fixes on the sick part and protects it, even idolizes it. In a similar way, it would be appropriate to develop the concept of the narcissistic wound for a group. A group feels narcissistically threatened when weaknesses, which it prefers to hide from itself, are brought out into the open; it prefers not to tarnish the ideal image that it maintains only at great cost. These two group mechanisms, the narcissistic cathexis of certain parts of their functioning and the defence against the narcissistic wound, constitute one of the major stumbling blocks to scientific group research. Indeed, these are not the only ones: during the course of this study we shall add to this list of resistances.

There are innumerable examples of defences against the narcissistic wound. It is the first and often insurmountable difficulty experienced by psychologists consulted by a sick group whose members stubbornly refuse to know themselves and want to get well without paying the painful – but nevertheless often the only – price: recognizing the truth about oneself. The gamut of such initial situations varies from intriguing to irritating. The psychologist has as much chance of making the group progress by laughing it off as he does by getting angry about it or by giving them learned analyses and detailed explanations of it.

Let us take the example – for which I was consulted – of closed

Jewish communities in Western Europe. They are fast disappearing: before it was too late Jews wanted to study them in order to know them better and to remember them more clearly. If they went to a non-Jewish psychologist, they were suspicious that not only would he not understand these communities but would even contribute, deliberately or inadvertently, to anti-semitic propaganda. If a Jew belonging to the community was given psycho-sociological training in order to carry out the study, it was feared he might lose his faith and his roots in the group. If there happened to be a Jewish psychologist in the community who was called upon, his results would have been indignantly dismissed: he would have been criticized for being blinded either by his own narcissism, by innate cruelty, or by current psychological theories that don't hold water. He would have been criticized for exaggerating well-known realities out of all proportion, or for giving encouragement to some faction trying to acquire power or reform everything.

## Bion's contribution

The psycho-analytic method, applied to both real and psychotherapeutic groups, has shed light on group phantasies. The contribution of the English school of psycho-analysis (essentially disciples of Melanie Klein working at the Tavistock Institute and the Tavistock Clinic in London) has been decisive.

The pilot experiment seems to have been that of Bion (1961), an English army psychiatrist during the Second World War. Bion was in charge of a hospital of four hundred men who could not be individually treated and who were undisciplined and anarchic. It occurred to him to see it as a psycho-analytic situation in which the patient is a community, to regard the attitude of the soldiers as a collective resistance, to adopt the analyst's attitude of non-intervention in this reality and to confine himself to purely verbal relations. His aim was to force the group to become aware of its difficulties, to constitute a group in the true sense and to become capable of organizing itself. Bion laid down rules for all: the men would meet in groups, each having a different activity: the members of each group were free at any time to stop what they were doing and return to their rooms as long as they informed the sister in charge; every day at noon the whole situation would be reviewed. After a period of hesitation, due to current habits and suspicion of the doctor's good faith, there were more and more genuine attempts at group organization, so many that one group could specialize in organizing activities for others. From the outset Bion criticized, using their own actions, the very inefficiency that they accused the army of; he refused to intervene in problems arising out of theft or malingering, telling the patients that it was *their* business not his. Gradually an *esprit de corps* developed: there were collective protests against malingering, attempts to find activities that would strengthen their sense of personal dignity and rapid progress towards rehabilitation. In turn, this spirit communicated itself to newcomers and affected their progress.

After the war, Bion worked in the rehabilitation of veterans and former prisoners-of-war to civilian life, using a method of group psychotherapy very close to the T group then being developed in the United States. In trying to understand the tensions that arose during sessions, he arrived at two fundamental conclusions:

First conclusion: there are two levels of group behaviour, that of a common task and that of common feelings. The first is rational and conscious: every group has a task, whether assigned by the organization to which it belongs or chosen by its members. Success depends upon an accurate analysis of the corresponding external reality, the judicious distribution and co-ordination of roles within the group, the regulation of activities by a search for the causes of success and failure, and the choice of goals in accordance with the means available by group members acting in a fairly homogeneous way. Here we are speaking only of what Freud called secondary processes: perception, memory, judgment, reasoning. These are necessary but not sufficient conditions. Persons who when alone can rationally approach a problem often have difficulty behaving rationally as a group. This is where the second level comes into play, the level of primary process thinking. In other words, conscious co-operation by group members, necessary for their success, requires a free circulation of feelings and unconscious phantasies. The first level is at times paralysed, at times stimulated by the second.

Second conclusion: the individuals in a group are combined instantly and involuntarily according to affective states that Bion calls basic assumptions. These affective states are archaic and pregenital; they go back to early childhood and are to be found in their pure state in psychoses.

Bion describes three basic assumptions that affect groups
without their being aware of them:

1 *Dependence* When the group functions in terms of this
assumption, it wants to be protected by the leader on whom it
depends for intellectual or spiritual food. The group cannot
continue without conflict unless its leader accepts the powers
attributed to him, along with the obligations they imply. The result
may appear to be fairly good, but the group may not really be
making progress. It is content to wallow in euphoria and
daydreams and ignore harsh realities. If the leader refuses, the
group feels frustrated and abandoned. A feeling of insecurity takes
hold of the participants. In diagnostic groups this dependence on
the group leader often takes the form of a long initial silence and
difficulty in finding a topic of conversation, as the group expects
suggestions from the monitor. Dependence is a regression to early
childhood situations where the infant depends upon his parents for
control over reality. Dependence corresponds to an eternal group
dream, the dream of a good, strong, intelligent leader who
assumes responsibilities in their stead.

2 *Fight-flight* If the monitor refuses to give in to the dependence
assumption, the group feels threatened and believes it will not
survive. Faced with this danger, participants usually band together
either to fight or to flee. In this sense, the fight/flight attitude is a
sign of group cohesion. Common danger brings members closer
together. Let us take an example. A free discussion group takes as
its topic: 'abandoned children'. The session is boring; an escapist
attitude prevails; few members take part in the discussions. Then
the group evaluates its work. Criticisms abound: 'we haven't done
anything', 'it was futile', 'we don't know anything'. The monitor
then observes that group members are escapists: the group wanted
to prove it was incapable of getting along alone. The participants
laugh. A lively critical discussion follows: flight is followed by
attacks on the situation and on the monitor. Fight/flight may
assume a number of different, more or less disguised forms.

3 *Pairing* Sometimes the fight/flight attitude leads to the formation
of sub-groups or couples. Herbert cites the following example. In a
diagnostic group the topic of discussion was 'crushes' in an all-girls
school. Only women spoke up. The men remained silent, saying
that the phenomenon does not exist in boys' schools. In the
following session only men spoke: there was thus a split between
the men and the women. However, during the next meeting, a

man and a woman teased one another about the preceding discussions: we were witnessing an entire session of 'aggressive flirting' (nobody else spoke). In this way a couple was formed. It may try to reform the entire group (Bion speaks of a 'messianic hope' aroused in group members), but the couple is dangerous to the group because it constitutes an independent sub-group.

The three basic assumptions do not all appear at the same time. One predominates and masks the others, setting up a 'proto-mental' system.

Bion provides only interpretations concerning the whole group and the basic assumptions underlying its collective experience. An interpretation is the 'translation' in precise terms of what the monitor considers to be the attitude of the group towards itself. The monitor in a diagnostic group, the chairman of a meeting, and the teacher in the classroom share the feelings of group members. If they succeed in analysing these themselves they can judge group phantasies by their own feelings. More than group members, the monitors feel the group's frustrations because they make it work and feel responsible for it; the group does not see itself when, for example, it sabotages the work. But the monitor, who is more sensitive to escapist tendencies, can recognize the true character of what may consciously be a friendly atmosphere. Interpretations must be timed right and must be to the point. The monitor has to struggle against the natural tendency to speak of his discoveries as soon as he makes them. Premature revelations, inappropriately presented, may hinder or divert the work of the group. Interpretations given by a monitor to a group are like the interpretations a psycho-analyst gives a patient. They must be selected, not communicated wildly. The patient or the members of the group must be able to accept the revelation, not superficially and intellectually, but actively and willingly. If interpretations are either accepted passively or refused, one must wait: either the interpretation is wrong, or the subjects are not yet ready for it.

## The monitor

For Bion, the real monitor is part of the group and shares its beliefs. He does not need to convince the group of his personal beliefs. 'If the group is conducted by an individual so caught up in the feelings of the basic assumption that he becomes like the leader of a work group, it is easy to explain the disasters of the group, for the qualifications of its leaders are only apparent.' The monitor must be able to stand back, to be at once inside and outside the group.

## The paranoid or depressed group and the psycho-sociologist

The merit of Elliott Jacques, another member of the British school, is to have extended Kleinian views to the understanding of real groups. According to him, psychological difficulties encountered in the functioning of economic and social organizations belong to two fundamental categories of anxiety well-known to child psycho-analysts: paranoid (persecutory) anxiety and depressive anxiety. It will be recalled that, according to Klein, the decisive change in early childhood takes place between the sixth and ninth month with the successive appearance of these two forms of anxiety. In order to illustrate Jacques's view by my own experience, I shall show how it accurately accounts for two phantasized representations that psycho-sociologists run up against in their work, that of the guinea pig and that of the spy.

The group regards the psycho-sociologist who has been asked to treat it as an outsider; he is not one of us; he cannot know our problems as we ourselves who live with them every day do; there are things he will never be able to feel. Indeed, he is not interested in us for ourselves, but rather because he is delighted to have an opportunity of applying his methods and his theories. Our group is for him no more than a laboratory in which he can apply his ideas. For him, the results will be highly instructive, even if the group is a failure. But *we* are running the risk of losing the definite, familiar advantages of our present functioning, of hurling ourselves into uncertainty, only to be rewarded with difficulties and disappointments. One must always be suspicious of the unknown. We don't want to be treated as guinea pigs by psycho-sociologists, economists, organization specialists or specialists in general.

The image of the guinea pig emerges when the group is satisfied with itself, when it is not in profound disagreement with the organizations to which it belongs and when its resistance to intrusion is low. The group is apprehensive about external intervention because it might bring its weaknesses to light; it dreads being shamed, humiliated and devalued. The group is in a depressive position; to bring its workings into question is to give in to the aggressivity of the 'out-group', to risk losing the love-object that it is for itself and being deprived not only of love, but also of its happiness and its victorious confidence in itself.

If the group is in a paranoid-schizoid position, if it projects its bad conscience on to the outside world, if it is in overt or latent conflict with the portion of society in which it finds itself, if it finds its cohesion in the struggle against an enemy, this is because it is diffusely overwhelmed by the 'spy' image. The intrusion of the 'out-group' is seen as destructive; it is, for the group, the equivalent of that invasion of the body by the bad object that Melanie Klein regards as a child's basic phantasy. This intrusion is greeted with suspicion and fear of persecution; it immobilizes group aggressivity and crystallizes it around the foreign body, encysts it and expels it violently. In this situation, nothing objective an outsider can say will be heard: the psycho-sociologist, the expert, is the villain *par excellence*; his words are poison.

But experience shows that natural or occasional groups behave quite unlike the model, which is as ideal and artificial as the myth of the biological community. Instead of discovering the laws and real functioning of groups, group theories are erected on the basis of how they *ought* to behave. This obstacle, which individual psychology took a long time to overcome, still plagues group psychology. Group self-analysis implies self-regulation, which in turn implies self-programming: here we find a pre-scientific schema that once served to explain individual will and moral conduct, just as the examination of conscience was supposed to lead to resolutions, which in turn were organized into a programme for life.

In group meetings the feedback of the feelings felt by certain members for others sometimes improves interpersonal understanding and resolves intragroup tensions. But this happens in a highly emotional or dramatic atmosphere and is accompanied by upheavals, internal psychological changes and changes in awareness. Such a feedback is of another sort than the mere adjustment of the information given and taken by senders and receivers. Furthermore, feedback within a group is often ineffective, interminable and ill-timed; feedback may in certain circumstances upset group functioning or divide group members; feedback may also be a manoeuvre used by a clique to impose its own opinions or to satisfy its wishes, or a manoeuvre by a minority to undermine the constructive action of the majority.

The notion of programme is similarly confusing. Who has ever seen a group stick to its original programme except for limited, specific activities? The programme of a machine is an automatic chain reaction of timed and measured operations determined in advance. The programme of a group is a guide for action, a general orientation, an articulation between short-range and long-range goals. Finally, even admitting that it is preferable that a group should fix its own programme in order to follow it the better, instead of having it handed down by a superior, it cannot extract its own programme out of itself. The programme requires information on the sector of reality in which the group acts and reacts with complementary, competing and antagonistic groups. This reality may be changing, the actions of other groups may alter; these groups may evolve: the programme has to be readjusted. There are then 'givens', imposed by reality, knowledge of which is in the hands of other groups. If these givens are ignored then the programme will be a mistake and a failure. Dealings with other groups, subordination to some, recourse to mediators and members of different groups who pass information from one to another are constant phenomena.

The idea of the self-programming and of the self-regulation of groups is a myth; like all myths, this idea expresses a hope, a 'programme', while its authors mistake their own wishes for reality. Self-regulating elements exist in any group; they function more or less without the group's being conscious of them. One may try to improve them. But to give self-regulation priority, to erect it into an absolute, to make it a tool to resolve all the group's problems is contrary to the nature of groups. Inter-regulation, on the other hand, is useful despite its difficulties and failures. To survive, to succeed, a group must rework its programme in accordance with the advice, criticism, needs, manoeuvres of other groups, formulated adequately or indirectly expressed by acts. A group that tries to avoid being regulated by other groups, which turns in on itself, which is deprived of the nourishment provided by society is a schizophrenic group. In the same way an individual who behaves as though external controls did not exist and who tries to keep his distance from others, like the obsessional neurotic, or to escape social control, like the delinquent, is pathological. One might sketch a typology of group pathology by studying the way in which groups strike a balance between the two necessities of self-regulation and inter-regulation. The suggestible group is ready to sacrifice self-control. The hysterical group is closer to the first; the paranoid group to the second. The normal group is able to recognize its 'normality' through its capacity to strike a compromise between these two necessities.

## 2 Summary: an introduction to phantasies in group work

The observation, organization and analysis of real or artificial human groups suggest a number of hypotheses and possibilities for research. What are the acceptable ideas about small groups in psycho-sociology. Lewin, interpreting group phenomena as an interplay of forces, was the first to try to represent these phenomena scientifically. Thus group behaviour could be reduced to the resultant of the external and internal forces to which it is subjected.

The validity of this schema is questionable, as few groups really behave according to this interpretation. Observation shows that, quite the contrary, group difficulties begin when what it wants to do corresponds neither to external nor to its own internal reality. In general, it is this 'crisis' that leads the group to call in a psycho-sociologist to improve its functioning.

So another hypothesis may be formulated: there is something more than an interplay of real forces between the group and reality, between the group and itself; there is, at its source, a phantasized relationship. The images that come between the group and its surroundings explain phenomena and processes that up to now have been neglected or attributed to other causes.

In this respect Lewin's 1942 experiment with his associates on changes in eating habits among American housewives warrants discussion.

The point of departure was the resistance of housewives to the viscera, the 'lower' cuts such as kidneys, sweetbreads or hearts, the price of which was distinctly lower than that of the 'nobler' cuts. The hypothesis was that this resistance was based on prejudice. The aim of the (non-directive) discussion group was to make its participants realize this and therefore to change their eating habits. If Lewin's interpretation was based on the dynamics of decision-making, it could not explain the psychological content of those prejudices. In fact, they touch a realm of phantasy which, in an individual's past, is associated with what is dirty, unclean and forbidden. Thus the giblets are 'bad objects' (Klein), which cannot be eaten without danger. During the discussion it was enough for the organizers to refer to the calorie value of these giblets or to ways of cooking them to objectify the associations underlying the prejudice (e.g. the smell of kidneys and urine) and to change the object from bad to good. The change took place in phantasy.

Certain more recent observations show that the group situation is perceived essentially in terms of the most archaic phantasies. To know what these phantasies are, we can follow up one fact: the very term 'group' is one of the most recent acquisitions of modern languages. Originally part of the vocabulary of the fine arts, it was imported from Italy to France in the late seventeenth century and referred to an ensemble of objects, in a painting or sculpture. In French literature it appears for the first time in a poem of Molière on the Val de Grâce. In the mid-seventeenth century, the French term *groupe* referred to any gathering of people, and from the nineteenth century it spread prodigiously (a musical group, a zoological group, a mathematical group, group psychology). Whereas the term could have designated the specific reality in which we live (family group, a group of friends, a cell, a union, a team), there is no distinctive term for this reality. Scarcely had the term come into existence than it took on meanings that disguised the psychological reality it might have designated. Moreover, no equivalent for 'small group' existed in the ancient languages, which amounts to saying that the concept did not exist. There was only the individual on the one hand and society on the other, and this opposition became one of the major themes of sociology. For the isolated individual is the business of psychopathology and it is difficult to look at an entire society without seeing groups, structures, institutions, through which norms and ideals find their way to the concrete reality of human activities and personalities. And if there is such a resistance to the notion of the group it must be related to specific psychological phenomena.

Research using the experimental method and content analysis of group discussions has shown that the only generally acceptable group is a group of 'buddies'. The work group or the group ascribed by the institution are seen as a threat to individual freedom.

The diagnostic group represents a purer sort of group to the extent that links with the outside are severed. Occupational and social roles remain in the dark, group members have never met previously and call one another by their first names. Experience with such groups or with any groups that recreate the same situation (such as polar expeditions, submarine crews, isolated patrols) has led us to the hypothesis that the group is felt by each of its members as a multi-faceted mirror in which he sees an infinite number of distorted and infinitely repeated reflections of himself. The group situation awakens this image of limitless fragmentation or splitting of the individual's body and personality. As in the psycho-analysis of children, the studies of early schizophrenia have shown that the dismemberment of the body image as such constitutes the core of mental illness. One of the deepest anxieties is that of losing one's physical and psychological unity. The group situation in which I don't know who 'they' are and they don't know who 'I' am is, as such, a source of anxiety. This is why the first meetings are devoted to struggling with this image and this anxiety. Let us cite as an example the extraordinary organizational effort required to 'structure' situations (to elect a chairman, to decide upon an agenda, or to get each person to introduce himself): the more participants feel threatened the less they speak of what they are.

Who am I? This is the most difficult question that the group situation forces on its members. Its difficulty might explain the resistance to living and working in groups, and to the very concept of groups. This hypothesis may be illustrated by several examples.

When a group has managed to overcome fragmentation anxiety, it is because it feels at last a shared emotion in an activity that binds it together, such as laughing or eating together: its unity, as a body, is restored. This metaphor of the body plays an extraordinarily important role in the history of ideas. It is significant that we base supposedly objective knowledge of social groups on this biological metaphor, whereas the *function* of this metaphor is to overcome the anxiety of the dismembered body.

But we should distinguish the different categories of images specific to different types of groups. Since the work of Le Bon, crowd phenomena have been a sociological problem: on the one hand, the crowd is passive, on the other, it behaves paroxysmally. The crowd is a place where beliefs and emotions are contagious (fear becomes panic, anger turns to lynching). Le Bon infers from this contradictory behaviour that the crowd is a woman. For Hugo this woman is drunk; for Zola she is a prostitute. The other metaphor is the oceanic image: crowds are associated with the risk of being swallowed up, drowned, the anxiety of being trampled on, lost. This comparison reactivates the child's primal relation with his mother, a relation that revolves around two antagonistic and complementary images: warmth, food, security, on the one hand, and the earliest representation of internal danger (the devouring mother), on the other. In other w .ds, men in a crowd are motivated by an image they hold in common, the maternal 'imago'.

The gang makes use of another type of phantasy relationship. In the gang, I am looking for others who will neither restrict, nor criticize me, others who are like myself. The image implied here is my own, multiplied, reinforced and justified by the others; it is a reassuring narcissistic image.

The last example is a personal experience that illustrates the psychologist's task when faced with these phantasized difficulties within a real group, the management committee of a company in provincial France. This committee worked so poorly that meetings were no longer held. There were four members: the general manager, the personnel manager, a technical manager and the works manager. Several individual interviews suggested that the problem of the committee was a problem of phantasies.

The former managing director and founder of the company had retired for health reasons and wanted to see his son succeed him. But the board of directors did not agree: it appointed the former sales manager to run the company and made the son personnel manager, out of respect for the father. Thereafter the members of the committee were unanimous in condemning the son's incompetence and blamed him for everything that went wrong. What is more the new general manager did not know the enterprise well, for he had previously lived in Paris where he handled orders: therefore he hesitated to take things in hand. As for the technical manager, he thought he was the only person capable of making the company work and believed that he would become general manager.

The psychologist consulted then discovered that the 'Old Man' was still living in the quarters of the company's managing director – with his son. Despite his retirement, he kept in close touch with what was going on in the company; he had a direct telephone line to his son's office at the factory. The study showed that the father had always run his business in an authoritarian manner. Although his son had wanted to make a career in banking, he had been forced to accept his father's decision and promised the position as managing director. When the board refused, the father told his son to accept the post of personnel manager anyway.

In these circumstances what was the dominant phantasy linking these various persons? It was guilt and remorse towards the dethroned king: the new boss believed that he had usurped the son's place; the son felt betrayed by his father and by his colleagues, so he unconsciously tried to sabotage the new general manager by proving that he was incompetent. As for the technical manager, he also felt that he had been betrayed. The real boss was not there; the image of the former managing director continued to dominate the entire committee.

The work of the psychologist consisted in making each person realize his own attitude with respect to the basic conflict. The new general manager came to understand that he was the boss and had to run things. The son realized why the others were against him: he was sinking his own boat by sabotaging his work and trying to prove that the others were right not to give him the post of general manager; he had to prove himself in the post of personnel manager. The father decided at last to go off on holiday.

In other words, this is the myth of *Totem and Taboo*: the symbolic murder of the father by the brothers allowed the brothers to draw closer together. As long as the father's image remained dominant, rivalry among the pretenders to the throne was the only possible behaviour. When this image was made conscious, the company's problems could be seen in their economic and social reality. (See chapter 6 for a detailed study of this episode.)

Such phantasies may constitute an obstacle to the functioning of the group, as measured by the aims accorded it by society, by its own statutes or by the motivations of its members; they may cause paralysis in the internal functioning of the group or errors in its attitude to reality.

### The group, a primary threat for the individual

Such experience led us to realize that the group constitutes a primary threat to the individual. A human being can exist as a subject only if he feels physically and psychologically coherent. Psychologists and psycho-analysts (Wallon, Gesell, Lacan) have shown the importance of the 'mirror stage' in constructing this coherence: the child plays with mirror images; when he realizes that these are images and not real persons, and that one of these images is his own, he is fascinated by this image that assures him of his own corporal unity and provides a visible support for the notion of his ego. The ego is now constituted as the ideal centre of the personality and is cathected by the subject; in his relations with the physical and social world, the subject relates everything to, and judges everything from the vantage point of his ego; in his relations with others, the assertion of this ego and the will to dominate others are apparent. The psychical life and interpersonal relations evolve and become more complex as the ego ideal and superego come into being. Successive identifications and new functions enrich the ego. Nevertheless, the archaic ego persists as a guarantee of personal unity with the characteristics indicated above, as a phantasmatic and therefore fragile guarantee.

In family life, love, friendship, in groups where there is a bond of identification or love with teacher or leader (in school, scouts, army, church) the ego is protected, even idolized, and relationships between subjects are ambivalent (interaction of hate and love towards the love-object).

The situation is a group (discussion, teams at work, communal life) whose members are at close quarters, but who scarcely know one another and who are far more numerous than in ordinary relations of friendship. There is no one dominating figure through the love of whom each member feels protected and united with the others. In such a situation the individual feels threatened; both his ego and his sense of personal unity seem endangered. In so large a group the others are felt either as identical to oneself or as having no individualized existence; in a very small group (couple, clique) each person feels himself to be a subject and tries to get others to recognize him as such and to satisfy certain of his wishes. In the face to face group, the number of members is limited. I have or may have an individualized perception of each of them; similarly, each of them tries or may try to subject me to his wishes; this convergence of half-dozen wishes on me is unbearable. Each member wants me to be for him what he expects and manoeuvres the situation so that I see things as he does, in order to subordinate me to his ego, reducing me to no more than an object of his wishes. Against one or two persons I can react by affirming *my* ego and *my* wishes. Against so many, I run the risk of no longer existing for myself, of losing all meaning by being torn by so many different demands; my ego is scattered, my beautiful phantasized unity is shattered; the mirror is broken into pieces, which send back to me distorted, different faces. In small groups, if no prior unity exists, either by common goals or attachment to the same person, this co-presence of un-united others arouses a particular sort of anxiety, the anxiety of lost unity, of the broken ego; it summons up the oldest of phantasies, that of dismemberment. The group draws the individual far into his past, to early childhood where he did not yet have consciousness of himself as subject, where he felt incoherent. What is more, by the absence of internal unity, the group imposes on its members a very concrete mental representation of the ego's dispersal.

At the beginning of a group, each person is ill at ease; some retire to their islands and others throw themselves into the heap with a view to taking over the group – two opposed ways of reaching the same goal: preserving the mythical ego (the shared image underlying its behaviour and anxiety) – which is not yet a group. Each person has his share in producing the image of the body dismembered, is frightened by it and seeks to run away from it. The group exists as such only when it can dispel this image by going beyond it. This is the first work (the *aufheben*), in the dialectical sense, which the group does on itself.

It is difficult, however, on account of the intense, primal anxiety aroused by the image of the dismembered body. This anxiety is reinforced by the fact that it is highly contagious in a group of individuals temporarily forced to be together and having no way of avoiding physical proximity. These two elements account for a series of frequently observed reactions. Certain individuals, frozen and 'absent' during the meeting, come to life and open their mouths in the corridors or in a café, after meetings or during breaks. They escape by retreating. Others escape by charging, by filling silences at all costs, by demanding a programme and continually proposing goals that the group is neither motivated nor ready to pursue. Others try to take over, in order to restore the illusory unity to the group and to their own egos. Thus certain ideas are heard again and again, formulated in an insistent, argumentative way. This merely exposes the underlying anxiety in the group. For example, one is told that the meetings are useless, tiresome, endless, nerve-wracking, a waste of time; that one could have worked more efficiently alone in the monitor's office or surrounded by one's faithful secretary and colleagues; that men work better individually than in a group. Or one is told that it is useless to discuss when there is no agreement (but what, then, does one discuss?) or that the meeting is not getting anywhere because the same people do all the talking, the same people are always quiet, and that things would go better if talkative members were quiet and quiet members talkative (which would not change the structure of the group).

This interpretation also takes into account the metaphor, for so long a part of political, moral and religious thinking, one that became a fundamental notion of the pre-scientific knowledge of groups, the metaphor of the living organism. This metaphor has been justly criticized by the pioneers of group psychology and by Sartre in his *Critique de la rasion dialectique* (1960) because it does not correspond to the objective reality of the group and constitutes an epistemological obstacle to a true science of groups. But these criticisms do not explain the persistence of this metaphor through history, the almost natural and ineluctable influence it has had on group participants and leaders. A group is born when a number of individuals bound together by, and anxious over, the omnipresent image of the dismembered body, manage to overcome this anxiety, to reassure themselves and see and feel themselves as human beings, to feel pleasant, common, positive feelings. These feelings may then give rise to concerted actions and thoughts, enabling them to describe the changes that have overcome them. When they come to feel themselves as 'us', when a unit superior to each individual, but in which each has a part, comes into being, then the group is born, like a living 'body'. Each person recognizes himself as a 'member'. The group that at last functions as such becomes differentiated and organized; the biological metaphor remains all-powerful: it gives itself 'organs' of decision-making, executive functions and control. It reaches its apotheosis when it is recognized by the state, institutionalized, acquires a legal status, and is funded: it has become an official body, like the large state 'bodies', themselves organs of the social 'body', as a whole.

If the new-found unity of the group suggests comparisons with living bodies rather than other possible examples of unity (arithmetical, chemical, sexual, architectural), this is because this reconstituted body is the dialectical negation of the primal dismembered body. The metaphor may be factually erroneous, nevertheless it is persuasive and effective, as high-powered ideas often are, because it corresponds to the *phantasized* reality of the group, because it expresses, as do myths, the transformation of the images that govern the underlying forces.


## Group metaphors

Certain collective representations of the group are highly idealized: they make the group the centre of certain values; they provide it with ready-made schemata that it is difficult to get rid of, even in scientific approaches to group phenomena.

1 *The group as living organism* The interdependence of the living body's organs has traditionally served as an analogy for the interdependence of individuals in an active, closely knit group. The origin of this metaphor dates back to the Roman consul, Menenius Agrippa, about 500 B.C. Agrippa put an end to succession by plebiscite, explaining that members could not live without a stomach (and vice versa) and that by feeding the stomach they got the false impression that they were working for someone else, whereas members and stomach are indispensable to the life of all. In Corinthians I (XII, 12-30), the apostle Paul, in decrying internal quarrels and enmities in the Christian assemblies, uses this comparison in an attempt to overcome these quarrels, a comparison that was to influence the notions of group and of society for centuries. Community and church members are, he says, at once diversified and united; no one member can play all roles; the least conspicuous are sometimes the most useful; far from arousing antagonism these differences must be seen in the light of interdependence: all members must help one another. The unity of these differences lies in the single spirit that animates them. Today we would call this spirit unity of beliefs and objectives. Paul concludes with a mystical vision: 'You are the body of Christ and individually members of it.'

The group is a totality, we might say today – a totality that is more than the sum of its parts, as Durkheim pointed out in the nineteenth century. This is quite true. But it doesn't include that internal finality observed in living organisms and for long deified, that which makes the parts act for the preservation of the whole and for the realization of its goals.

Christianized in this way the biological metaphor was enlarged to include a spiritual meaning alongside the original utilitarian one. Just as the soul expresses and guarantees the unity of the body, so a group, or rather a tightly knit group, gives rise to a spirit that expresses and guarantees the morale and efficiency of the group, what is called *esprit de corps*. The truth of the Roman fable and the text from St Paul (group life and activities require division of labour, complementarity of roles, hierarchy of functions and therefore of the persons who perform them, and, if this internal organization is accepted by the members and effective in practice, it helps to forge a high collective morale) lead to a communal mystique. This calls for a high morale, regardless of the cost and the necessary conditions. The large social groupings born in the Middle Ages (the church) or the Revolution (the Army) exalted this mystique.

The progress of biology has further reinforced the metaphor. We learn that one organ, the brain, watches over the unity of the entire body and directs all the others. Leaders become the brains of the group; the classes in power, the brains of the society. We discover the equilibrium of the outside world: neither sociologists nor social psychologists hesitate to speak of a homeostatic function in groups, to assign this function to discussion of meetings and to dream of a permanent social regulation produced by conversations altogether worthy of chemical exchanges within the organism.

This organic metaphor is both tenacious and insidious. Familiar words convey it without our having to think: member, body, corporation, organ, organism, nucleus, cell, symbiosis, etc. However, the difference between the human group and a living organism are essential. In a living organism there are several quite specific functions: nutrition, breathing, circulation, digestion, excretion, reproduction, locomotion. These functions have no group parallel. Furthermore man does not behave like an organ or a cell belonging to a larger unity: he seeks first what is in his interest, what gives him pleasure, he belongs simultaneously to several groups or groupings; he does not necessarily die if cut off from his group; he may change groups or functions in a group, or create new groups. Man is a mobile, mutable organ; groups of men are organisms whose structure changes. These difficulties do not weaken the organic metaphor, so much as lead it to renew itself: if the beautiful unity of the body proves inadequate the beautiful unity of animal societies will provide the moral example people need. For, in this case, what matters is not to know how groups really function, but to forge a myth that captures the energy of individuals, which goes beyond natural human selfishness, which establishes belief in a social order, as did the Platonic archetypes, and makes it easier for men to conform to this order.

Reference to social insects has become a common theme in moral and political literature. The hive is a model of hard work, discipline, organized effort, division of labour, cohesion and the defence of the common good. The good group is a humming swarm that builds, amasses food, and is thrifty with its capital; when it becomes too numerous, part of the group emigrates and colonizes, builds a new city, which reproduces the civilization of the metropolis. By contrast, termites, no doubt because they do not produce nourishing, delicious nectar for men, are the prototype of the bad group: an invading prolific mass, a sinister destructive force.

These are anthropomorphic views. Man is not an insect, governed by instinct, with an undifferentiated nervous system, whose physiological structure changes several times during his lifetime as does his social function, and who lives in a society of females whose queen is the only one able to reproduce. The problems of co-ordinating minds, bringing the males into the picture, of finding an effective balance among the unequal capacities of individuals (whether innate, acquired or socially inherited) are altogether different.

2 *The group as a machine* Let us begin with the socio-analysis of J. and M. Van Bodstaele, who worked with natural groups and organizations, using psycho-sociological methods of investigation. They were influenced by a cybernetic model, which they worked on with the help of a systems specialist, G. Senouillet. The group is a black box, i.e. an opaque system of mechanisms that elude conscious control. The role of a team of socio-analysts is to understand how the black box functions and to enable the group to come to the same understanding. The socio-analysed 'natural' group is encouraged to project its mechanisms on to the team of socio-analysts. This projection enables the team of socio-analysts to provide the group, once more a black box, with an analysis of the way it functions, and so forth. The intervention of the socio-analysts constitutes a feedback or control system.

The artificiality of this schema is obvious. It has, moreover, been abandoned. The principal danger of such schemata is to mask an empirical practice of psycho-sociological work and training behind a pseudo-scientific theory, and to invite 'hit-or-miss' analysis of individuals and groups.

Let us examine more closely this model of the group as a machine. Though fairly recent it harks back, on the one hand, to the Cartesian theory of animals as machines, and, on the other, to Taylorian projects for the rational organization of work. The human organism is regarded as a machine; the problem is to perfect this machine, to maintain it, to adapt it and to make it function as efficiently as possible; like all machines, the human machine is used for the intensive and rationalized exploiting of natural resources. But the human organism is a mediocre machine, which responds only to conspicuous signals, is not watchful, and which tires rapidly.

Under the influence of cybernetics, this schema has been applied to human groups. The group is thus seen as a structure in equilibrium, as a system of interdependent functions, the inter-dependence of which is thought more important than the individuals composing it. The energy that makes this machine work is the motivation of the group members; the programme is drawn up after the perceptions each member may have of the goal have been discussed; the maintenance of the machine is taken care of by discussion; the regulatory mechanism is the scoring of members' satisfaction and dissatisfactions with respect to objectives pursued and the feedback obtained. To train team members to produce and receive feedback and to work in a programmed manner thus becomes the preparation *par excellence* for team work. Group psychologists and trained monitors have devised training courses for work and diagnostic groups based on this schema. Inviting a 'natural' group to project its own image of its functioning on to psycho-sociologists, who then send this image back to them, becomes the model for psycho-sociological work in organizations and for controlled social change. The 'natural' group (management committee, board of directors, etc.) would compare the goals with the results obtained, but until that time insufficiently understood, and would learn to use a control system that would transform the arbitrary or blind functioning of the group.

But when a group functions efficiently, there are also phantasies that enable it to be closely-knit and to work well. When one phantasy is banished, it is replaced by another. The psychologist's job is to recognize these phantasies and, with the group he is working with, bring them to light, and to bring the group itself to elucidate those that impair its functioning.

But removing unconscious images for an individual, a group or a culture is always the most difficult and dramatic of tasks. Moreover, expressions to describe this process such as 'bring to light' are inappropriate positivistic legacies. For the shifting of unconscious images comes about only in crisis situations and through a dramatic process that Hegel tried to conceptualize as *aufheben*, i.e. at once to negate, to overcome and to preserve. These preserved images that one has gone beyond constitute in the end the essential reality of human groups.

# Chapter 6
# The analogy of group and dream: wish-fulfilment in groups

This chapter seeks to apply psycho-analytic theory and practice not only to artificial, temporary groups (psychotherapeutic or training groups), as is often done, but to real or natural social groups (associations, organizations of all kinds, professional meetings, etc.). There are two major obstacles. Professional psycho-analysts are often worried when psycho-analysis is applied outside its natural setting, the individual psyche and its disorders. As for the majority of psycho-sociologists, they have trouble admitting that in real groups, as in therapeutic groups, the role of the unconscious is essential.

Let us begin with Freud's first great discovery: that dreams are wish-fulfilments, that the primary processes are dominant in them despite their intermingling with secondary processes. In other words, the dream, like the neurotic symptom, expresses underlying phantasies. Human beings go into groups as they go into dreams. My thesis is that, in terms of psychological dynamics, the group is a dream.

My first argument is drawn from contemporary attitudes towards groups. For certain specialists in social work, teaching, or management training, for example, the 'group' has become a fetish; groups are formed on the slightest pretext; they are expected to come up with solutions to the problems of economic and administrative organization, higher education, mental health, scientific research, etc. etc. In short, it is a new best of all possible worlds. Perhaps such zealots should be called 'groupites' and the illness afflicting them 'groupitis'. For them the group is a fulfilment in phantasy of their wishes. None the less, resistances to group work, to thinking in group terms, are widely recognized. Freud spoke of the resistances to psycho-analysis. What can be said, then, of the resistances to group dynamics? The concept of the group emerged slowly and painfully. Psycho-sociological studies of collective notions of the group have shown that, for most people, 'the notion of the group is non-existent . . . the group is ephemeral, essentially random in nature. Only interindividual relationships exist' (AFAP, 1961). The group is generally represented as alienating individual personality, freedom and dignity.

The spread of group methods is felt as a threat to individual equanimity and social order. It is inevitable that the group, the privileged locus of wishes, should arouse the ego defence mechanisms of company bosses and union leaders, of psychiatrists, psychologists, teachers and psycho-analysts themselves.

The group situation is thus perceived as anxiety-arousing with the same intensity as it is perceived as phantasy wish-fulfilment. This confirms our notion that the group, like the dream and the symptom, is to be linked to both wishes and defences.

There is nothing original about the notion of the group as a fabulous place where all one's wishes come true. There are many variants of this theme in the history of ideas – Sir Thomas More's Utopia, Rabelais' Abbey of Thélème, Fourier's phalanstery, Jules Romains' 'Les Copains' and enduring legends built up around real situations – the Tahitian paradise, the island of the *Bounty* mutineers of which the anthropologist Alfred Métraux dreamed all his life before committing suicide.

Fourier's phalanstery expresses this perhaps most clearly: man is governed by a dozen basic emotions, which, according to the individual, are of greater or lesser importance; this gives 810 possible characters on the basis of a hierarchical classification of these emotions; the ideal group or phalange is made up of two of these 810 possibilities, a man and a woman: thus each person is sure at all times of finding the task and the partner best suited to the economy of his wishes. The dream of a group that would satisfy all wishes immediately and unconditionally, where each member would find wishes complementary to his own, is the dream of a society ruled exclusively by the pleasure principle, by a communal life in which the primary processes would act in their pure state. This is the dream of a dream. In the gang, a real group, we can see at work the attempt to bring this Utopia to life. The group maintains the mirage of the imaginary fulfilment of this wish that is so fascinating for its members, but it is, of course, an unattainable wish, the absolute qualities of the impossible wish.

Such a wish, as the psycho-analytically informed reader will have recognized, is the forbidden, Oedipal, wish. As we see it, this accounts for the anti-group attitudes and reactions that have always existed everywhere: for individual and for society, both of whom defend the stability of their psychical structure, the group evokes a danger, the danger of forbidden wishes. Hence, the accusations, usually without foundation, that have been levelled at groups, sects, ghettoes, clans, orders of chivalry, freemasons, etc.: those who meet in secret are suspected of evil-doing; any factional activity is felt by others as an expression of the wish to escape the wishes repressed by the censure of prohibition. It is always the wishes repressed by an individual or a society that are projected in such suspicions: those who meet behind closed doors must be indulging in sexual debauchery, sadistic cruelty, exhibitionism, defilement or conspiracy to murder. As, from time to time, this is true, the reality is used to give credence to a phantasy, a natural human tendency that culminates in neurosis or psychosis.

This also explains why the group often constitutes a privileged dimension for the practice of perversions. It has long been noted how easy it is for perverse individuals to become group leaders and how easily groups become pathogenic or criminal: rather than being realized in phantasy in the group, forbidden wishes lead to acting out or the phantasy finds a specific mode of fulfilment. For example a relatively new form of crime has recently attracted the attention of police and courts because of its rise among rich adolescents in large cities: collective rape. One can guess what the underlying imaginary quest for such behaviour might be: the fulfilment in common by brothers of incest (wished for and prohibited) towards a sister or mother substitute.

The often raised question of the influence of individual personalities on group dynamics would get farther if the specific ways in which the hysteric, obsessive, paranoid, depressive, homosexual or those with character disorders made use of wishes were compared with the phantasized wishes of these persons in *group* situations. This would enable research to go beyond the intellectual or socio-economic level of group members.

Some of these inter-relationships are already known: a group, like a gang, weakens the defences and strengthens the wishes of its members; it favours the pleasure principle over the reality principle; it is thus attractive to, for example, lost souls, psychopaths, and the emotionally stunted. Others to whom it might be attractive include disturbed individuals at the limit of psychosis, with archaic underlying anxieties and phantasies, for example, an important man struggling with a tendency towards depersonalization and 'hyperactive overcompensation', diffuses through the group so strong an anxiety of having been abandoned that he becomes either its tyrannical leader or a deviant to be rejected. In the first case, his authority over the group derives from the fact that it is he who sharpens each member's own anxiety at being abandoned; in the second, he is really inflicted with the abandonment that the group fears and arouses.

We also know that obsessives are all too pleased to chair debates: indeed they often feel a vocation as monitor of training sessions, since they then avoid any possibility of being subjected to questioning themselves and, by programming the meeting, controlling its progress, they constantly lie in wait for any wish that might spread contagiously through the group. When a brilliant, narcissistic and perverse individual with a character disorder belongs to a group, such phenomena as the cult of the personality, disparaging adversaries or those who hesitate, or lyrical, even prophetic, exaltation, an intellectualized homosexual excitation becomes dominant: his phantasy becomes a trap for the entire group. 'Follow me and I will lead you to the end of the world, to the end of knowledge, to the heights of power.' Translating this into psycho-analytic terms: the first, lost love of the mother will be regained by us all forever; the prohibited possession of that which the Oedipus complex made it necessary to give up has become possible again.

One last example. Some psychologists teach training group monitors to observe without participating and to consolidate their position as observers by filling up observation grids made out in advance. This is the approach of a pyromaniac who lights fires to watch them burn; it encourages the consciousness to distance itself from wishes: I don't have wishes; as a voyeur, I 'eat up' the burning desire of others. Such a monitor lives death and wants to see the others living life. In other words, he wants to see living wishes in others, not in himself. One can imagine the difficulties that such a death phantasy expressed by the monitor, in a nonverbal way, induce in the group. No psycho-sociological techniques can get rid of them if nobody in the group formulates the phantasy of the group's death and the corollary phantasy of the monitor's death.

Let us return to our analogy of the group and the dream. It can be summed up as follows:

Firstly, wishes in groups and wishes in dreams are repressed and unfulfilled whether in terms of inter-individual relations, private life, or social life. This is illustrated by a few everyday observations: a group of teenagers breaks up with the advent of girl friends; the imperialism of both the couple and the group make coexistence difficult, as each tries to take over the individual as completely as possible. One of the resistances to group life derives from the fact that the theoretical equality of the members forms an obstacle to the Oedipal wish of group members to have sexual relationships with their women, shared in common with their leader.

But one must go farther still. The wishes in groups and in dreams are repressed wishes from early childhood. This is an important and novel idea and one that enables us to account for observations that presented difficulties previously. In play, groups of children imitate adult activities, they play at football, war, cops and robbers, mother and father; in short, they play at being adults. Conversely, when adults are gathered in a group that leaves them a certain liberty, as in a training group, or a friendly gathering, they become children again and behave like children (see Muller, 1965).

Collective monologues, puns and stories, dirty jokes, speaking louder than the others, settling grudges, needing a leader to undertake any task – all this is rampant. The group psycho-analyst has always known that the free group situation produces regression: this regression provides the material necessary for his curative technique. But how can the psycho-sociologist using this technique resolve the antagonism between his aim of training (not curing) adults and the method that he uses, which makes them become children again?

Thirdly, wishes in groups and dreams may be not only wishes frozen into a symptom or a pathological structure, but also the emerging desire of the unconscious, a desire whose meaning is still not understood, but heralds real undertakings in which it will seek fulfilment. Freud explained premonitory dreams in this way. Alexander the Great, exhausted by his siege of Tyr, dreamed of a satyr, which he interpreted as 'SA', the Doric form of the possessive adjective and 'TYR': Tyr is yours. The following day he took Tyr. The dream had revealed to Alexander his own confidence in victory: all he had to do was attack in order to be victorious. The same thing holds true for groups. Some dream their wishes and, content with hallucinations, don't *do* anything. Others act out their wishes, but with a substitute or derivative object. In groups, as in dreams, what happens is the result of the displacement, condensation and symbolic representation of wishes. In any case, it is well known to sociologists that the real activities of a group seldom correspond to its avowed or official goals. Moreover, it would be easy to describe certain aspects of a group's ideology or beliefs as a rationalization, overcompensation, a reaction formation, or even an annulment of wishes actually fulfilled in practice.

Neurotics have permanent symptoms; normal persons have a few occasionally. But both dream: phantasies are part of the psychical apparatus in all human beings. It has been said that neurosis is individual symbolism, poetry or myth. Sanity also has its own symbolism. Some individuals choose activities and partners that reveal their phantasies and indicate their destinies. In a similar way, all groups have their symbolism, their myths. In other words, the group is an arena in which the unconsciouses of members interact and produce phantasized constructions that may be short-lived or stable, paralysing or stimulating. Here we part company with Bion (1961), who recognized that when a group is blocked, one must look for the core of phantasized ideas that hinder its rational functioning. But he seems to think that a group functions rationally when its phantasies, once formulated, disappear. Our experience has shown the opposite: where there is a group there are phantasies that circulate among its members; these bind group members together both in their activities and in their anxieties. Freud knew this too. In the only article he wrote on the group, *Group Psychology and the Analysis of the Ego* (1921), he showed that religious or military groups are closely knit, that they have a high morale and that their energy level leads to the success of their activities when members identify with their leader and when a common ego ideal has counterbalanced differences between individual egos.

Let us take an allegorical example. In the eleventh century, Western Christendom set out on the Crusades to reconquer the Holy Land in order to forget about poverty, plague and brigandage. The Crusades were to change relations between East and West, between feudal lords and vassals. Each group, we believe, relives in its own way the mythical model of the Crusades (or the quest for the Holy Grail): its wish defines a holy place that it has been deprived of and which it intends to recapture (to convert, take over a market, make a product, change habits, create a new style). This holy place is the re-possession of the mother, whom the Oedipus complex and incest taboo have taken away from us. We do battle with the infidels who illegitimately occupy this territory; in the group, members play complementary roles in re-conquering it. Some advocate a crusade, others organize; some carry the flag, others arms, others give money; all leave their families, their countries and, if they don't die on the road, meet with the plague, that is to say, to translate my mythical tale into clearer terms, castration anxiety.

Gangs of children illustrate this schema with great simplicity. Their main activity, failure in which makes impossible all further activity, is the building of a hut (in the middle of a forest, for example) where they meet for various ceremonies, from picnics to initiations and wars against rival gangs. The hut is also the place where the gang hides its treasure. Of no value to adults, this treasure – a few stones, provisions, the booty of ransoms or raids – is valuable to them, for it is what makes the hut sacred, by expressing wishes and bearing witness to a common dream. The rival gang is in no doubt about it: to get back at the enemy, the rival gang tries to destroy the hut and scatter the treasure, the unifying group phantasy. In natural or temporary adult groups, the hut is often replaced by the café, where the participants, as subordinates, can get together without their monitor or leader and speak together freely and happily, i.e. can share their dreams and set some phantasy group in opposition to their real group. In training seminars, the interpretation of the phantasy of a café-hut is necessary.

This phantasy that underlies real groups is accessible to the psycho-analyst who remains a psycho-analyst when trying to understand a real group. It often escapes the psycho-sociologist when he has not been trained and is not motivated to recognize it, as in the case of Kurt Lewin's (1942) interpretation of changes in the alimentary habits of American housewives referred to earlier.

The psycho-sociologist who runs a diagnostic group or who is consulted by a company finds himself in a psycho-analytic situation: the moorings of the secondary processes (perception, judgment, reasoning) are cast aside and phantasizing comes to the fore. Whether he be a psychiatrist, a psychologist, a psychoanalyst or a sociologist in a real group – from the simple everyday meeting to a learned conference – the person responsible for understanding what is hidden and for telling the truth, that is to say, for putting the phantasy into words, by his very presence, arouses what has been up to that time repressed, immobilized and frozen in the unconscious of group members. Through what is said to him, and indirectly through the official or informal requests addressed to him, phantasies begin to take a grip on the group. If he allows this to happen, if he consents to the communication of the unconscious, if he allows himself to be affected by the phantasies, but welcomes them, shows that he recognizes them and communicates what he knows, the inter-individual unconscious will begin to change. And the psychiatrist in his asylum, the psycho-analyst in his meeting, the psycho-sociologist in his enterprise will be the participating observers of these changes in the unconscious processes underlying the group or institution. Particularly easy to observe will be the change from a state where the phantasy is frozen in a symptom, when the group is sick, to the freeing of its phantasizing.

A diagnostic group run in this spirit often enables one to witness the freeing of creative energy previously captivated in phantasies, if, as in psycho-analysis, the interpretation of the phantasies underlying resistance has been accurate. This was the case with a diagnostic group I ran in the South of France. For an hour and a half, it spontaneously composed a sort of prose poem on the nearby Camargue; just as Homer's epics told of the exploits of warriors at Troy and the adventures of their return, this poem narrated the wanderings of the group, its anxieties and adventures in allegorical, that is to say, metaphorical, language through the lives of animals and free men; in doing so, the group found its Camargue, its sacred place, the phantasy object of its wishes.

The group, like the dream, deals with the same basic drives: the libidinal, the aggressive and, we believe, the death drive. In fact, although the hypothesis of such a drive is controversial among psychoanalysts themselves, certain group phenomena seem to support this hypothesis. Phantasies are unconscious constructions in which the psychical representatives of the drive are imprisoned by the ego's defences: the strength of the wish is entirely located in phantasy. But the phantasy, endowed with such force, does not remain inactive; it penetrates the body (for example, a symptom of hysteria), our waking thoughts (for example, obsessional mulling over), action (in which it may be released), external reality (on to which it may be projected). In the group the only psychical processes are those known and described for the individual's psychic apparatus. The major difficulty in all groups – considering their action while taking into account the segments of reality surrounding them and which they wish to act upon – stems from prevalent individual phantasies. These come from certain members, filter through the thought patterns, acts and perceptions of reality and, in the others, either become contagious or arouse resistance. The errors of judgment and internal dissension found in groups are due principally to this. But to get a group to see its relation to the phantasies that deform its thought and action is not an easy thing to do. I know of two ways, though there may be others: either a prestigious personality – who fulfils the role Freud described for the ego ideal – modifies the conceptions of the group, which then adopts these modifications; or people begin speaking freely among themselves *outside* the collective situation in which omnipotent unconscious phantasies paralysed them; when they do begin to speak freely words that were frozen begin to thaw out (this is non-directivism) and a fresh analysis of reality emerges. But in both these cases the process of disengagement requires mounting tension culminating in a crisis, dramatic upheavals, even rifts, which eliminate the most rigid persons or those whose defence mechanisms or anxieties coincide most closely with the dominant phantasies. The film *Twelve Angry Men* provides an example of such a collective crisis and of the final resistance of a member of the jury who relived the rejection of his own son while following the acts of the accused.

I include here two examples of the importance of phantasies in groups.

In another diagnostic group that also took place in the south of France, and which lasted three days, I went out of the room at a break on the second day. The rest of the group remained and worked on a drawing on the blackboard. In this drawing the group is a boat in which everyone is rowing except the monitor, who is at the helm. From the mast flies a flag depicting a heart, the symbol of mutual love. The boat is going to Cytherea. At the other end of the blackboard it has landed on the island. A naked man and woman are separated by a tree. On the tree above them, the monitor appears in the form of a snake.

This drawing reveals the phantasy that had hindered the progress of the training group. But the understanding of others was blocked by the mutual declaration of love symbolized by the flag; the group obstinately refused to analyse itself. Cytherea is a dream of exclusively libidinal human relationships. But Cytherea becomes Paradise where Adam and Eve, ashamed of their nudity, are together under the tree of knowledge of good and evil: they know that the wished-for love is prohibited and they are standing apart.

I was thus able to interpret the phantasy underlying the group's resistance: knowing one another, knowing group phenomena is eating the forbidden fruit of the tree of knowledge, knowing the secret of birth, the mystery of procreation; for the child, it is witnessing the primal scene, i.e. the act by which his parents conceived him. The feeling of guilt is so strong that it makes a thirst for knowledge unacceptable. The psychological knowledge that the participants had come for was felt to be an inaccessible secret, a forbidden mystery. The need to understand, freed in this way, led to a joint request for an extra session, where it was possible to clarify certain aspects of the group's experience.

A word on group anxieties. The group situation arouses certain specific anxieties. While Elliott Jaques (1955) and Max Pagès (1968) have recognized this, we agree with the criticism that Pontalis (1963) has made of their work: to identify anxiety is not enough if the phantasies underlying it are not elucidated at the same time. In addition to Oedipal anxieties, which we have already mentioned, the group arouses pregenital anxieties.

The anxiety of breaking apart physically and psychologically comes first. In an anonymous situation each person feels this anxiety. But non-directive groups reveal here anxieties latent in all groups, real or artificial. The Kestembergs (1966) cite the case of a girl who had miraculously survived Auschwitz and whose psychotherapy proved difficult for Edith Gyomroi, her psychotherapist: 'This adolescent willingly spoke of events and actions that she imputed to herself and which were manifestly contradictory.' She spoke of having seen or done things at the same time that could not have happened simultaneously. The analyst took this for a mythomaniac attitude. 'In fact, thanks to progress in the analysis, the adolescent realized that the events and actions that she had attributed to herself belonged in reality to another child in the group: she had felt that she and the other children were one: she had identified herself with each of them, without being able to isolate her own identity.'

The anxieties and phantasies of groups that stem from early childhood and are prior to ego-formation remain to be studied. The fact that the unified group calls itself a 'body' and those who compose its 'members' seems to us to be the survival, in everyday language, of the fragmentation anxiety aroused by the group situation.

Other group phantasies revolve around what Melanie Klein has described as the paranoid-schizoid position and the depressive position. A psycho-sociologist working with a real group or institution arouses one of these types of primitive anxiety and must first of all deal with the group's defensive reactions towards him. He is powerless as long as he has not been able to formulate, in serious discussion, the underlying phantasies of a spy sent to destroy the group or a disparaging judge who expects the group to conform to his dictates. The group's request is aimed at the psycho-sociologist – or the expert generally speaking – either as someone who is able but refuses to give back the good lost object (depressive anxiety) or as a bad object to be expelled (persecutory anxiety).

The parental imagos discovered by Freud play a role in structuring certain group situations. How, for example can one understand the apparently so disparate phenomena to be observed in a spontaneously formed crowd without the concept of the unity underlying an imago? The density of the human aggregate, that mass in which each person feels small, at once drowned, lost, threatened by suffocation, fearful of being crushed and buried, but also sheltered, enveloped, warmed, the long periods of replete apathy, paroxysmal periods of collective anxiety, the panic of collective excitation (convulsions dances, drinking parties, fornications, mutilations) or of collective anger (lynchings, wanton destruction of objects and persons). Does all this not point to the central, unconscious presence of the maternal imago in human groups, reduced to an infant's mouth, to devouring teeth, to the warmth of breasts and to a gigantic stomach in which swarm hundreds of digested substances and beings waiting to be born?

Popular imagery and texts on crowds confirm this if one takes them literally: the crowd, it is said, is a capricious, changeable, sentimental woman, ready to give herself to the first person who knows how to please or to dominate her; the crowd is a drug that puts conscience and reason to sleep, frees the imagination, emotions and instincts; the crowd is a strong drink that makes you drunk; the crowd roars like the ocean, breaks into waves, destroys like a tidal wave. The crowd is compared to a drunk, delirious, dangerous woman, to an orgy ending in human sacrifices; the crowd, a man-eater or quicksand, swallows up those imprudent enough to fall into her midst; the crowd exerts the attraction and arouses the fear of vertigo; it is a gaping void that fascinates and captures by the thousand those who hurl themselves into it; the crowd is a suckling child, wailing, yelling, expressing himself in monosyllables, humming, who demands to eat, to drink and to bite, who flies into a rage, defecates, bares its teeth, stamps, kicks, screams, goes to sleep suddenly, exhausted by exercise, pure milk and fresh air. The emotional instability, physical impulsiveness, proneness to anxiety, the concrete, intuitive, syncretic character of its ideas, the thinking in terms of pairs of opposites, etc., described by Le Bon (1895), can be explained only by the presence of this imago. This also explains the well-known solution to the dangers of a spontaneous crowd: surround it, infiltrate it, organize and discipline it, in other words, establish the supremacy of the paternal over the maternal imago.

Is it possible to apply the second Freudian meta-psychology to groups? Do the id, the ego and the superego have meaning for group dynamics?

The id is present in a group in the following way: the number of individuals produces libidinal and aggressive drives in each of them; drives achieve greater intensity in groups. From a structural psycho-analytic point of view, there is no other problem in a group than that of satisfying these drives. This seems to corroborate rather well the clinical observation of groups.

The drive or id is formed at the same time as the ego, which, at first archaic and physical, becomes better able to carry out the functions of control, of choice between the drives and of the reality sense. The archaic ego, which the group takes on to defend itself from its own drives and to take reality into account is the leader or the chairman of the session. But, starting with the individual egos of members, groups tend to construct a common, fictive, relatively autonomous ego, which can make the group self-regulating and guarantee both control over drives and a perception of reality, accompanied by a critical sense.

With this fictive group ego the group builds a superego – rules born of common consent and binding on all – and a group ego ideal, whose functioning in the army and the church was described by Freud. If one adds the additional distinction between the ego ideal and the ideal ego, we should describe the primacy of the ideal ego, that is to say, the ideal of narcissistic omnipotence, in certain gangs.

In conclusion, let us say there are two very different ways of studying groups depending upon the level of analysis.

In the first case the small human group is seen as a miniature society: in fact one finds in it, in a nascent state, magnified or simplified, certain fundamental social phenomena: the circulation of information, the exercise of authority, variations of 'atmosphere' and 'morale', resistance to change, negotiations, pressures, tensions between the common interest and the satisfaction of individual needs, conflicts between the requirements of organization and the preservation of individual differences and of creative spontaneity, norms, codes, beliefs, a common language, commemorations, hesitation between toleration and ostracism of deviants and cliques that weaken the collective unity, antagonism between outstanding personalities, generally re-enforced by those of corresponding sub-groups. Much revolves around such themes: as majority-minority-unanimity, scapegoats, heroes, leaders and masses. In this experimental society, restricted in size and duration, and from which certain reformers have extracted a model of utopia, it is possible to live and study several problems of political philosophy, sociology and social history, so long as these studies do not relate to the size and duration of real societies. Such studies might well be called 'microsociology'.

But a small human group is also a place where people meet, a place of confrontation and of bonds between these people outside of any social reference. Affinities and clashes of personality thrive. Individual wishes, always just beneath the surface, cry out violently to be fulfilled: a call for help and protection, the lust for power, exhibitionism, denigration or contradiction, curiosity, admiration, idolatry. The narcissism of each individual meets with sweet victories and bitter defeats, victories over others where they can be treated as the objects of my wishes, wounds that other narcissistic beings, willy nilly, give me by their very existence. Anxiety common to the group arouses the oldest individual fears. The fear of being a group, of losing one's identity in the group, is no doubt the first difficulty encountered. In the depths of these fears are phantasies, unconscious imaginary scenarios in which the most secret wishes meet the most archaic defence mechanisms.

From these vulnerable points emerge works of art, madness and crime as well as dreams and day-dreams. Here the group is the laboratory for other experiments: over and above the programmes, the avowed goals, the work done together, the group arouses the resistance of all these individual phantasies. Because unconscious can communicate directly with unconscious, the disparity between these phantasies produces group disunity; the anxiety aroused by predominant phantasies produces the paralysis of the group; the convergence of phantasies may produce an ideology even a mythology, both defensive and peculiar to the group, or it may provide the group with the energy for its work. To succeed in the latter is the goal of the psycho-analytic study of groups, whether they be temporary (e.g. training and psychotherapeutic groups) or real.

# Chapter 7
# The group illusion

To the three major social forms of illusions that Freud described in *Totem and Taboo* (1912-1913) and elaborated in subsequent works – the religious illusion, the artistic illusion and the philosophical illusion, which I would prefer to call the ideological illusion – I propose to add a fourth: the group illusion.

It now seems to me that the analogy between the group and the dream may be carried farther. First, the dream, individual illusion *par excellence*, is produced in sleep, a state in which the cathexis of external reality is withdrawn. But training groups also take place in a situation of cultural isolation, outside social and occupational life during a period that interrupts the rhythms of everyday life. External reality is suspended. To this withdrawal of object cathexis corresponds, in economic terms, an over-cathexis of the group, that is to say, freed libido is cathected in the only reality present: the here and now. The group thus becomes a libidinal object. The observation of real groups confirms that there too one finds the same economic equilibrium as Freud discovered in the individual psychical apparatus between object libido and ego libido: there is an inverse correlation between group cathexis of reality and narcissistic cathexis of the group.

Second, in groups as in dreams, the psychical apparatus is subject to a triple regression: chronological, topographical and formal or structural. The group situation produces a chronological regression not only to secondary narcissism, but even – and this is one of my theses – to primary narcissism. To limit myself to the example of secondary narcissism, confrontation with others is felt as an anxiety-arousing threat of the loss of ego identity. This in turn produces narcissistic counter-cathexis, which leads to well-known difficulties in communication and cohesion in group work or life. The group situation opens the narcissistic wound in its members. Some react by protectively withdrawing, others do so by obstinately asserting their egos.

Like the dream the group produces topographical regression. Neither the ego nor the superego is able to control sufficiently the representations of certain drives. The id and the ego ideal then control the psychical apparatus. The ego ideal, inadequately differentiated from the id, tries to realize a symbiosis with the breast, source of all pleasure, and the introjective restoration of this first part object of lost love. In the eyes of its members the group becomes a substitute for this lost object.

The third type of regression, formal regression, is to be seen in the use of archaic expressions close to primary processes, like figurative thinking (mytho-poetic discourse, puns, interjections, onomatopoeias, gurglings) or infra-linguistic signs (gestures, looks, smiles, postures, mimics) taken from the expression of the feelings of – or the first symbols discovered by – the child playing with his mother and his surroundings. From this stems the difficulty of maintaining discussion between members at the level of secondary processes, a difficulty frequently encountered in school or in learned societies.

Regression in group situations or in sleep is expressed by other spatio-temporal characteristics. Our observations have led my colleagues and myself to note that the group's phantasy space is the projection of the mother's phantasized body, with its internal organs, including the phallus and children-faeces. Time also becomes regressive: it loses its chronological character and becomes reversible, thus allowing for repetition and the eternal return, and the phantasy of a return to origins and a new beginning.

Human beings come to groups as they might come to a Utopia. The spatio-temporal category specific to the group is elsewhere. If it is true that the unconscious is eternal, indestructible, it is also other. It is an ever-present realm that each of us always situates elsewhere. To its members, the group appears in phantasy as a place outside time, as the other side of the mirror, where the unconscious will at last be represented and realized so long as it is what the group shares in common.

The group's elsewhere, its collective Utopia, for example, serves as a defence mechanism for each individual against his unconscious; in groups the unconscious is grasped not as an intra-individual reality, but as one that is inter- and trans-individual. However, it can be apprehended by a common code, as I have shown (Anzieu, 1970b); each part of the world makes sense in terms of a phantasy and vice versa; each unconscious process is named as metaphor or metonymy of a natural phenomenon. Thus, while being defences, group psychical productions fulfil a transitional role between internal psychical reality and the natural, external social reality.

I have just shown that a group may produce an illusion just as can an individual. I shall call the 'group illusion' a particular psychical state to be found in both natural and therapeutic or training groups and which is spontaneously verbalized under the following form: 'We get on well together; we are a good group; our head or our monitor is a good head, a good monitor.' I will study this group phenomenon by presenting three cases. These have guided by reflexion and practice working in true psycho-analytic fashion with training groups.

## Case 1

I was monitor of this diagnostic group held in the South of France over a period of four days, during which time there were twelve sessions of one hour and a half each. I am grateful to one of the two non-participant observers, René Kaës, for having written a detailed account. Thinking over the functioning of this group, I began for the first time to be aware of the existence of the group illusion.

The thirteen participants, six women and seven men, were all 'psychists', as William James called them; in other words all were persons who worked with psychical, not external reality; they were psychologists, psychiatrists, teachers and social workers.

The first session was held on the afternoon of the first day. It began with a protest against the role of the observers; it continued with a presentation by each member of his expectations. On several occasions the idea of knowledge of others, which would 'level differences, set everyone on a equal footing', appeared. The only explicitly mentioned difference was between the monitor and the other members. Nicolas, one of the participants, wanting to play psycho-analyst, drew the latent aggressivity of the group to himself. The session ended with an admission that deeply affected the group. Léonore, who had already aroused the attention of all the men when she introduced herself as a woman doctor, declared that she was a family planning specialist and had previously belonged to a group of social workers: for a long time this group went on meeting ('we didn't want to die,' she said) and each of its members had been very satisfied ('we all got on well together').

The group's destiny was decided there: the negative transference, which members did not dare direct to the monitor, was displaced on to Nicolas, who retained this function to the end. Léonore, by presenting herself as family planning specialist, was unconsciously perceived by most as the one who knew the secrets of life, birth and sex and had mastered them. Later I was to interpret her function as the group's good mother, but this interpretation was ineffective because it did not go far enough: it seemed to me in fact that the group expected nothing more of me now that it expected knowledge from Léonore, that is to say, the revelation of the mysteries of seduction, of the primal scene and of sexual differences. The group was to express this clearly later in a drawing on the blackboard. I was to interpret this drawing, by a narcissistic counter-transference, as related to me, whereas it expressed the group's relation to Léonore from which I was excluded. In these circumstances, the Utopia that Léonore proposed of the 'good', inseparable group in which everyone loves everyone else was naturally adopted: we are going to be a good group, too, and Léonore will become the good monitor. In fact, after the end of the course, the group was to get together regularly and for a long time, without either its monitor or observers (all three male).

The following sessions, the evening of the first day and the morning of the second, dwelt on the silent and frustrating neutrality of the monitor, a neutrality that Léonore also adopted for a time. She explained why in a revealing fashion: she had been psycho-analysed. The other psychists spoke of their professional powerlessness in their jobs. Then they described the group as a sphere without an opening, in which each member was suffocating, isolated and exposed to the dangers of an internal struggle without rules. They dreamt of the opposite, a group where monitor and observers lived together with group members and mingled with them. They forced the monitor to speak, then, fearing a breach, were divided for and against what he said. Participants who got on well together began to pair up, men with men, women with women. Only Léonore chose a partner of the opposite sex. The presence of two bearded group members (Nicolas and Raoul) gave rise to the anguishing question: who is wearing the beard, the pants, here?

The group illusion made its appearance during lunch on the second day, after the fourth session, as often happens. The group members were together without observers or monitor. At the beginning of the fifth session, in accordance with the rule of restitution, the participants explained that, for the first time, they had eaten together and had been pleased to sense the cohesion of their group; they also unanimously expressed their dissatisfaction with their monitor; some proposed to exclude him altogether, although he would be paid.

The monitor interpreted the dependency on and ambivalence towards himself that members had expressed. Some felt that interpretation came from an awe-inspiring father who was to be got rid of. Others said they were satisfied with its tone and content. At once the collective aggressivity was directed towards the substitute: after a mock vote, the notebook in which Nicolas was writing his observations was taken from him (nobody criticized the monitor for taking notes). Nicolas was asked to speak of his prior relations with the monitor when he was a student. From here, group members were quizzed on what they knew of the monitor before the group. Léonore declared that from the beginning she had not needed the monitor: she ignored him before the course and had continued to ignore him since. The group phantasy of excluding the monitor appeared to several persons thereafter as the group's fulfilment of Léonore's wish. She denied this. The monitor interpreted the group's desire to have a good mother instead of a male of dubious powers. As I said, this interpretation was correct but incomplete and was not enough to make the group grasp and go beyond fascination with the phantasy of a narcissistic collective fusion with the image of an all-powerful mother. So ended the afternoon of the second day.

During the seventh session, on the morning of the third day, there was a discussion about the perturbing effect of parental conflicts on children, an unconscious allusion to the struggle for power over the group between Léonore and the monitor. Suddenly the theme of equality from the first session reappeared: 'Let the mountains and valleys be levelled, kings dethroned, everyone reduced to a common denominator.' Except for the monitor and the observers, who introduced distance, judgment and difference, everyone must belong to the ranks, nobody should set himself apart: in such conditions, all group members like one another.

A few men tell Léonore how attractive she is. This arouses the jealous aggressivity of several female group members. She is so put out that at the break several persons try to boost her morale.

In the eighth session the group illusion intensifies: in a burst of warm feelings the group 'takes back', by paying attention to their anxieties, those members who had 'suffered' most during the course, Léonore and even the monitor, who was spoken of as a 'most important member'.

At lunch the warm feelings begin to ebb away. As they did the day before, the participants go to the university caféteria; it is late; the waitress wants to have them fill up the free seats instead of putting them at two clean tables. Raoul tells her off so vehemently that she bursts into tears, and lets them sit together. The other participants stayed quiet. Thus the group, which pretended to be loving and strictly egalitarian, was capable of tyranny over an employee in order to eat together, i.e. to preserve its group illusion. This second meal together was gloomy: members admitted that they were feeling defeated and bogged down.

When he learned this, the monitor took advantage of the situation to stress the group's avoidance of any situation in which it might lose its unity and equality, by avowing either affinities that might lead to heterosexual couples or internal antagonism.

Raoul said something that was to have considerable impact: apparently he and Nicolas owned a boat; their experience as co-owners had much in common with their experience of the group; each of them felt that there were more disadvantages to it than advantages. Raoul's comments gave rise to intense phantasizing. We are together on the same boat, it was said, for better or for worse. The group became a galley in which everyone was rowing at his own rhythm; it was advancing blindly, in heavy seas. Then, at last, came the question: Could the plague victims remain? Yes, they had the plague on board. Only then was the incident with the waitress reported, briefly and factually.

During the break in the middle of the afternoon, before the tenth session, a few participants drew a galley on the blackboard from which projected a dozen oars of equal length; from the mast fluttered the yellow quarantine flag; death was on board. The commentary was provided at once: love is a plague. The figure-head is a woman with large, naked breasts. Two fishy observers are coming out of the water. The group then indulged in associations of collective ideas: the monitor was at the helm; the boat might be a crusadership on its way to reconquer the Holy Land or that of lovers setting out for Cytherea.

The monitor related the episode of the drawing to the caféteria incident. There was a desire in the group for a superficial unity to plaster over the contradiction between declared principles and actual behaviour. A heated debate broke out over the caféteria incident. Léonore vehemently reproached Raoul for venting his temper on the waitress, whom she admitted she had identified with. Are women mere servants of men? Suddenly, it was realized that this abhorred domination functioned here and now; the youngest and, if I may say so, most spinsterly of the female participants had expressed this clearly in her refusal to row with the others; nobody paid any attention to her and from then on she stayed out of discussions altogether. When the monitor intervened it was discovered that in the group the women spoke less easily than the men, the single men and women than those married. The monitor also stressed the importance of sexual rivalry. Raoul mentioned that one day a woman pulled so hard on his beard that she pulled some skin off. Anxiety over sexual differences was intense: who was a man, who was a woman and what made the difference?

The two last sessions were held on the morning of the fourth day. The eleventh began with the words: 'At noon we will go our separate ways'; it continued with expressions of death anxiety alternating with attempts to grasp the experience of the three preceding days. Participants recognized that they had agreed to see themselves only through the ideal image of a phalanstery, a boat or island where love and order, now made compatible, would enable each of them to fulfil his wishes.

During the pause before the final session a few participants again went to the blackboard. They drew the Paradise of the Garden of Eden, the supposed goal of this group. A man and a woman are standing naked on either side of a palm tree, the Tree of Knowledge, in which sits the serpent-monitor. After a long silence it was explained, with some difficulty, that the woman might be Léonore. Her arms were amputated, 'in order not to be able to defend herself against the sexual advances of the man'. After another silence, participants add that the two are pure, naïve, innocent.

The anxiety of the 'end' of the group returned; the drawing was forgotten and the summing up continued. Nobody was listening to what the monitor said. Another theme appeared: an afterlife for the group. 'The group dies, but it will bear fruit . . .'; 'When I was a Catholic, the mystical body was a very potent idea . . .'; 'One has to feel that there is something beyond death!' The participants decided to meet in the future and declared that the session had helped them to live better, progress had been made; they hoped that 'the world we are now going to return to has changed on account of the experience in the boat'.

Nicolas, however, was not euphoric; he was isolated, silent, excluded: 'Since his tongue was cut off he keeps quiet.' The group, it is added, began to exist by putting him down, because he did not accept its law. He had to be 'castrated, his notebook taken away'; what was condemned in him, it was repeated, was his identification with the monitor.

Bringing up the matter of difference again gave rise to an aggressive, deprecatory judgment on the course: the experience was artificial, the presence of the monitor introduced inequality, elsewhere there were groups where inter-individual relationships could be satisfying both for a group and for a couple. Léonore's suggestion that the group should go on meeting was accepted.

The monitor announced the end of the session and of the course, but the participants asked to stay around the table, and compelled the observers and monitor to set up a thirteenth session during which three questions were to be discussed.

The first was directed at the observers: how had they experienced those three days? Their answer removed the fear that they had been spies. This proved that the persecution anxiety had been present in the group all along and that it had been linked with the group illusion.

The second question was put to the monitor: how did this group compare with others he had worked with? I answered by repeating that in this group people had tried above all to get to know one another, hence the fact that group tensions had been treated as conflicts between persons rather than analysed as group processes. There too, in writing up my notes, I now realize that I had not fully understood the transferential character of this second question, whose latent meaning was: have we been a good group, loved by a good monitor, or an unborn, bad group indefinitely kept in the womb of an indifferent monitor? Among the monitor's other group-children, are we the favourite or not?

Finally, the last question: what have the participants learned about groups? As at the time I was working with Lacanian models of the imaginary, the symbolic and the real, I suggested interpreting the group imaginary expressed by the drawing of Paradise: only the monitor could have the knowledge prohibited to ordinary participants; the armless woman in the drawing was armless not so as to be unable to resist the man's advances, but so as not to be able to pluck the forbidden fruit and give it to him. In the hope of enabling participants to move from the imaginary to the symbolic register, I added that only the whole group, by sharing the individual evaluations of all participants, could know what the group felt, that the self-knowledge of a group is not a matter of initiation or guilt or secrets; that the monitor is neither a serpent nor a god. So ended the course.

Later we learned that the participants continued to meet. After two months, one of the observers received a postcard signed 'the group'. All that was on the card was the drawing of a white flag with a red heart. The card itself depicted a peasant, pitchfork in hand, who had surprised a man and woman naked behind a hedge. Below was printed: 'Eh, pretty one, you shouldn't have got up for me, I was only looking.'

What I failed to interpret in this group was the anxiety of the primal scene as manifested in the second drawing, the third question and the postcard. This sheds light on the refusal to broach the matter of couples in the group, Léonore's refusal to be the monitor's partner. It also sheds light on the refusal to admit that the group's existence was based on the initiative of monitor and principal observer, and on the affirmation that everyone was equal, that is, the negation of sexual differences.

In one way the group's illusion functioned as a defence against the phantasy of the primal scene, that is, as a defence against explaining the origin of human beings from the sexual union of a man and a woman. The group illusion reflected the unconscious idea that groups lie within the body of a self-fertilizing partheno-genic mother. This accounts for the unconscious wish that incites so many of our contemporaries to 'form a group'. This wish is at bottom a wish to heal one's own narcissistic wounds and to prevent any re-opening by identifying with the good breast.

## Case 2

With the agreement of a recording studio, a diagnostic group of eight participants (four men, four women) was held in the East of France. I include here only those circumstances pertinent to the appearance of the group illusion.

The group developed in a regular fashion until the tenth session. In the eleventh the atmosphere was heavy, there were long silences and there was no thematic unity to what was said. I lost the thread of the conversations. In the twelfth and last session, I tried to give the participants something of what they had come for and threw myself into the conversation. However, none of my lengthy points contained an accurate and effective interpretation.

What had happened? The group illusion had appeared in the tenth session, as it had appeared in the group from Provence.

First Daniel, a specialized teacher, an Alsatian and proud of it, and a devout Catholic, became the group's scapegoat just as Nicolas, obviously Jewish, bearded and charitable, had been the scapegoat of the Provence group. Both were irritating for one sensed a certain masochism behind their good feelings. Avowed admirers of the monitor above all, they drew upon themselves the collective aggressivity towards the monitor. For them, as Freud described it (1921), a group is the identification of all members with its chief, an ego ideal. But this was not the belief of the other participants, who had come to experience a group as a group and not as a satellite around a central figure. Thus the first condition for the group illusion is split transference. The group must find a bad object on which split negative transference may be projected before it can become the good introjected breast.

The second condition is an egalitarian ideology. In its drawing of the galley the Provence group expressed this wish to level differences. Except for Daniel, the Alsace group was made up of teachers, psychologists, those whose profession was to train. They were all French living outside Alsace or Alsatians so well assimilated that nobody could tell where they came from. They developed a Jacobin belief in democratic liberty, equality and fraternity in the group, threatening the Terror to suspects and asserting centralized power over regional, particularly Alsatian, differences. Their explicit intention was to feel the group as an experiment in political philosophy, not in psycho-analysis. In the ninth and tenth sessions, they devoted themselves to a Utopian project, similar to the drawing of the Garden of Eden in the Province group: they wanted to become a self-governing polis.

But why should an egalitarian ideology be a condition for the group illusion? Regression provoked by the group or crowd situation often goes beyond the Oedipal structure on which Freud based his application of psycho-analysis to culture. English followers of Melanie Klein have noted that this situation mobilizes archaic persecutory and depressive anxieties linked to the dual relation with the mother. The group illusion in this regressive situation is precisely the counterpart of these archaic anxieties, just as for the infant the phantasy of fusion with the good mother is the counterpart of the phantasies of the bad breast and the bad object. 'We are all good objects in the womb of the good mother and we all love one another in her as she loves and gives birth to, feeds and cares for us.' There is thus an equality of penis-children in their relation to the breast as part object. Such an equality is very different from the hierarchy that Freud saw in social organizations where the leader or king is supposed to love those under him equally and where subordinates, symbolic children of the same father, feel united in fraternity. With the group illusion, on the other hand, we are dealing with primary or narcissistic identifications: the group elicits the phantasy that participants are equal at the all-powerful and self-sufficient breast of the mother experienced as part object.

A third feature shared by the Provence group and the Alsace group was the refusal to admit the sexual difference, the rejection of couples, of psycho-analytic explanations, in other words, a refusal of supposedly sexual knowledge. In the Alsace group, this came out in the tenth session in the observation that the project of self-sufficiency was male and the female members wondered whether there was room for them in a City in which love had no place. This led us to believe that the group illusion triggers off primary phantasies. Laplanche and Pontalis (1964) have often shown that primary phantasies are related to three phases in the sexual cycle: phantasies of seduction, arousal and expectation of pleasure; castration phantasies and phantasies of the primal scene.

In both groups the egalitarian ideology functioned as a defence against castration anxiety, since this entails difference *par excellence*. The rejection of couples is a defence against the phantasies of the primal scene. The rejection of a psycho-analytic interpretation is a defence against the phantasy of the group's seduction of the monitor or vice versa.

Nevertheless, the group illusion is itself a phantasy: 'We are born of parthogenesis, we live in the mother's womb by continuous conception, we are conceived but will never be born as our mother wants to keep us and we want to stay together with her.' Here more is at work than Laplanche and Pontalis's classification leads one to believe. We are dealing with a primal counter-phantasy (against the three phantasies mentioned) or a counter-primal phantasy. This sheds light on the indifference of both groups towards the monitor and their refusal to accept him as founder: 'We are born not of a father, but out of our own group; we are a womb-group that gives birth to itself.' Descartes, in discussing proofs of the existence of God, reformulates the ontogenetic argument by saying that God exists because he causes himself to be. Thus, in the group illusion the group is *causa sui*, and exists in the circular time of unendingly repeated fusion, like the phoenix that feeds on itself and is born from its own ashes. Semantic analysis has stressed two metaphors used in groups, the bond (or knot) and the circle (or round table), the second of which comes out in collective discourse.

## Case 3

Two considerations are pertinent to the psycho-analytic treatment of the group illusion. First, the group illusion is an inevitable phase in training or natural group life, which group members sometimes try to prevent. Second, psycho-analytic work is required to 'dis-illusion' the group, as it is required to 'dis-illusion' the individual in psychoanalysis (see Favez, 1971).

How then must group experiences be handled so as to foster psycho-analytic work along these lines? One method, which I and my colleagues have used for several years, is the alternating group. The following case concerns a group of this type run by staff members at the University of Paris at Nanterre for students in psychology.

Several characteristics of this training seminar were out of the ordinary. Participants were of course volunteers, but knew one another previously. They had worked in small psychodrama groups, each made up of friends. These groups went on meeting three times after the end of the seminar. The seminar lasted four days with one plenary meeting and three diagnostic group sessions each day and took place on the university premises. Students knew the monitors, as they were taught by them. Finally, although I knew my colleagues and worked with them in research on small groups, this was the first time we ran an alternating group training seminar.

The unconscious processes in the seminar situation – split transference, the making of a myth or ideology, the denial of primal phantasies, and the group illusion – were essentially the same as in any group.

We did, however, discover more about the group illusion from working with this group. On the fourth and last day, at the daily morning meeting of monitors and observers, we compared the three diagnostic groups with one another and with the plenary meeting and found what we expected: withdrawal of cathexis from the large group and over-cathexis of the small group. But we found more. For participants, the small groups, which were also psychodrama groups which, moreover, had for months been highly cathected, functioned defensively in two ways: as a defence against inner psychical realities (the unconscious), which these psychologists in training had come to learn more about, and a defence against the hard socio-occupational reality, because they symbolized the end of a university career and the beginning of a job with its adult responsibilities. In fact, the seminar situation was nothing new for these students, who since 1968 had become familiar with seminars in the university. They had encountered the group illusion in small friendly gatherings, were the same age, had had the same experiences, were studying the same subject. Since the reforms of 1968 they had felt happy with their *alma mater*, this motherly university with its liberal, understanding faculty, which even ran free experimental seminars. Many said that not having to pay the fees was one of the causes of their passivity in the large group sessions. The real price is in fact that of weaning, or rather object loss, the earliest form of castration (see chapter 9).

The interpretations given on the last day in both the large group and the small groups suggested these elements, but without formulating them systematically, so as to enable the participants themselves to do the work. One of the three groups grasped this during the psychodrama where the theme adopted was: must one tell the truth to a patient if he is fatally ill? The acting between patient and doctor and patient and her mother reached a peak of dramatic intensity that some participants could not stand. For this reason the collective analysis was put off to the following week. This session began with a question: 'Who did you want to die? The monitor? The group?' At the end of the session it came out that the truth so feared was death, the death of childhood, or adolescence, and of university life. Thus the group entered social reality by verbalizing its experience of disillusionment.

The second group refused to continue with the psychodrama after the seminar and devoted the remaining meetings to analysing the effects of the diagnostic group on its members. Whereas the first group realized that it had used the group illusion as a defence against 'the shadows out there', the second group realized that it had used the group illusion as a defence against recognizing the individual unconscious.

The third group, containing several pre-existing couples who were somewhat defensive with respect to the group, finally understood that pairing up was a defence against collective regression. Because there were so many couples in the group, instead of being faced with the group illusion, they were faced with phantasies of the primal scene, which assumed overwhelming proportions from the second psychodrama session on and blocked further work. This blockage was expressed in several psycho-dramatic themes (for example: striking truck drivers block highways), the meaning of which still remained unclear.

## Psychoanalytic explanation

To conclude, we shall complete and systematize the theoretical references scattered in the commentaries on these three cases. In psychoanalysis to explain is to grasp unconscious processes from four angles: dynamic, economic, topographical and genetic. Let us apply these here.

From the dynamic point of view, the group situation presents the threat of a loss of ego identity, and the fact that members are not previously known increases fragmentation anxiety. The wish for security, the wish to protect ego identity, gives rise to the group illusion, which displaces the preservation of individual identity on to the group; the group illusion is a reaction to the threat against individual narcissism. Thus the group discovers its identity at the same time as individuals assert that they are all identical. Everyday language confirms that the conflict is at bottom the struggle against the fragmentation anxiety since groups have an *esprit de corps*, and are 'bodies' with 'members'. These observations go beyond those of Pontalis (1963) in his paper 'The small group as object'. For the group may become a libidinal object in the psychoanalytic sense.

In considering the economic point of view, we must turn to Kleinian concepts. The group situation arouses a phantasy that until now has been encountered in the psycho-analysis of children: the phantasy of the mutual destruction of faeces-children in their mother's belly. Others are rivals to be got rid of. In a group participants adopt various individual defences against such persecutory anxiety, for example by keeping obstinately quiet or by trying to take over the leadership or splitting off into sub-groups. The group illusion is a collective defence against common persecution anxiety. As Béjarano has aptly pointed out to me, it is a hypomanic defence. The euphoria experienced by the participants proves this. Once the death drive has been 'projected' (on to the scapegoat, the large group or the shadows 'out there'), participants are able to feel a purely libidinal bond between themselves. The group becomes the lost or destroyed object, which, newly found, produces feelings of exultation.

From the topographic point of view, the group illusion illustrates the functioning of the ideal ego in groups. This notion, not accepted by all psychoanalysts, but indispensable for those working with groups, designates an archaic state of the ego, heir to primary narcissism, and not a new level of the psychic apparatus. In abandoning the first topography (conscious, preconscious and unconscious), Freud first referred to the ego ideal, then, instead, to the superego. Some of his followers, Nunberg and Lagache in particular, kept both notions in order to designate opposite poles (that of the forbidden and that of the model to be realized) within the superego. Moreover, they differentiated between an ego ideal and an ideal ego. The ego ideal, which is formed with the Oedipal organization, is essentially representative: it suggests projects to the ego and guides it in what it does (whereas the superego hampers it). The ideal ego is precocious; it is formed earlier, along with the child's first object relations; its function is far more affective than representative; it affects the individual primarily through exaltation at finding the part object, which was the first source of pleasure (the breast and its substitutes). Consciousness of these intra-systemic conflicts (between the superego and the ego ideal, between the superego and the ideal ego, between the ego ideal and the ideal ego) is extremely important for an understanding of psychopathological syndromes (see Lagache, 1965). To come back to the ideal ego, it is constituted by the interiorization of the dual relation of mother and child on which it depends and by which it is protected. This image, narcissistic omnipotence, it uses when an individual tries to maintain a symbiotic relationship with another in terms of this primary identification. The group illusion derives from the substitution of a common ideal ego for the ideal ego of each member. Hence the stress on the close relationships between members, on their reciprocal fusion, on the protection the group offers, on the feeling of being part of a sovereign power. Often, the group illusion appears during the group meal, which may symbolize the collective introjection of the breast as part object. This is quite different from the totemic meal in which the father, the total object, murdered collectively, is incorporated and interiorized as the superego and the ego ideal. Lagache has stressed the sado-masochistic aspects of the ego ideal. One example is the humiliation of the waitress during the second meal of the Provence group. Others include the tyranny of the group when it looks at itself: deviants like Nicolas or Daniel, are made to suffer. Lacan, linking the ideal ego to the mirror stage, places it in the register of the imaginary. Observation of groups confirms this: the group illusion is the particular form under which the mirror stage appears in groups – the mirror having as many sides as participants, like the polygonal room of mirrors in Orson Welles's film *The Lady from Shanghai*, in which the pursuer and pursued, who find themselves shut up in this room, struggle with repeated images of one another. I believe, to conclude our topographical analysis, that psychoanalysis applied to group life can make progress only if it deals with the types and levels of identification that come into play in the principal group phenomena. Freud gave an example by analysing the role of the ego ideal in groups, but instead of continuing along these lines, work on groups has been too limited to the ego ideal.

From the classical genetic point of view, the group situation produces regression from the Oedipal position to the oral stage. Fear of revealing one's own castration to others in the group leads participants to avoid this phantasy by regression, a reversible, temporary neurotic defence. As I have already described the split transference that accompanies passive incorporation and oral sadism, I need not treat the matter further here. However, a genetic study cannot be limited to classical positions. Winnicott has provided a missing theoretical link. The withdrawal of cathexis from external reality, the short-circuiting of the superego-ego ideal dyad, the suspension of reality testing, together put participants in an intermediary state between pure phantasized fusion at the breast and recognition of the existence of reality as such. In the group illusion the group is a common transitional object, at once external reality and its substitute or, more accurately, a substitute for the breast. Winnicott stresses the fact that, while tending towards an object relation properly speaking, the transitional phenomenon gives the individual something of fundamental importance, i.e. a no-man's land between external reality and inner reality, which Winnicott calls the field of illusion. In art, religion or scientific creation, we experience intensely the field of illusion.

What I have tried to show, then, is that in addition to what Winnicott has recognized as the individual illusion and the cultural productions that it sustains, there is a group illusion, a protective regression that affords a transition towards either inner unconscious or outer social reality. By immersing themselves in group life human beings sometimes rediscover their creative powers and sometimes share a bewitching self-destructive illusion. In the latter case the death drive, split off and inaccessible, is projected not on to the outside, but rather on to the group itself. When this happens, the group stagnates in the vicious circle of repetition.

# Chapter 8
# The group is a mouth: oral phantasies in the group

The group is a mouth. This truth explains both the present success and the methodological difficulties of group training. Abundant and varied proof may be called upon in support of this thesis. At a time when psychoanalysis, through popularization and intellectualization, tends to become a dry nurse for the collective imaginary, the group, for many, is a wet nurse, a mouth that feeds.

What accounts for the growing need in learned societies and in television programmes to replace lectures by round-tables discussions? Or for the belief, ingrained in participants in training sessions, that because the course is non-directive, they must be arranged in a circle? Why should free and fruitful discussion require that participants be arranged in a circle? A pseudo-psychoanalytic mythology has been erected to account for these facts in sexual terms: the group is essentially female and maternal. In that womb, swarming with potential children, the monitor's interpretations introduce the male principle, the phallus of the father. Jokes on these themes are commonly heard in the corridors and during the sessions. Such pseudo-Oedipal 'explanations' are defensive. The situation of the group in general, and of the free group in particular, provokes a regression to oral sadism, a correlative anxiety of loss of personal identity and a compensatory search for fusion with the imago of the good mother. As is also often the case in individual analysis, stress on genital sexuality in collective discussions is aimed at silencing the increasingly insistent pregenital sexuality. This is a hysterical defence: while the uterus emerges explicitly in group metaphors, latent content revolves around a fellatio phantasy, a sexual theory of the oral origin of children, a dream of bisexuality for all human beings.

The child who nurses at the breast sees his mother's mouth as she speaks to him, if she is not seriously inhibited or pre-psychotic, of her love for him. The nursing group dreamed of by participants in training courses represents this mouth-breast that the child hungrily gazes at. But object splitting is inherent in this stage of development: as the mouth sucks, the child imagines that he is biting and tearing.

For the participants the group situation is often a mirror that reflects the image of this childish phantasy, the image of their own fragmented body. One of the most active, or rather paralysing, unconscious group representations is that of Hydra: the group is felt to be a single body with a dozen arms at the ends of which are heads and mouths, each functioning independently of the others – an image of the anarchy of freed past drives – incessantly searching for prey to be squeezed and suffocated, and ready to devour one another if they are not satisfied. Conversely, in moments of great relief, each member stops speaking for himself and against the others, and the group succeeds in speaking coherently with many voices; these are moments when the imago of the unifying and good maternal mouth gives to each the fulfilment of a common symbolic order.

'Do you have cannibals in your tribe?' asks a young anthropologist studying cannibalism in Africa. 'No,' replies the chief: 'There aren't any more. We ate the last one yesterday.'

This joke was a turning point in a one-week group training seminar that I monitored using psychoanalytic theory and technique. Each person was to formulate his feelings here and now as he felt them. Silence, passivity and paralysis are frequent during the first sessions. Participants and monitors baulk, complaining that the large group, in contrast to the small group, does not work. Participants blame monitors and vice versa: participants say that the method is too difficult and that they are not helpful; monitors say that participants are not providing the associations they have been asked for and that consequently they (the monitors) cannot function as psycho-analysts.

The story of the last of the cannibals epitomizes the two complaints. The 'savages' see to it that the curiosity of the anthropologist is not satisfied. The anthropologist – the psychoanalytic monitor – asks the primitives (the students in training) to drop their civilized veneer, to show their teeth and eat.

The anecdote told by the monitor as an indirect interpretation of the collective experience was an immediate success and was thereafter referred to by numerous participants with various meanings: the naïvety of the monitors; the guilt-feelings of the students in training who felt judged; the cunning of the latter in the face of the supposed cunning of the former; allusion to participants who don't open their mouths or to monitors who don't give them anything to eat; the rule of restitution felt as a duty to confess one's sins, etc. 'Anxiety in the face of the sadistic-oral drive was obviously implicit,' we observed when describing this seminar for the first time (Anzieu, 1972, p. 212).

Here we are dealing with an interpretation, with its specificity in a group. The interpretation is given from the point of view of the transference, but the transference is not that of one patient on to one psychoanalyst, but rather that of a number of participants on to a group of monitors; hence the allusion to a 'tribe'. The style of the interpretation is related to the mechanism of a pun. Such words, rare from patients in individual analysis, abound at certain times in group situations: these are most commonly hypomanic defences, but they are also attempts to short-circuit the pre-conscious by symbolizing archaic phantasies and anxieties. Relying on them periodically the psychoanalytic monitor facilitates the removal of depressive anxiety and the establishment of the process of symbolization. In the example mentioned, the release brought on by this indirect interpretation disguised as a joke was expressed by the abundance and growing ease with which the trainees verbalized their anxiety at being destroyed by the monitors and by their (to them) odd training methods, their anxiety at becoming destructive themselves having been trained to use such methods. This is what we have called 'fragmentation phantasies', the group transposition of the anxiety of oral castration.

The material normally gathered in training courses with partially psychotherapeutic goals led us to observe that an oral model of the group operates unconsciously in the participants. This material may be divided into three categories: the behaviour of individuals in groups, collective behaviour and collective discourses. We shall provide examples of each.

When the sadistic-oral drive is common in only one or two members of the group, it is expressed not by words but by silence. The group situation, as we have said, often arouses phantasies of a hydra with many heads and sucking or devouring mouths. When a participant is overwhelmed by such phantasies, he is seized by an unconscious fear of being eaten by the others if he opens his mouth; in other words, he projects on to them his own repressed wish to destroy the love-object by swallowing it. He lives an archaic form of the law of retaliation: 'The others, who have not stopped talking, have shown me, by opening their mouth incessantly, that they would be ready to devour me if I hint that I want to devour them by opening my mouth.'

A study by Jeanne Souchère-Gélin, under the supervision of Jean Maisonneuve, confirms this explanation. She interviewed individually trainees who had been quiet during most of the sessions. They turned out to be as at ease and as cooperative in a one-to-one situation as they had been inhibited in the group. They spontaneously verbalized their representation of the mouth, terrifying as a swallowing-up organ, rather than one of speech. Persons silent in groups keep quiet because they are afraid of being devoured.

Here are a few extracts from two of Jeanne Souchère-Gélin's interviews. One female participant who had spoken very little and who said she confined herself to the role of observer, exhibited violent vaso-motor reactions and left the course before the end. She explained that others are so dangerous that before speaking, one must be sure that what one says is appropriate. To manage to speak to others, she needs to know them well, to know what they are thinking, what they are, and then to feel aggressive towards them, for aggressivity 'pushes' her. Speaking is for her a weapon with which to attack others: 'I noticed that aggressivity was always latent and that it is much easier to express oneself when one is aggressive; saying shocking things provokes an immediate reaction.' The non-directive group situation was particularly painful for this participant; it is not to be found in everyday life, where one can say silly things with people one knows. Here, where contact with unknown persons is constant, she is continually afraid of being judged; afraid of being 'dissected'. Thus through speaking she can dissect others; by speaking they can dissect her. She feels others are devouring beings who are going to gobble up what she says and that she will not be able to find herself afterwards. At the time of the interview the psychologist commented: 'She seems to feel that if she speaks, the others would jump on her as on a child coming out of her mouth – as an erogenous zone giving birth to words. . . . During her "child birth", her "work", she would not find herself. . . . Speaking was highly cathected for her, orally and anally, and was accompanied by castration phantasies.' In this context she reacts to others as she feels they react to her: she must devour or be devoured. But this reaction arouses guilt feelings, which in turn lead her to project on to others her own wish to devour. This vicious circle intensifies her anxiety. Hence her passive opposition to the group, a sign of extreme dependence upon it. She expected that by speaking for her, the group would take over complete responsibility for her. She could not stay to the end, because the death of the group, with which she totally identified, was felt to be her own death.

Let us go on to the second interview, this time with a young man in the same group who at times appeared totally indifferent to what was going on around him and at times syntonic. He reacted to the psychologist who had come to interview him as to a friend come to chat with him; he helped her to set up the tape recorder and was co-operative – though once or twice aggressive – throughout the interview. His silence in the group was related to the intense and repeated frustration he had encountered: frustration at being called on to speak in his turn which he took as manipulation, at the group situation and at the monitor's non-directive approach: 'When I found myself faced with this thing, thrown in with other people I didn't know, I was disgusted.' It took him two days (the course lasted three) to get an idea of the group; he saw the group as a maternal lap and the monitor as a castrating father. He refused to 'let go' in the group because he was afraid of living symbiotically. The training reminded him of other groups (summer camps particularly) in which he had never been able to be integrated, as he wanted to know only certain persons of his own choosing, not all: 'I have never managed to accept the group as such, as a whole. I have always chosen people who interested me, without taking notice of the others or of what the others might think of me. That was of no interest. Only the people I had chosen interested me; those I hadn't chosen were of no interest whatever to me.' In a group, he allows himself to be completely absorbed by one-to-one relationships. If the relation is positive, he talks; if it is negative, he keeps quiet. With persons of the same sex his relations tend to be negative and aggressive. He attributes his silence to the desire to 'preserve his integrity', to be logical with himself, keep his head high: 'I didn't want to start. I thought that if I spoke first I would be integrated into the group, and I wasn't interested in that.' However, on the third (and last) day he accepted the situation, 'the rules of the game', speaking . . .

and the rivalry with other men.

A comparison of these two interviews is instructive: the first shows intense, primitive anxiety at being devoured; the second shows how anxiety over oral castration may, if it persists, intensify anxiety over phallic castration.

How can we consider this material? It would seem that a veritable symptom of group anorexia is at work in the silence. The experience of being the one spoken to is split: either it is felt as a threat, when the person is anonymous, changing and chameleon-like (which helps the situation of the training group where, as a general rule, participants do not know one another) or it is a sign of the esteem, confidence and love of someone with whom a special relation may be established (as in the case with an individual interview). What psychical dynamics underlie these two reactions? In the first instance, the fear of freeing one's own destructiveness is projected onto the unknown strangers: if they give free reign to their drives (the instruction to say everything that comes to mind is understood in this sense) and if they are all-powerful (at this level, others are the heirs of the archaic maternal imago), these unknown strangers, whose number increases the dangers, will use their omnipotence to destroy me. In the second instance, the one-to-one relation receives the dual relationship with the nursing, speaking mother, from whom the child learns his first words.

Seen in this light, one understands why silent subjects in groups are even more uneasy when the others, worried or irritated by their silence, use them as scapegoats whom they can hold responsible for the unsatisfactory progress of the group. They are invited to speak, badgered to participate and accused of spreading paralysis to the rest of the group. Reality thus confirms phantasy: silent subjects are really threatened and become all the more rigidly counter oral-sadistic. The only way to get this to change is to use the one-to-one dialogue in which one (and only one) group member speaks encouragingly and understandingly to silent participants and if the other trainees are careful not to interrupt. But the complexity of the situation grows out of the fact that the taciturn members are not even approached as long as they do not hinder the group, as long as their use of archaic defences against an archaic drive remains their own problem. Rather, they are put in the dock precisely when most members share their oral phantasies. In fact groups have a knack of detecting at any given time which of their members 'fit' the gist of the conversation and problems raised; such persons are singled out at once, so that a general, group problem may be placed squarely on them and so that the symbolization and working-through of the group may be indirectly aided. The accusation addressed to the silent member may be partly justified and partly not. Their paralysis may spread like oil to the entire group: the excessive anxiety of one member may wreck the collective defences against a shared phantasy. But, on the other hand, silent members do not cause, but rather reveal, problems common to all. This paralysis of certain participants by the anxiety of being eaten is even more prevalent in the large group. Turquet (1974) has shown that because of the more lasting anonymity of the situation and the larger size of the group, the bad parts of each participant, split and expelled by the ego, are more difficult to project on to the outside because it is difficult to distinguish between the group and the outside. These unwanted portions are projected on to the central space, on to the *inside* of the circle formed by participants. This circular, internal space is verbalized as a spittoon, as a bad, dangerously contagious mouth.

Another remark concerning this type of phenomenon. The equation seeing=eating is common. Geza Roheim, an anthropologist and a psychoanalyst, has noted this equation in 'primitive' beliefs concerning the 'evil eye'. Our everyday language contains such expressions as 'to eye greedily'. Anxiety dreams of patients in psychoanalysis often associate threatening mouths with red eyes. Missenard (1972, p. 228) has stressed the importance of this equivalence in groups: looks are feared; some group members intensify looks; others try to avoid them; most ask themselves anxiously: 'What do they want from me?' 'The moment I look at some, the others I know nothing about have a hold over me in some way.' In our view, this link between seeing and mouthing is established during the positive primal experiences alluded to earlier in which the child looks alternately at his mother's eyes watching him and at the movements of her mouth. This link is reinforced later by negative experiences in which the mother, angry and irritated by her child, scolds him with words and looks. We have tried to show how this double experience provides the basis for interpretation.

When oral phantasies spread to most group members and the defences against them lower, the theme of shared discourse sometimes emerges, in which a sort of daydream evokes anxiety by playing with the drive to devour. Collective free associations hit on a series of animals – muraenas, sharks, piranhas, Brazilian ants, rats, vultures, etc., – where cultural references – the *Raft of Medusa*, Sartre's *Huis Clos*, the devouring dogs of Athalie's dream, the sacrifice of children to the god Moloch, Bunuel's *Exterminating Angel*, Pasolini's *Pigsty* or *Medea*, etc. – are important. In a diagnostic group held at Aix in 1965, which I monitored, members devoted a whole session to listening to one member talk about her life in the Camargue among animals in their natural habitat. She told of their fights, their capture, their training, of a jungle with its own laws, customs, rituals and sacrifices. What she provided, albeit unconsciously and unintentionally, was a portrait of the group with its tensions, organization and dreams of a 'natural' free, life. But this rhapsody also produced the anxiety of being bitten, of being torn apart. It had a cathartic effect and was received with laughter and cries of admiration. As the narrator spoke, postures grew more relaxed and verbalizations more spontaneous. In short, there emerged the first profound feeling common to all members – except the narrator. This emotional discharge together with the absence of a correct interpretation on my part (at the time I was oblivious of the importance of oral phantasies in group situations) temporarily satisfied the participants, but lowered their motivation for subsequent work. As a result, the group had difficulty progressing thereafter. For analogous reasons the 'whale' group analysed by Max Pagès (1968) was satisfied with an allegory. In other words, participants limited themselves to a conscious phantasy; they restricted themselves to a certain defensive immobility against the handling of their unconscious cathected drives.

References to the Christian myth of the Last Supper and Eucharists are, in our experience, rarer. Is this due to a prudishness, a shyness, deriving from a religious upbringing, even when religion has been cast aside? Is it the monitor's defence against the temptation to abuse the power that transference gives them and to give in to an unconscious collective demand for a group substitute for religious faith, to stand up, and say: 'Take, eat; this is my body', and 'drink of it, all of you; for this is my blood'? Indeed the counter-transference is, at this point, indicative not of the wish of the female group for an Oedipal relationship with the monitor as father, but rather a pregenital, ambivalent wish to eat the monitor as mother, to incorporate him, to identify with him so as to enable the participants to become themselves good monitors. Before the incest taboo (and parricide), the taboo against eating the mother is at work, enforced by weaning. Clinical experience with training groups confirms this. More accurately, sharing the mother's body is the most archaic form of incest, an incest indistinguishable from matricide. Because it is regressive and collective, the non-directive group situation fosters phantasies of such incest and strongly arouses the oldest childhood prohibition, that against precisely this sort of incest: one cannot freely open one's mouth, or it will tear apart the very object for which one is hungry or thirsty.

Although phantasies of the eucharist-group do not frequently appear in the discourse of participants, they do appear as unspoken phantasies in behaviour, in the scenario of a transgression. The trainees' compulsion to eat together is a well-known fact. If they participate in a live-in seminar where everyone comes together in the evenings, each diagnostic group tends to reconstitute itself around the dinner table and if members of the same group go out, generally all go together to eat or drink. One who doesn't is looked at askance. Monitors are often asked to join them. Until psychoanalytic rigour brought them to respect the rule of abstinence, they joined in this lay communion, which ended, as we have seen in the preceding chapter, in a group illusion. Why are these meals eaten together most of the time in a festive spirit? Participants literally eat the group, about which they continually speak while they down food and drink. No longer do they feel paralysed or serious, as they do during the sessions. They speak more freely, joke, flirt, exteriorize much of what they previously kept to themselves. A ban seems to have been removed: the prohibition against biting the mother, she who loves you and whose power, knowledge and immortality one would like to ingest. The training illusion, the 'purest' form of which appears in psychoanalytic training (Anzieu, 1973), aims at obtaining these three attributes by projective identification with the phantasized all-powerful mother.

The Freudian myth described in *Totem and Taboo* (the primitive horde, the father's murder by his sons who, tired of his despotism and refusal to share women, band together, and the feast at which the father's body is eaten) may be illuminating if it is altered slightly. We find this myth in virtually all groups at one time or another in varying forms. Béjarano (1972, p. 132) has suggested that this myth corresponds to a phantasy specific to group situations; we will deal with the phantasy of murdering the father in a later chapter (see chapter 12). Freud stressed the Oedipal aspects of this phantasy, to show that the Oedipus complex is at the root of culture as much as it is at the root of child-rearing and neuroses. This author believes that the Freudian myth is a restructuring at the Oedipal stage of an earlier oral stage phantasy. The proto-group is not a real horde, but a phantasized horde composed of the mother (or both parents) and her children, born and unborn. Certain insect colonies might serve as metaphors. The mother is a part object, with which the child is in symbiosis. The proto-group develops during a series of equivalences: breast=penis=child=excrement.

Participants' experience with such phantasies might be summed up in the following inverse and complementary propositions: 'the group feeds us' and 'the group eats us'.

Oedipal phantasies in groups are quite different. The monitor appears as the central figure, to whom a leader of resistance is opposed. The monitor's authority, his rules and his interpretations are disputed. Central transference becomes more important than group-object transference. One is less apt to transgress in a meal eaten together with or without him than in amorous pairs that develop under his nose. Seduction, provocation and exhibitionism are prominent. The dinner table is not an end in itself, but fore-pleasure. The symbolic murder of the father, the fraternal, judging society and the differentiation of the sexes and of roles may then be observed in groups – but in this case without a trace of devouring.

The preceding considerations concerning certain peculiarities of group phantasies among trainees need to be completed by an evaluation of the role of oral phantasies among the monitors themselves. This subject has been dealt with by René Kaës (1973a), who speaks of the 'training breast' of the 'pelican phantasy' and of 'envious training'. Melanie Klein's concept of envy and gratitude is to Kaës a key to understanding monitors' phantasies. 'Identified with the nursing mother, the monitor phantasizes the pleasure and anxiety linked to the breast at weaning. In exchange for the food that he may, as could his mother, give or refuse, monitors expect love or gratitude from their infants.'

In training seminars, many monitors derive great satisfaction from their practice and work with team members, particularly when they use psychoanalytic theories and techniques. Monitors who pretend not to have any wishes concerning those they train are in fact motivated by an unspoken wish – like the death drive from which this wish derives and of which Freud noted how much it operates in silence – the wish to keep their 'infants' unborn although they are supposed to do just the contrary: keep them to be born again.

These phantasies cease being obstacles if monitors become conscious of them, in which case phantasies contribute to the inter-analysis among colleagues. Monitors' phantasies may then be used to understand patterns of latent phantasies in training groups. Kaës (1963a), Gori (1973b) and Anzieu (1973) have concluded that these patterns are always group versions of the infantile sexual theories described by Freud (1908). Indeed how could they be otherwise?

# Chapter 9

# The breaking-apart phantasy: anxieties aroused by the group situation

## 1 Presentation of the case-history

In training groups, the fragmentation phantasy is the specific form under which castration – or rather destruction – anxiety appears.

This case-history concerns a live-in training seminar lasting one week at which I was chief co-ordinator. There were ten or so monitors and observers and about thirty participants, who were all by profession engaged in training activities in industry, specialized education, mental health and social care. Throughout the seminar they were divided into three groups of about ten persons each. On the same day seminar participants met in diagnostic groups (twice a day) and psychodrama groups (once a day). Monitors and observers were different for the two types of activity. At the beginning of each afternoon, the monitors and observers of the diagnostic groups and psychodrama groups got together under my direction to talk about what had gone on during the previous twenty-four hours and to enable the team to 'grasp the seminar in its totality', for such was the explicitly stated goal. At the end of each afternoon there was a general meeting, which brought together everyone, participants, monitors and observers. This was how the 'large group' began.

I wrote the case-history, which I include here *in extenso*, in the days following the seminar, from notes taken during the two meetings for which I was responsible (the general meeting and the meeting of the monitors and observers). In fact the interrelation of large group, small groups and the group of monitors was one of the important and unexpected features to emerge.

## 2 The case history

### *The first day*

I The first day ended not with a large group, judged to be premature at the time, but by way of transition, by a lecture I gave on the history and problems of training. A debate followed in which participation was low, but one began to see the preoccupations of the participants and their motives in signing up for the seminar. I gave the lecture in a slow, dead-pan manner and said it had no inherent interest. This provoked frustration on the part of the participants and disappointment on the part of colleagues who had expected more.

### *The second day*

II(a) There were two large group meetings on the second day. Before dinner was the first. Encouraged to speak of their problems, the participants began by asking the organizers questions: what are the rules for dividing the participants into three diagnostic groups? Were any candidates refused? Can the result of such training be evaluated? Are groups composed of psychologists not different from 'naïve' groups? Why do people come to such seminars? How do they hear about them? Are there stages in the development of diagnostic groups? Are there differences between the three diagnostic groups of the seminar?

Each of these questions was discussed, first with the chief monitor, then with the other organizers and participants. Several of them pointed out that the discussion remained 'academic' (the 'teacher' was questioned for his knowledge), and the seminar experience as such was not discussed.

There was a discussion of the comparison between the diagnostic group and the psychodrama, between their organizers and their functioning, as well as advantages and disadvantages of changing the group make-up from one sort of activity to the other. Participants demanded that this be justified from the outset (instead of basing their opinion on experience). As no justification was given, they objected.

The possibility of participants' changing the programme of the seminar came up. Why did they want to change it? Would the 'staff' of monitors allow them to? If not why would they refuse?

Latent content appeared as the seminar went on: Are we participants capable of changing? Are the monitors capable of changing? Were only persons capable of changing selected? But what will happen to those incapable of changing? Was the group formed so as to foster the greatest change? Participants asked whether they could have objective scientific proof of their changes. Would psychologists not have more trouble changing than others? Would the three groups change in the same ways? And were the participants there to change or just to learn something? But will the monitors tell us what they know? These were the questions in the first phase of the discussion.

The second phase revolved around the unconscious collective preoccupation: how will changes in this seminar differ from those of preceding seminars of the same type?

The third phase was a minor image of the first: will the monitors let us change them? Is not resistance to change stronger in the one who performs an experiment than in the guinea pig?

Thus phantasies and anxieties about change are two-sided: 'Are we free to change?' is mirrored by 'Must we change?' One aspect is the fear of being incapable of changing, of being judged and rejected as such by the jury of monitors. The second fear of changing, of being metamorphosed is analogous to the child's fear of being changed into an animal, a recurring theme in folk tales and legends. This double fear is projected on to the staff of monitors. The first affect remains conscious: 'Does the staff allow us to change?' becomes 'Can we change the staff's programme?' The second affect, the fragmentation anxiety, remains unconscious, that is, unformulated. It will not be verbalized until the fifth day, when it appears as a projection: the staff is at sixes and sevens with itself, divided and coming apart; it is breaking up.

II(b) After dinner there is another plenary meeting. In Reichenbach's film, *The Marines*, the subject is methods of training American marines. A sergeant at the military school ordered his students on a night march, which led to a number of them getting drowned. The film ends with the question: if you had been a member of the jury that judged the sergeant, what would your verdict have been?

The discussion that followed got bogged down in the problem of how to train men to kill. Was the most effective method not that illustrated by the film: change the candidates' personality, teach them to make others afraid so as not to be afraid themselves. Is not all training an initiation, the tearing away of childhood in becoming an adult? Is not all training imposed by the outside alienating to the individual? Although favouring methods contrary to those of the American marines, does not training in human relationships not try to form a certain type of persons, defined in advance?

It is hardly worth pointing out that these questions reflect certain preoccupations of the seminar.

However, it is important to note that the discussion avoided Reichenbach's question: is not a certain 'breaking in' inevitable in training? This omission was a sign that shared phantasies were at work. The monitors, however, did not catch the omission until the following evening: what sorts of 'accidents' are likely to happen when one 'submits' to training? In fact group monitors, even psycho-analysts, have difficulty in immediately identifying castration anxiety when it is collective. As we shall see, the monitors had to share the anxiety in order to recognize it and to have it recognized by the participants.

## The third day

III(a) On the third day there was a plenary meeting before, and a long meeting of the 'staff' after, lunch.

In the plenary meeting, one participant asked what effect a table had on diagnostic group sessions. In the discussion that followed, as is always the case in non-directive work, a particular group problem was transposed into other terms. The group does not admit its own problems or speak of them in a concrete manner: it defends itself by making the problem general and abstract. What is the real, concrete problem here? It is a fact that diagnostic groups meet around a table, whereas large groups do not (the participants are placed in two concentric circles around an empty space). The group problem is clear: what is the difference between diagnostic groups and this large group? Are we really in a diagnostic group?

Let us return to the plenary meeting itself, which now discusses what happens when trained people find themselves in a situation in which they cannot use their training? For a number of participants this question was one that they had had to confront in their professional lives. But it was also a generalization of the '*hic et nunc*' problem of the seminar: why can't participants transpose to the plenary session what they have learned in the diagnostic group? What is the use of hard work if we cannot use what we have learned in our professional lives? Is this training not apt to tear us apart, leave us powerless and unhappy? Is there not a fundamental contradiction between the training received here, which obliges us to change, and the organizational structure of our professions, which we cannot change however well trained we might be?

The mirrored questions at the end of the first plenary session appear clearer in the light of these questions. The well-known alternative, 'change oneself or change the world', is caught in a dilemma: 'If I change myself first, such a change will be no use to me because the world cannot be changed. If the order of the world is changed, I won't have to change myself. So whatever the case, let's not change.' All this is expressed in a projection: it is the 'staff's job to change its organization and methods; not ours to change our habits and ways.'

The discussion is stopped by a comment by one participant whose position is ambiguous, half-monitor and half-participant: he gives a brief interpretation as though he were monitor (he's training to be one), but it is untimely and incomplete. He says, quite rightly, that the discussion concerning training difficulties is an escape from the here and now situation; what needs to be done in the plenary session is to speak about the experiences of the seminar (diagnostic and large groups). The observation is accepted, but ineffective. We cannot, and do not know how to do what we would like to do (*say* what is going on). A number of practical manoeuvres are attempted: the monitors of the diagnostic groups are asked to speak; the monitors are compared (anxiety over being torn apart appears in group discourse for the first time); participants are asked to speak about their groups (infantile curiosity about what is going on in the next room also appears for the first time).

The failure of the large group to do what it is supposed to do (i.e. deal with matters of general concern) gives rise to protests: the large group doesn't work; something must be changed. It is the structure that prevents our functioning, as it prevents those who have been trained from using their training in what they do. The informality and non-directive character of such a large gathering must be changed: a table is needed, discussion must be organized. Several participants suggest returning to the classical methods of a panel or of the 'Phillips 66'. Moreover, it is suggested that the monitors don't know what they are doing. A wave of fear sweeps through the assembly. What if Anzieu is losing control, if the person we came to learn from knows less than we do? One perspicacious participant formulates the diffuse anxiety of the group and finds a scapegoat: 'If things don't work, it's Anzieu's fault.' It is time and timely to end the session. I do so.

The latent content is this time displaced, not condensed. What is interesting here is not so much the mechanism of the general upon whom the fault of defeat is laid, of the prophet dragged through the mire, that is to say, one of the innumerable variants on the group myth of the murder of the father. In passing we may note, however, that in training one cannot take what is given without having symbolically killed the authority of the giver; in group phantasies what is 'sacred' may become 'grotesque'. But the failure of this larger, regulatory session requires a more specific explanation. The phantasy that paralysed the group was now obvious and the true cause of the failure of that session was that this phantasy had remained present, but unexpressed. In a group that is not working there is always a silent phantasy. Here there is a series of repressed questions: can there be training without breaking apart? How much fragmentation is there usually? How much will the monitors tolerate? Fear of breaking apart while being trained is inverted as fear of a desire to break others apart when one is responsible for training. For the group, this complementarity of fears and wishes concerning phantasies of breaking apart is facilitated by the identification of the participants, many of them responsible for training of one sort of another, with the monitors of the seminar. . . . Only at this point does the scapegoat mechanism become clear: fear of being broken apart is unexpressed (hence the greater importance of the theme of deaf mutes in a psychodrama group than in the large group seminar); only the wish to break others is expressed verbally: 'Anzieu intentionally makes the seminar fail; he wants us to break apart; this is what he calls training; and once we have been trained by him, we will, in turn, as monitors, be responsible for training, be carried away by our own wish to break apart those we must train!' This is probably the latent content of: 'things aren't working, it is Anzieu's fault'.

III(b) After dinner the staff met. Meanwhile participants peeked through the crack between the doors, talked jokily of drilling a hole to see what was going on, and then locked the doors from the outside using the doorstops: since the monitors want to be closed off together, in among themselves, well, let's *really* close them off. The monitors did not realize what had happened until they tried to get out.

Staff discussion is tense. Several monitors are afraid the seminar will fail, afraid they won't be able to stand it. The phantasy of breaking apart was soon recognized and spoken about. But one fear remained that I was to learn about later: the staff's fear that its leader was tired, and unconsciously wanted to sabotage both the seminar and the team of monitors. In short, they unconsciously did not want to be broken apart.

I remained deaf to this reproach, explicit among the participants and implicit among the staff members. I reproached the other monitors for speaking too abstractly in large group sessions, of not using concrete material from the small groups. In short, in complementary and symmetrical fashion, I reproached them for not giving me enough help.

Two tendencies emerged inside the team. One of the monitors put in a plea to keep the methodology of the seminar 'pure'; the monitors had, in fact, in their working with training seminars, gradually eliminated 'refuse': lectures, mythological asides, case studies, various exercises in running seminars, etc., in order to limit themselves to three indispensable activities in group training: diagnostic groups, psychodramas and plenary sessions. Another monitor objected, saying 'purity' could lead to suicide, and that effectiveness was more important: what counted above all was the seminar's success: the participants, many of whom had paid large sums for the course, must leave satisfied; let us give them what they want (panels, etc.) and preserve our reputation. These two monitors were opposed on principles, on methods, on tone, as well as for reasons that had to do with their own characters.

I then dropped my role as chairman and told my colleagues how I felt the regulatory large groups should be conducted. First, whatever the criticisms, I insisted on keeping the plenary sessions and on remaining their regulator. Secondly, the criticisms, like everything else in these sessions, were transference phenomena and had to be understood as such. Thirdly, if participants did not say what they had to say as the seminar proceeded, it was up to the monitors to stick more closely to the *hic et nunc* of the sessions in what they say. Finally, I noted several times in the past I had successfully used a psychodrama staged by two or three monitors in front of participants in which both staff discussions and seminar problems were acted out. Naturally all this came out in more confused and complicated fashion at the time than it does here.

My first two points were accepted, but the last two were not. The third produced objections from the monitors of the diagnostic groups: to speak up in plenary sessions would violate the rules of technical 'purity' needed to run diagnostic groups. One purist would rather not have been present at the plenary sessions at all. My fourth proposition was rejected because it was not believed to be 'efficient'.

I was not happy about the rejection of the last two proposals, vainly tried to defend them, but felt like a voice crying in the wilderness. In fact, it was an unformulated phantasy at the time that there was a desert that made all declarations (except for the correct interpretation of the phantasy) seem disagreeably predicatory.

We later learned why the monitors had resisted the proposals: a prey to collective castration phantasies, they defensively phantasized that I was powerless. I shared the same phantasy, because I thought them timid and weak.

The compromise reached by the staff consists in (1) delegating me to tell the participants in a plenary session what had gone on in the staff meeting, by interpreting particularly phantasies of breaking apart and of the fear of changing, (2) setting up a panel consisting half of participants and half of staff members and (3) proposing that the subject for panel discussion be 'how to understand our training responsibilities in the light of the seminar experience'.

The selection of the only female member of the staff to preside over the panel was, like an authorized signature, the final sign of the murder of the paternal imago and the institution of an egalitarian brotherhood.

## The fourth day

IV(a) The third session of the large group was held at the end of the fourth day. I spoke, as was agreed at the staff meeting. But I spoke for too long (45 minutes) in a professional manner. During my lecture, I unconsciously protested against the laxity of my colleagues and against what I felt to be an accusation of impotence.

My talk bored the participants, who told me so. Nonetheless they accepted the idea of a panel, made up of five volunteers and three psychodrama monitors. The panel took up two themes in turn: the risk of breaking apart, both for an individual and his enterprise, in in-depth training seminars; the discrepancy between the goals of training (greater individual freedom) and the goals imposed by 'efficiency'. After it was over trainees and monitors alike were utterly exhausted.

IV(b) The 'staff' held a short meeting while dining in a separate room. Members were satisfied that the breaking apart phantasy had been dealt with and decided to continue large regulatory groups as planned, i.e. to reply firmly and negatively to the request to change the programme of the seminar. However, they still rejected my proposition of provoking a catharsis of the phantasies concerning the seminar by a psychodrama put on by the monitors. They wanted to continue the panel, but in a more flexible form: participants and monitors would be able to take part or not during the large regulatory group meeting; the subject proposed would be decided on freely: saying what one had to say about the state of the seminar (that is, a return to the principle of the enlarged diagnostic group, which had been rejected twenty-four hours earlier). But the unfortunate impression given by my talk was not mentioned. Thus, the phantasized fear that the seminar would fail was repressed.

I went home (there weren't enough rooms for the monitors to sleep in) with an intense feeling of weariness and solitude, all too well aware that a diagnostic group of forty people could not function. During a night of insomnia I finally admitted that I couldn't work the seminar. In other words, as I understood afterwards, I finally gave the trainees freedom to progress as they wanted. But for the time being I felt 'broken apart'.

## The fifth day

V(a) On the next to last day the progress of the diagnostic and psychodrama groups was encouraging to us all: collective phantasies were shifting; problems had ripened in the minds of others as they had for me. But is fatigue not the price paid for refusing to allow phantasies to ripen and be articulated?

It is interesting to see how the subdivision into distinct small groups helps this ripening. One of the three groups devoted this fifth morning to the following themes: men are wolves (the monitor's fear of becoming a fierce beast who breaks the training enterprise); how to change boats in mid-stream (resistance to change); is the staff made of stucco or granite (fear of the staff's inconsistency, incoherence, disagreements). And underlying all this: if monitors are hateful and use their powers to break participants apart, then the seminar is an abortion, a failure.

A second psychodrama group, borrowing the Christian myth of God chasing Adam and Eve from paradise, acted out a scene in which 'Anzieu' passes two 'participants', a man a woman, in front of the seminar door. 'Anzieu' accuses the excluded couple of (1) not distinguishing between phantasy and reality thus going against the spirit of the seminar and (2) sleeping with one another during the seminar, trespassing the fundamental rule according to which what happens here should be verbal and not acted out. The accused couple then appealed to the 'people' and tried to 'cut' Anzieu off when he spoke (an allusion to my too lengthy discourse, which nobody, I observed, had dared to interrupt). One of the group members concluded: Anzieu's trial is our own trial as trainers or educators.

The third group chose as a basic idea the pitfalls of a liberal education: a girl tells her mother that she is pregnant ('it's your fault, you brought me up'); a young man tells his father that he has got pregnant the one girl with whom he did not want sexual relations. The free associations that follow lend meaning to these scenarios: the staff purposefully made pedagogical blunders; one can only accept having children by 'screwing' one's own parents; lax parents give their children only one way of shaking off their influence: getting into trouble.

Putting the phantasies of the three groups together allowed us to group the latent unconscious content: the staff wanted to allow their children radical freedom (they want a 'pure' seminar in which the experience of freedom is pushed to the extreme); if the trainees want to become trainers ('parents') in turn, what freedom is left except to turn the liberty allowed them back on to the monitors? Phantasies of the seminar's failure can be broken down as a wish to retort. Through its methods the staff wants to train trainers capable of dealing with pure freedom: the participants showed the staff the dangers of this approach (becoming 'wolves', 'breaking' everything they attempt), by destroying first of all the seminar itself. The staff is perceived as a conglomerate of vindictive, ignorant parents who don't know their job and who keep secrets; the seminar they 'conceive' can be nothing but a monstrous, sexless child who breaks everything.

V(b) The plenary meeting was thus facilitated. What is more, during the afternoon recess each small group prepared what it was going to say at the meeting, as did the monitors. Several participants let me know in the halls that there was an 'abscess to drain', and I repeated this at the opening of the session.

The panel functioned effectively in its more elastic form, dealing with the intentions, methods and attitudes of the staff, particularly of Didier Anzieu. Everyone was attentive; discussion was tense and self-disciplined. The phantasized temptation to put the staff on trial was replaced by an exchange with them on the nature of training in the light of the seminar experience. Staff members and I entered into the discussion equally and naturally and could thus communicate our interpretations of the phantasized dynamics underlying the seminar. This was in fact a fundamental difference of style, and technique between individual psychoanalysts and the psychoanalytic handling of groups.

In the discussion it was clear that the staff conceived of the regulatory large group as an enlarged diagnostic group. The ambiguity of a 'model' trainer or educator, which most participants had come in search of, was analysed. It was not recognizd that the staff and particularly Anzieu were perceived simultaneously as models to be imitated and parents to be got rid of; only in this way could participants become monitors or persons otherwise engaged in training, capable of training people who would then be autonomous. The 'sabotage' phantasy was explained in the light of the psychodrama (to which reference was made for the first time during a plenary meeting) as the wish to catch the trainer-parents in the wrong in their handling of their trainee-children.

I analysed Anzieu's mock trial put on by one of the psychodrama groups that morning as a symbolic transcription of the training process. Participants had come to the seminar fearing and wishing that their training would be judged. Similarly, in their work, they felt judged by their superiors on the one hand and by their trainees on the other. The Kafkaesque myth of an imaginary defendant who accumulates objective proof of his guilt and finally brings on his own trial and condemnation – was one of the mainstays of the seminar. Hence a hypersensibility to the problem of 'breaking apart'.

After the end of the meeting discussions continued in the corridors in small, spontaneous groups of participants and monitors.

V(c) A round table was organized for the evening, to which a specialist on mythology (a woman) and one on problems of training people to work with juvenile delinquents had been invited. The two guests sat in on the preceding regulatory large group, by way of 'initiation'. The woman told an old Irish myth of an aggressive and warlike hero, and spoke of structural similarities with certain types of the knight, the agreeable outlaw and the bellicose saint in medieval Christianity and with contemporary heroes like Saint-Exupéry or James Bond. The second guest spoke of the training of counsellors dealing with juvenile delinquents: an initiation with delinquents could be either stimulating or destructive; if the hero won (if he slew the monster), the educator or counsellor could be a structuring model for the juvenile delinquent disturbed by a terrifying or inconsistent, but excessive paternal ego.

Innumerable echoes from the seminar could be heard throughout the evening: some were brought out by participants or by myself; others, which remained latent, would provide occasions for inner individual work. For example, let us take the alternative of an overwhelming or inconsistent authority, the tendency to project inconsistency on to the staff, which uses non-directive methods; the double face of the mythological hero terrifying on one side and grotesque on the other: the alternative of a warlike hero, who kills to defend society, but is doomed to die young and the cultural hero, who defends himself with words, but who uses them in a two-edged way, truthfully and cunningly.

## The sixth day

The fifth and last regulatory, plenary meeting was held at the end of the morning on the sixth day, and closed the seminar. There was no longer any need for a particular spatial disposition nor a pre-arranged agenda. Each person took his place around the 'ring'. The female monitor and I chair the proceedings when necessary:

this represents the reconciliation of children with their parents. The session runs a half-an-hour over time but the crux of what the participants wanted to say about the staff and vice versa seems to have been said.

In the official seminar programme it was decided that for the last meeting there would be a round-table discussion on the presuppositions of training. However, during a short break that morning, the staff decided to make room for a new final large group session. I announce this at the beginning of the meeting

Around the round table are five monitors, myself included. Our discussions stress training and change. Training is changing knowledge and attitudes. Why train? To prepare members of an organization for the changes it and they must undergo. In this sense, monitors, or trainers are agents of group change. One of the postulates of training is that if man cannot be made perfect he can be made to change, and can be led to become conscious of himself and others in new ways. Another postulate is that such changes are good for both the individual and society. The training of monitors must give them insight: one can only give what one has experienced and felt oneself. But the staff are not super monitors who don't need insight themselves: monitors continue their own training while training others. Once trained an individual becomes more autonomous, more responsible, but also more alone. Reference was made to a psychodrama where the theme of solitude was particularly intense: one person must go through a doorway guarded by genies of Good and Evil; they demand his reasons for going through and warn him that once on the other side there is no returning. This door, a point of no return, symbolizes the very operation of change. One may get others to do many things, even wish that they change rather than oneself. But when one has to change, one does it alone; or perhaps one can only change for oneself alone.

The solitude of the monitors necessitates his silence. A monitor keeps silent until he can speak the truth at the right time. Little by little he carries on a primordial language with the participants that enables them to begin changing and to get away from his solitude. A seminar like this one teaches monitors and participants alike to speak and hear this primordial language; to know and to deal with it. As Foucault has said, words have several meanings and meanings have several words. This dimension of language is the opposite of the role of simple signs to which the monitors in

*Marines* reduced it; the only words that they required of and allowed their student-soldiers was the sign of unconditional obedience: 'Yes, sir.'

From there the discussion became general and I spoke more frequently. First I called attention to the link between the kind of problems discussed during the seminar and the kind of concrete situations actually experienced. For example, the antinomy between training goals (to heighten personal autonomy) and institutional or company goals (to increase output) was intensified to a point at which, in the manifest content, one had to call the institution wrong and the training right. However, in the latent content, the converse was true: participants complained that the plenary, regulatory sessions were not productive; this lack of productivity appeared serious, whereas participants hardly recognized the too great freedom allowed them by the very method of the seminar. Our meetings were more productive as people felt freer, freer of their phantasized fears and freer to speak of them. Moreover several participants pointed out that modern organizations, which must and can change rapidly, necessarily aim at both greater individual freedom and increased productivity. This in turn gives the organization the additional resources needed to give more freedom to its members, through training, culture and leisure.

I also spoke of the internal dialectic of change, as opposed to attachment and uprooting. Trainees' admiring attachment to the team of monitors was the reason most participants signed up for the seminar. This attachment sought to make the staff take on the role of the ego ideal, the importance of which Freud has shown for collective psychology. The 'staff' disappointed them because it didn't live up to this ideal, but above all because it didn't wish to play this role at all. Tearing participants away from this ideal was difficult and painful. The process was marked by a displacement of aggressivity on to Anzieu, the scapegoat, the attempt to 'screw' parents, and the phantasized murder of a dangerous, inconsistent father. I admitted to the trainees that just as they tore themselves away from this ideal, I gave up trying to make them change.

At last one participant asks: were there disagreements within the staff during the seminar? I try to answer it as a psychoanalyst. A psychoanalyst keeps quiet on questions that are misleading; but to a true question he replies by unveiling the phantasy behind it. However, I reformulate the question in order to reach the latent content. The question I will answer is, I say, 'What does this question represent for the seminar?' Then I try to interpret the anxiety at confronting the primal scene, but attempt to do so without explicit reference to psycho-analysis, in that 'primordial' language in which the group may recognize what in its own experience has until then remained incomprehensible. In effect, I ask: 'Do your parents agree or disagree?' If they disagree, the results for the child will be catastrophic. The seminar is the monitor's child. If the monitors disagree, the child cannot grow, the seminar cannot progress. In one of the diagnostic groups a similar question arose: Is the staff made of stucco or granite? If of granite it is monolithic; it is Anzieu together with little sub-Anzieus; participants can aspire to no more than being a sub-Anzieu. If of stucco (torn by disagreements), it is inconsistent with the ideal image participants have of it, and of their conceptions of their own training functions. (I implicitly linked the anxiety of breaking apart with anxiety over the primal scene, which appeared later; but I did not tell the group this.) My interpretation produced a sigh of relief in the seminar and was followed by a series of free associations confirming it. I could now say what everyone knew from start: the staff is composed of different personalities sometimes opposed on matters of technique and theory or even by differences of character, but who are bound not only by ties of friendship but also by a common attitude to diagnostic groups and psychodrama as the methods best suited to bringing to light latent group phantasies.

I had one more thing to say concerning transparence and appearance. The staff's wish was to act like a glass house: it eschewed secrecy as a matter of principle and believed that the work of training could take place in the open. Participants wanted primarily to see the staff at work. This inevitably led to a situation involving mirror-images. The window between staff and participants became a mirror in which participants saw their own problems reflected; they projected their own images on to the staff. The participants learned an old philosophical lesson; appearances are deceptive, reality is permeated with phantasy and appearances block or hide the truth.

Free associations take up the image of the glass house. Upon nods from myself and the female monitor we get up. The session is over. Each person by leaving assumes the death of the seminar in silence.

## 3 Comments

This case was written up in 1967. Since this time our theories and techniques have naturally changed. We no longer stress the relation between manifest and latent content. Instead of common group phantasies, we distinguish between the imaginary narcissistic or mirrored dimension of groups and their strictly phantasized dimension. We use only psycho-analytic methods. Moreover, the concept of split transference has enabled us to understand the singular contrast between the dissatisfaction of participants and monitors with large groups and their satisfaction with small groups.

The above case describes, but does not explain, phantasies of breaking apart. Such phantasies are the group form of castration anxiety. The intricacy of individual anxieties is related to psychotic, narcissistic and neurotic aspects of personality.

The psychic life in group situations is first organized around individual phantasies, or those of a prominent participant or monitor. The phantasies of others echo these. The group then progresses in this manner until conflicting intra-group phantasies develop. But these are not tolerated. Moreover, each individual tries to impose his phantasies on the others. In training groups, as in any group, there comes a time when the group is united by primal phantasies. Primal phantasies are those shared by all human beings (see Laplanche and Pontalis, 1964). Some are of the primal scene; at times participants feel themselves to be 'females' possessed by the 'male' monitor, or, as shown in session II(b), at times they phantasize that the monitors are indulging in coitus behind closed doors. Some are of intra-uterine life; the group goes on a sort of voyage inside the mother's body, making ecstatic discoveries and facing fearsome monsters. Some are seduction phantasies, with libidinal activation among several members of the group, public declarations of love, exhibitionist comments, voyeuristic complicity on the part of certain participants, etc. Some are castration anxieties pertaining to sexual difference or difference between male and female group members: some are phantasies of breaking apart as we have just seen. Sometimes groups have several primal phantasies simultaneously, as though they took all possible phantasies of group members into account. Sometimes phantasies are organized around primal counter-phantasies; this is the group illusion, in which differences among members are phantasized in symbiotic fusion.

The anxiety aroused by breaking-apart phantasies exists on several levels. At a pregenital level, it is a separation anxiety. The child who grows up resents his dependence on his mother and projects on to her his wish to be rid of her; he phantasizes a bad mother who rejects her children as a bad object or lets them kill one another. What is 'broken apart' here is the symbiotic bond between mother and child. To be trained is to feel exposed to breaking apart repeatedly. Initiation in traditional societies does just this to novices. Another breaking apart phantasy is that of wild beasts who tear one another apart. Group training experiences foster this phantasy, whereas individual psychoanalysis arouses fear of breaking mother-child bonds (which is also called oral 'castration').

# Chapter 10

# The phantasy of the group as machine: persecutive-seductive groups

In the phantasies of the group as a machine participants feel carried away by an apparently inexorable psychical process. Metaphors used to express these phantasies vary: monitors are compared to the sorcerer's apprentice, unable to stop what they have set in motion, participants to navigators caught in a maelstrom: their raft is sucked down by a deepening funnel of water. Or monitors are believed to have programmed everything in advance; what happens is scheduled without giving participants time to catch their breath. Hence the participants' extreme tension, overwork, and intense psychical and physical fatigue. In short, participants feel they are a prey to an overpowering force over which they have no control. This impression is accompanied by mixed feelings: anxiety at not being able to control the mysterious, terrifying force, at being swept towards an unknown destination, but also satisfaction that they are being confronted by an exceptional experience, because they are entering a world of dark, powerful forces that they had never known before.

We have three interpretations at our disposal. In religious terms, this transcendent force surrounds us and acts within us: 'My brothers, kneel and pray . . .', group monitors are sometimes tempted to say. In sociological (Durkheimian) terms the force is the result of group unity: we feel surrounded, transported by a collective force of greater-than-individual wills, thoughts and emotions. In psycho-analytic terms, this force is that of the freed primary processes of the unconscious, freed of defensive repression and the ego's watchful eye; it is proof of the indestructible energy and existence of these unconscious drives.

However, these three interpretations are too general to be satisfactory. One principle of all scientific explanation is, first, to account for specific facts and, second, to account for their inherent over-determination. Let us return then to an account of the facts.

Firstly, this phantasy of the group as a machine which is getting out of control is rarely verbalized during the initial sessions. This is because group phantasies, at least at first, are not expressed verbally.

Let us analyse the representations and affects that accompany the phantasies of the group-as-machine. There are two sorts of representations: (1) the diagnostic group, the psychodramatic group or the large group is a *machine* whose cog-wheels catch up most members; and (2) it is a *machination* of monitors against participants to get them to lay themselves bare, to spy on them, to take them apart, to transform them into guinea-pigs, objects, things, to reduce them to something purely mechanical.

The affects are also bipolar. One pole is that of suspicion (they may change us into an inhuman mechanism); the other is that of passive submission (we are dealing with something stronger than we are and cannot avoid being dominated, but by letting ourselves be carried away by this power, we will get some share of it).

Putting these representations and affects together, we can shed light on the question at the root of our phantasy of the group as machine: Is what is going on good or bad? This question applies to the method, to the particular group, to the type of training and to the monitor(s). Is what is going on going on inside or outside – inside *and* outside – myself inside or outside us? In other words: where are the limits between me and others, the group and the outside world, good and bad? Our hypothesis is that the phantasy of the group as machine is an expression of persecutory anxiety.

Scaglia (1974b), the Argentinian psychoanalyst, has defined the initial period of a group as a situation of primal paranoia. In fact, this is the period during which participants most often feel a prey to the machinations of the monitors. First series: 'they' take down notes about us, 'they' judge us, 'they' dissect us, 'they' keep their observations to themselves. Second series: we have to do as 'they' want, but 'they' refuse to give us what we ask of them; we cannot influence them with words, but they can influence us with their silence. Third series: in any case, when the monitors speak, it goes in one ear and out the other and we promptly forget it. Scaglia uses the Kleinian notions of breast-penis – the power of the phallic mother is attributed to monitors and observers – and of a part-object relation (the breast-penis is separated from the total person and lives an independent existence).

In the first series, by complaining that they are cogs in a machine that can be dismantled, participants express their projective identification with an image of the maternal belly phantasized as a container for independent pieces: sex organs, breasts, the father's introjected penis, the unborn children-faeces. In the second series, being influenced without having influence oneself, we can find the archaic equation: to be frustrated = to be attacked. In the third series monitors and observers represent a disturbing alienness, a bad projected double. Let us note in passing that monitors and observers are not always lumped together; the observer is often felt to be more persecuting than the monitor. This protects the monitor, for a paralysis of his interpretative functions is inevitable if collective persecutory anxiety is massively concentrated on him; this would equally inevitably lead either to relieving him of his functions or to the dissolution of the group. This is one of several reasons why observers are necessary in training groups.

Roland Gori's (1973a) analysis of words as objects in training groups sheds further light on the third series: the part, autonomous and destructive breast becomes the voice-penis of the monitor-mother who (in their phantasy) penetrates the participants through the anus: this explains the terrifying anxiety of a schizophrenic towards words spoken to him, well illustrated by Louis Wolfson (1970). This phantasy is reinforced in large group meetings where participants have more trouble getting to know one another than they do in small groups and where there are several interpreters. This analysis confirms Melanie Klein's criticism of the succession of stages in the psycho-sexual development of children: oral, anal, urethral and phallic. In fact, observation of young children shows that the phantasies accompanying these stages are simultaneous and overlapping, not successive. Group observation confirms this: in phantasy the monitor's voice penetrates the participants anally; the sadistic-oral and sadistic-anal drives are the same, a destructive drive that comes from an autonomous organ that bursts the body that it enters. What is more, a link of symbolic reciprocity exists between mouth and anus: what goes into the mouth and comes out of the anus is generally good; what comes out of the mouth and goes into the anus is generally bad.

Up until now we have analysed participants' projections on to monitors and observers. What happens to relations among participants at the beginning? The anonymity required by the rules of training groups, or instituted in certain circumstances in natural groups, means that others are not differentiated from myself and above all that I do not feel recognized as a total person by them. Others are anonymous and interchangeable for me, and vice versa, I am nobody for them. I want to be desired by the monitor and group. But the participants tear one another apart in the womb of their mother, the group. At least this is the latent content. The manifest content was well expressed by Sartre (1960): there is a struggle against scarcity; each person is afraid of being *de trop* for others, a 'useless mouth'. Hence, at the beginning of a group, so many mouths stay shut: participants feel useless and do not want to attract the attention of their exterminator-rivals by speaking.

Let me sum up. A 'persecuting' monitor and/or observer. Participants who do not know one another. Why under these conditions should the group be represented as a machine? Let us recall the differences between the depressive and persecutory positions. The depressive position, phenomenologically speaking, is the experience of chaos, the internal chaos of the subject. Only towards the middle of the course of a diagnostic group or seminar does the experience become chaotic for all, monitors and participants alike. The paranoid-schizoid position, by contrast, is the experience of the robot. Participants mechanically obey the rules. The monitor's counter-transferential belief in his group-machine leads him to want to explain and even anticipate the way in which his well-oiled machine will function. In seminars where several small groups function simultaneously, participants insist upon the similarity of discussion themes in various groups, as though everything had been planned in advance.

But to explain the phantasy of the group as machine by the arousal of persecutory anxiety in group members is necessary but not sufficient. We have come to the point where we should consider the particular character of the group reactions, as group members feel them.

First, however, a terminological and theoretical consideration. The psychical ego is not the same thing as the corporal (body) ego. Psychologists, psycho-analysts and group therapists often confuse these notions. The distinction would appear to be due to Freud's ill-loved disciple, Victor Tausk (Tausk, 1919). Before committing suicide, Tausk wrote an article which, even today, has lost none of its originality. In a sense, it deals with the phantasy of the body as machine among psychotics. Tausk studies the delusional belief of certain schizophrenics in an influencing machine made up of pieces, wheels, electric wires and levels corresponding to parts of the body, so that if a seducer, doctor, etc., manipulates a machine part, he directly influences the corresponding part of the body. The influencing machine is a particular instance in such ideas: the influence is attributed to a machine. Moreover, although elements of persecution are evident, the persecuting figure is not believed to be threateningly hateful, as he is in paranoia; he only wants mastery over the patient's body, only wants to control his physical sensations. Of course, these are primarily sexual, specifically genital sensations (erection, ejaculation to weaken male virility, exciting caresses for women to hold them at his mercy) are more frequent at the beginning of the illness; other sensations, to which psycho-analysis has drawn attention, derive from certain body zones, skin surfaces or internal organs. Tausk shows: (1) that what is projected – in the psycho-analytic sense of the term – in the delusion of influence is the sexual drive, which the ego cannot tolerate (whereas in delusions of persecution, it is the aggressive drive), and (2) that the body is projected in the neurological sense, as a reality outside the subject; sexual and sensual impressions felt physically can then be interpreted as having been produced by an alien influence, a disturbing alienness, willed by a seducer-persecutor.

The paranoid makes a distinction here between the psychical ego, which continues to function, since the subject always recognizes it as his (the ego defends itself against any dangerous wishes and rationally interprets what it perceives) and the corporal, physical ego, which also continues to function, but unrecognized by the subject as his.

From the economic point of view such a dualism can only be understood on the basis of an internal dualism of the libido. Here, this dualism is the sexual drive (the body image is cathected) and the narcissistic drive (the psychical ego is cathected).

Let us re-examine several features of the situation of training groups in the light of this comparison with individual psychopathology. First, the familiar world of family, occupation, social life, with its own time and space, is suspended. External reality is bracketed; the body becomes the only external reality of the psychical ego. Second, the participant is not alone watching his body function; he is forced to live with others in the same situation who are also told to speak what they feel. This is a para-psychotic situation: the limits of the ego become hazy; individual thoughts and emotions become transparent to others; when others speak, they speak for me, about me; and when I speak, I talk not of what *I* feel but of what one feels, despite vehement insistence from the most hysterical participants to say 'I'. In a note, Tausk speaks of Freud: 'Freud particularly stressed that the source of the child's belief that others know what he thinks is rooted in learning to speak. For the child receives others' thoughts through words, and his belief seems based on facts, just as is his feeling that others have "made" language and wish its thoughts' (*ibid.*, p. 224, no. 2).

It is often said that the non-directive group situation provokes regression. This is correct but vague until one specifies what regression is towards. If there is a chronological regression to archaic psychotic anxieties and phantasies, as the Kleinian school has shown, there is first a topographical regression to a state in which neither the super-ego nor the ego ideal has been formed, but in which the ego is already differentiated from the id. This enables the libido, undifferentiated in primary narcissism, to divide itself between two objects, two movements, sexual libido and narcissistic libido. Regression, then, brings group participants back to the stage of secondary narcissism and auto-eroticism.

The phantasy of the group as machine constitutes a defensive operation, like the syndrome of the influencing machine; it is a defence against the mobilization of the auto-erotic sexual libido in a situation cut off from the outside world; but it is also a defence against the danger of symbolic wounds inflicted by the group situation. At the same time, it provides an 'interpretation' of the trans-individual thoughts, experiences and verbal expressions, which are felt and explained as though they came from a 'manipulation' of the group by monitors or observers. One can thus understand why in such a phantasy monitors and observers are not destructive persecuting figures, but rather seductive persecuting ones. At the same time, one understands better the counter-transferential reactions of certain monitors who lead the group sometimes towards persecution and sometimes towards seduction phantasies. Moreover, in the present state of our knowledge of group methods, splitting tends to occur according to this pattern: verbal methods are experienced as persecutory and feared; methods involving physical contact are experienced as seductive and more and more sought after. As there is nothing new under the sun, here we are, working with the latest group techniques and methods in a pre-Freudian situation (the hypnotic approach to hysterics) – suggestion, seduction and influence.

Participants come to training groups in order to change. Thus they often expect to be changed by the monitors. At the same time they fear they will lose control over changes taking place in them and fear these internal changes will be manipulated at will by monitors and participants alike. To feel the group as an influencing apparatus is then one of the forms of resistance to change. It is inevitable until the participants' psychical ego is able to integrate changes taking place in the psychical apparatus and in their corporal experience.

To conclude, the phantasy of the group as machine, when it no longer astonishes group members in the early stages of a seminar but circulates in what is said, connotes the beginning of an acceptance of the unconscious processes brought into play by the situation. The group illusion becomes possible when the group is no longer a persecutory, seductive part object but rather a good, cathected object, a whole, united body which each person feels part of. The body is no longer a monstrous machine over which the ego has no control: the body's physiological structure, recognized as such, is a usable, but controlled projection; it may be compared to other structures.

# Chapter 11
# Paradoxical resistance

## A new form of resistance: rigged psycho-analytic work

The history of psycho-analysis in general, like that of any individual analysis, is the history of the resistances that the psychic apparatus opposes to the investigation of its functioning when this involves seeking forbidden pleasure, avoiding anxiety and the formation of symptoms of character traits. The development of theory or technique has no sooner allowed for the treatment of a new form of resistance than this resistance is displaced, transformed and reorganized. Thus, having overcome his horror at the crimes of Oedipus through an analysis of his dreams, Freud learned to analyse the corresponding complex in his patients; resistance became linked to more archaic processes and contents until Melanie Klein deciphered a good many forms. Thus pathology changes, as though to throw therapy off the track: conversion hysteria, so prevalent in the time of Charcot and on which Freud worked, has now practically disappeared in developed countries; by contrast, personality and behavioural disorders have developed that are neither neuroses nor psychoses but are due to deficits, failures, excesses of narcissism against which the psycho-analyst, armed with his usual theory and technique, is rather helpless. Finally, the popularization of knowledge has affected the psycho-analytic situation: it has become familiar whereas it was previously unknown. Paradoxically this reinforces its arresting strangeness and makes it easier to refuse while encouraging it. This does not happen only with patients. Many trainee analysts are no longer young Oedipuses in quest of the unconscious and triumphant over what is forbidden as were Freud's first disciples: what interests them is not the unconscious but psycho-analysis,

195

and it does so through their own narcissism.

The example of resistance to psycho-analytic work we are going to take comes from the field of applied psycho-analysis which today is rapidly gaining ground. Members of a group, many of them psychologists, psychiatrists or social workers resist by ostensibly coming to see the team of monitors at work; as a result, they do not enter into the experience sufficiently themselves to set off a process of individual and group change, and the team of monitors has little to work with.

In such a situation if psycho-analysts react with standard techniques they are trapped. Either they can keep silent, hoping that something will emerge, but nothing does, because the situation is jammed; there are signs of deterioration (absences, acting-out, individual psycho-pathological episodes and the spontaneous organization by participants of a counter-seminar). Or they can interpret the phantasy that they believe underlies this resistance. But even if all phantasies are mentioned (a sort of world's fair or festival of phantasies) the effect is null, because the interpretation of phantasies is precisely what has been most popularized for the present generation of 'psychists'. Thus the conscious social representation of the unconscious is used as a defence against individual insight into unconscious representations.

This problem is not only practical and technical. In a more general sense it stresses the inadequacy of psycho-analytic conceptions of conflict. In these conceptions the psychic apparatus represents its intra- and inter-systemic conflicts to itself. These representations are at once wish-fulfilments and compromise formations. For example, the theory that the ego is the centre or brain of the person is in fact, for the psycho-analyst, a phantasized fulfilment of the ego's narcissistic wishes; the 'beaten child' phantasy appears as a scenario in which the subject's internal conflict is dramatized, where fraternal rivalry is satisfied (my rival is beaten, not me) and where the defence (the threat of punishment) is personified at the same time as the drive (the eroticization of the sadistic drive). Thus spontaneous theories of the psychic apparatus about itself – often echoed by philosophical theories – are variants of infantile sexual theories, as Freud realized. The aim of treatment is to substitute a true representation, free of affect and cathexis, for a symptom of dream-like internal conflict.

## The case of the reflective bull

In the seminar mentioned above, the participants were split up into several small groups, alternating between discussion and psychodrama. The following is an account of the last psychodrama of one of these groups.

After several rejected scenario propositions and commentary on preceding psychodramas, it became apparent that in this group the same persons spoke and played, thus preventing the others from expressing themselves. The monitor interprets the participants' dilemma: they want to identify themselves with the monitors (i.e. to remain silent spectators), but also want to obey the rules proposed (enter into discussions actively). One of the silent members could then express his discontent. He wanted to find a play in which everyone had a part.

One of the members – who frequently suggested themes so that the group could get going, so it could reach a compromise between opposed suggestions – proposed a bull fight with one matador and two bulls: 'The bull who played the game would be killed; the other does not play along, wonders what he is doing there, why the matador brought him, what he [the matador] is going to do to him.' Everyone laughed at this suggestion, which represented a well-known difficulty encountered in the seminar. At once, everyone or nearly everyone, could take part. One trainee known for his provocative statements at the beginning of the sessions chose to be the charging bull. Another called attention to himself by leaving the room during the second session to join a strike of the personnel of the institution at which the seminar was being held; after this he progressively engaged in the activities proposed; he chose to be the reflective bull. The participant who had initiated the theme gave himself the role of matador. Several other participants said they would be the crowd which calls out 'Olé!'. However, once the play had begun, nobody thought of doing so.

The first part of the psychodrama was a mime. The two bulls came on stage. One of them sat down to think, despite the exhortations of the other. Suddenly, without a word, the first bull charged the matador, who, using his cloak, stepped aside. Furious at having been lured by the cloak, the bull stopped and realized that by charging the cloak he had missed the man: he then charged *him*. There followed a third which the actors later interpreted. The 'bull' thought he had hit the 'matador' and the 'matador' was convinced that he had avoided him.

The second scene was purely verbal. The charging bull sat next to the 'striking' bull and asked:

'Why did you come here?'

'I was told to come. We were caged. I thought we were being freed. And you, what are you running after? You blindly charge at nothing.'

'Red for me is like a green light. I feel alive, breathe freely.'

'I am quite comfortable where I am as a spectator.' The matador joins the conversation:

'I have to wave my cloak and get out my sword, since I am paid for that' (reference to the sum paid by participants and to the supposed fees of the organizers).

The matador is asked what he thinks of the bulls.

'Some are not nice or friendly, but are real cows.'

'Yes, but when you have to deal with a bull who doesn't move, you seem ridiculous.'

'I am going to tell you what I feel for the bulls I kill' (allusion to a large group monitor who was criticized for not entering into plenary meetings and who then, to everyone's surprise, said he was lonely). 'First I get ready. I must have a doctor with me, because we get gored. I get dressed. Then I go to the corral, smell animals' smells, I love them so much I want to kill the animals.'

'That is the point. I don't want to die.'

'Perhaps we can reach an agreement. When the bull has been brave, I can ask the crowd to spare its life. We can pretend to fight: I will let you be brave and you will be saved. But you must seem to play the game, otherwise the public will get even. You must also remember not to take the game too seriously. . . .'

'No, I won't accept your terms. I wouldn't even chance it.'

'Then the picadors will come and you will see what they will do to you.'

'I won't play the game.'

Having said that, the reflective bull got up to leave.

'Why don't you want to play the game?'

'Because I don't want my ears and tail cut off . . .'

This remark, quite unpremeditated, caused a sensation among actors and observers alike. A discussion of what just took place began.

'That reminds me of Ferdinand the bull who preferred to chase flowers.'

## The Palo-Alto School and pathogenic communication logic

The Palo-Alto school has attempted to rethink mental illness as a disturbance in communication. Indeed there is an implicit logic in parents' attitudes, or an explicit logic in what they say, which can imprison the child in contradictions, thus impairing the development of his relation to himself and others. The extent of this impediment depends upon the precocity, strength and permanence with which this logic is imposed. Following Bateson, psychiatrists and logicians of the Palo-Alto school at Stanford have identified three types of pathogenic logic: (1) tangentialization and disqualification, (2) mystification and (3) the double bind. All three are at work in varying degrees in psychodrama. All three imply that the outcome is vital for at least one of the two interlocutors involved.

In tangentialization and disqualification the listener brutally refuses to consider the speaker's desire to communicate irrespective of the content of his message. The speaker, who takes the initiative and expects an answer, sees himself neither praised nor criticized for what he says, but degraded for having taken the initiative to speak. At the very moment he tries to speak meaningfully, it is implied that he is incapable of doing so. He thus encounters primordial semantic frustration. Such is the child who, happy to play, calls his mother to manifest his contentment: 'Look how well I play,' he says, but she only replies, 'Go and get washed, you filthy thing.' This is the disqualifying mystification implicitly denounced by the reflective bull: 'What is the use of exchanging views when I will be beaten?' He then turns it against the matador: everything you say to me is meaningless. Underlying this manifest content is a latent meaning that relates to the seminar: participants cannot take seriously the apparently serious intention of the monitors to communicate with them; even the encouragement to speak is seen as a trap to disqualify them. In this game participants will be 'cut off': their tails will be cut off (they cannot take initiatives) as well as their ears (willingness to listen).

*Mystification* is also a denial of the speaker's message: what he feels, thinks, perceives and tries to communicate in his message is not considered to be what he feels; what he thinks and perceives is false; the other – the mystifier – knows the truth about him better than he does. Such was the case of a child whose mother plunged him regularly in a scalding bath so that the water temperature would be just right for his little sister. When the child tried to protest and complain of the intolerable heat, his mother insisted that the water wasn't too hot, that he was simply being awkward, that he didn't feel hot and uncomfortable, so he shut up. One day, however, he passed out. The bull fight, and the seminar activity it symbolized, were represented in the psychodrama as a mystification. If one acts out a bullfight, one is, in fact, arguing, reasoning. Whether one was actor or spectator, whether one was engaged in what was happening or reflecting upon it (allusion to the two tasks the monitors had given participants), it was nothing but a game. Charging is wrong; observing and interpreting are wrong; discussion, communicating is pointless. There, too, we find the mirror image: monitors who claim to decipher the real meaning of the feelings and experiences of the participants can only reflect the false impressions those participants give themselves, withholding their true feelings.

The double bind (paradoxical communication) is the best known of the types of pathogenic logic described by the Palo-Alto school. Whereas in the two preceding cases a weak subject, in his attempt to assert himself as speaker, runs up against frustration, here it is the speaker who is in a strong position, who takes the initiative and traps the listener by making his position as listener unbearable. The bind is double not only because the speaker says two things, but above all because it is paradoxical (the two statements are mutually contradictory). Paradoxical communication is an argument in which the enunciation contradicts what is enunciated: 'I order you to be spontaneous' or a road sign that reads 'Do not pay any attention to this sign.' The corresponding form of logic is the dilemma: the subject is obliged to choose between two branches A and B; but whether he chooses A or B, if he thinks about it, the consequences contradict his initial choice (the purest example is the affirmation 'I am lying', which, if false, is true, and, if true, is false); if he must act, things will go wrong. Like the mother of a schizophrenic who liked to repeat to her child, 'You are a monster; only a mother could love you', leaving the child with the alternative of either becoming a monster, so as to be loved by an impersonal mother, or not remaining a monster and being nothing.

The paradoxical injunction – a necessary condition for the functioning of a communication trap – is addressed to one for whom what is at stake is vital and who thus finds himself in a weak position (child, patient, prisoner, lover, etc.). A number of additional handicaps go with it. These prevent the subject escaping from the paradoxical situation. He could, in fact, get out of the bind if he used his head, by criticizing the internal contradictions in what is being asked of him: but all criticism is reprehended; he is made to feel guilty at any attempt to realize what is going on. He could also escape by externalizing the excess aggressivity inevitably produced in whomever is forced into a paradoxical situation and by breaking the Gordian knot by some violent reaction: but all expression of resentment is condemned by the person in the strong position as an act of ingratitude, as shameful behaviour, as serious disobedience to the established ground rules. If, finally, he turns in on himself, if he takes refuge in passivity, he is accused of selfishness and indifference; if he uses neither his intelligence nor his aggressivity, he is criticized for being stupid and weak. A paradoxical situation is such that one is prohibited from not reacting; yet it is impossible not to act paradoxically: which is used to criticize the subject, to discredit him still further.

## Paradoxical injunction in the scene of the reflective bull

The psychodrama session described is a series of variations on the theme of paradoxical communication, as the monitor pointed out when he first spoke, on the subject of the discussion preceding the act, about the participants' alternative between identifying with the neutral, uncommitted attitude of the monitors and obedience to their rule of participating, letting themselves go, throwing themselves into the seminar.

It is not surprising that the psychodrama (about the reflective bull) enacted the form of paradoxical injunction already mentioned, namely, 'I order you to be spontaneous.' In the paradoxical situation of the reflective bull a mirror was held up to monitors who spend their time thinking and never act. Several criticisms were condensed in this injunction. First the monitors keep their thoughts to themselves or communicate them so rarely and in so elliptical a manner that they are of no use to anyone. The logical aporia attacked here belongs to the following category: be spontaneous in what you say, but keep what you think to yourself. Second, if the monitors think without acting, it is logical that the participants act without thinking. In this case the aporia is: think before acting and do not act after having thought. Third, the monitors appear to reflect, keep to themselves and leave us free; in reality, they are bulls, power and strength are on their side. This aporia may be expressed as: Do what you want so long as I decide what it is. The internal contradictions of these different aporias are reflected in a remark of the charging bull faced with the stimulus of the red cloak waving before him: 'Red for me is a green light.' With greater logical purity, this could be stated: the red light gives me the green light.

Paradoxical resistance is expressed throughout the psychodrama in many different forms. The reflective bull agreed to come into the arena because he was closed up and thought he was being let free. This illustrates the aphorism that men believe themselves free because they are ignorant of what makes them act. The charging bull strikes at the cloak, but there is nothing behind it. This illustrates another aphorism: the lust for life is the veil of Maya, the lure that causes all our suffering. These aphorisms, one due to the 'wisdom' of Spinoza, the other to that of Buddha and Schopenhauer, do not appear by chance; they are, like many philosophical aphorisms, a resistance to the life drive, to the affirmation and development of the psychical life: we shall return to this point shortly. By basing their two contradictory arguments on these aphorisms, the two bulls enable us to witness in its purest logical form the dilemma mentioned above: we who come to be trained either play that game as it is proposed and run great risks, or we don't and nothing happens; in either case we lose. This dilemma was expressed by the same group in an earlier psychodrama session in the following form: a man condemned to die is offered freedom on condition that he accepts being inoculated with an incurable disease, so that he can be the guinea pig for a new treatment whose effectiveness has not been tried. In the performance, the actor who played the condemned man had refused the proposition: he considered that by remaining a prisoner he had as much chance of being saved as he had of getting well once he contracted the illness. Science fiction has developed infinite variants of this same fundamental dilemma. In training activities using the small non-directive group, it is often condensed in the theme of the guinea pig; the monitors use us for their experiments; instead of working on laboratory animals, they raise human guinea pigs. The underlying dilemma takes the following form: either their intentions are suspect, or their intentions are praiseworthy, but they are not technically in control of the process they initiate (they are sorcerer's apprentices); in either case we are in danger of being, if not destroyed, at least mystified. Let it be noted that it is the argument of mystification that mystifies, since it is resistance to training.

The experience of psychoanalytic work in training groups confirms the results of the Palo-Alto school. Parents who enclose their children in logical aporias at an early age make them psychotic. The regression that a psychoanalytic type of situation produces in participants leads them to relive psychotic anxieties and to project corresponding pathogenic reasoning on to the monitors. Dismantling these aporias involves the recognition on the part of participants that they are false and the possibility of escaping from their grip: the psycho-dramatic sequence dealt with above well illustrates the disentanglement necessary at the close of a seminar. A new field of research into group dynamics is thus opened up; drawing up an inventory of reasonings used by groups as resistance to training, and classifying them according to the level of collective anxiety and the individual psychopathology of its members.

## Logical paradoxes are figures of the death drive

Where we disagree with the theoretical orientation of the Palo-Alto school is where they hold that their logico-psychological perspective replaces the psycho-analytic approach. Obviously, the two are complementary; having concentrated on flushing out of the undergrowth primary process thinking, too many psycho-analysts have ended up by forgetting the existence and the importance of secondary processes. But, on the other hand, for the psycho-analyst, there can be no explanation of a psychic process as long as the motive, the wish and the drive behind it are not understood.

Let us take up the case of the reflective bull from this angle. We have studied above all the dilemma of the bulls and insufficiently that of the matador. Either the matador does what he does only because he is paid or he is a matador because this role fulfils a profound wish; in either case the result is the same: he kills. Whether he kills coldly, because he is paid or passionately as an artist, the outcome, death, is certain.

But what is one submitting to or revolting against? The object that alternating submission and revolt aims at is not only the supposedly strong, non-castrated adult. It is equally and perhaps above all the internal destructive drive. If I give into the destructive drive I become destructive for others. If others abandon themselves to the destructive drive, they become destructive for me, to destroy or be destroyed – such is the fundamental dilemma posed by the existence of the death drive, of which the castration anxiety (alluded to in the final remark of the psychodrama 'I don't want to have my ears and tail cut off'), is a particular case.

Thus an analysis of the logical mechanism at work in this psychodrama does not go as far as a psycho-analytic interpretation. In fact this logical mechanism is a particular form of resistance. Resistance to what? To transference: in this session the transference, more on to the group than on to the monitors, is persecutory. As in the phantasy of the group-as-machine, where the group is at once persecutor and seducer, the participants tend to be paranoid. But in this phantasy there is no element of seduction. The monitor of this psychodrama session understood it as a burlesque on the activities of the monitors among themselves, in other words as essentially a sadistic primal scene, and only incidentally as a reflection of the mystification or marginalization that participants perceived in the monitors' interpretations.

In his article on 'Negation' (1925), Freud showed that negative forms of verbs are imbued with the death drive. Refusing or denying are symbolic equivalents of destroying. But neither Freud not his successors pursued this study of the logical forms in which the death drive finds a representation that it tries to impose on the subject and get the subject to impose on others. An unfortunate phrase of Freud's in which he refers to the silence of the death drive, has assisted resistance to the analysis of its representation. We believe it is necessary to affirm that the death drive is indeed not silent. With the acquisition of language it speaks with sound and fury, aspects of the logic of which we have tried to indicate, following the Palo-Alto school. Resistance to psycho-analytic work in training groups can now be pinpointed. Psycho-analysis has remained for the public what it initially was for Freud, the investigation of conflicts stemming from the sexual drive. This serves as an ideological cover enabling the death drives to be omitted from the field of analysis. However, training consists of holding a discourse, on oneself and on others, in which the two categories of drives – the life drives and the death drives – are represented in complementary and opposed relationships (see Kaës, 1975).

## Resisting representation

All representation is at once of external and internal reality. To be more specific, as Freud discovered through dream analysis, the drive, the internal reality, attracts perceptions deriving from the body and the world, cathecting them, and thus giving them meaning, in order to get themselves represented in the psychic apparatus. But this must be extended from perception to reasoning. Secondary processes are always infiltrated with primary processes. All reasoning processes are at the service of one or another drive. Only true psycho-analytic thought is a reasoning process which, while respecting the demands of logic, represents not one drive but a dualism of drives. Each uses the logic of its representations as a defence against the representations of the other.

Changing, like leaving, is experienced as dying a little: hence resistance to change. To do what is necessary so that nothing happens where one comes with exceptional expectations is the fulfilment of a self-destructive wish: let nothing happen. But this wish does not come out so simply. Its representations are formally structured as the mystifying dilemma whose contradictory terms block possibilities for the renewal of thought and personal development. Hence representation becomes resistance. The exit from this dead-end demands that the subject, with the help of the analyst, turns things round so that resisting the representation is no longer given in to but rather is reconceived as representing resistance. This work entails the dismantling of the formal structure and taking the specific organization of the secondary processes into account. This is why interpreting a phantasy directly, without taking into account the conscious mediations specifically related to it, cannot be effective.

# Chapter 12
# The group and the superego

## (A)  The phantasies of the father's murder: clinical observation of a group disorder

The managing director of a medium-sized metallurgical company came to consult us concerning a double problem of management: the management committee was not functioning properly and there was a crisis of conscience after firing a colleague. The company headquarters and factory were in northern France.

There are four persons on the management committee:

Bernard, about forty years old, has been new managing director for a year. He is a graduate of a business school. He was sales director and lived in Paris because most of the company's clients are there. He was appointed managing director by the board of directors, composed largely of members of his family: when the former managing director had to resign for health reasons, Bernard retained his functions as sales director, but came to live in a town near the factory.

It was intended that Jean-Denis, son of the former managing director, Jean-Albert, would take over. Jean-Albert's financial errors in managing the firm, the rather limited ability of Jean-Denis and the fact that a majority of the board members favoured Bernard, on whom they were counting to put the company back on its feet, thwarted Jean-Albert's plans to have his son succeed him. Jean-Albert got the board of directors and Bernard to agree that, as Jean-Denis was not given the position of managing director, they would promise that he would stay with the company as a director. Jean-Denis is thirty-two, has a law degree, is on the board of directors and is personnel director.

Robert, sixty years old, is works manager. He does not rank as a director, but he regularly attends management committee meetings because of his knowledge and experience. He is one of the longest serving of the firm's employees, having begun work in it forty years ago, shortly after it was started by Jean-Albert, who took notice of him, promoted him and considered him his right-hand man.

Xavier, forty-eight years old, an engineering graduate, is production director. He was hired by Jean-Albert twelve years ago, when the company was expanding. He rationalized the work in the factory and functioned as management consultant, leaving Robert to run production. He has taken courses in how to run meetings, so Bernard lets him run the management committee meetings.

Meetings of the management committee had been interminable and inefficient; Jean-Denis, Robert and Xavier could not agree. As a result Bernard was forced to ignore the committee and made whatever decisions he himself thought best and then informed the others. He scheduled meetings less and less often, and then did away with them altogether, preferring to meet individually with each of the other three members. He believes his relations with them are good and that the problem lies in their relations with one another.

Robert and Xavier have the same excitable, authoritarian temperament. They have arguments every day, but work them out and respect one another as working colleagues.

The same cannot be said of Jean-Denis. He has the reputation of being lazy and incompetent; he loses files, forgets to take care of matters for which he is responsible (hiring personnel, raising pay, preparing office space), which exasperates those in other departments who have to suffer the consequences. Robert and Xavier have had violent arguments with him, which have only reinforced Jean-Denis's individualist attitude. Rober and Xavier work together at Jean-Denis's expense; whenever they think it necessary to short-circuit him so that their departments can function properly, they do so. Jean-Denis knows this and at every possible occasion blocks them. Each one wants to put the blame on the other. Things are so bad that Xavier and Jean-Denis communicate largely in writing, despite the fact that their offices are adjoining. Robert and Xavier have little by little convinced Bernard that Jean-Denis is incompetent and demand that he be fired to save the company.

Bernard has tried in vain to help Jean-Denis organize his work and act as mediator in conflicts between colleagues. He came up against the same difficulties: Jean-Denis's negligence and procrastination. However, relations between them remained courteous. Bernard is in a moral quandary that troubles him and from which he sees no escape.

He is torn between keeping his promise to the former managing director and making the company function properly. He wonders whether Jean-Denis is intellectually 'all there', whether some childhood illness has not impaired his mind; he asked us to run a psychotechnical, psychopathological examination of him to answer these questions. But it is doubtful whether Jean-Denis would willingly accept such an examination. Bernard doesn't feel that he has a right to force him to. Given Jean-Denis's university career and the emotional tone of the conflict, this curious request on behalf of a third party seems to us to be a way of displacing the problem of a sick group on to a single individual. Moreover, it makes us wonder whether Jean-Denis is not a scapegoat for the sick group.

I suggest to Bernard that the first thing to do is to meet with each of the four members of the management committee. These meetings are accepted, because the atmosphere is so poor, the management's cohesion so threatened, that its members are willing to try anything. The request for an individual consultation takes on its true meaning; the sick group realizes that in fact it is the group that needs a consultation. We intend to sort out what is objective and what is phantasy in this conflict by speaking to each of those concerned. To grasp the phantasy element in the situation, however, it seems indispensable to contact a fifth person around whom we intuitively feel the group phantasies have focused, the former managing director, Jean-Albert. The latter, saddened by the problems of a company that means much to him, is flattered by our visit: moreover, our going to see the individual whose image has remained central for the other four, lends force to our function as consultant and helps to make it acceptable to Robert, Xavier and Jean-Denis.

Jean-Albert lives in a large house near the factory: it is the house of the managing director, which, however, he was allowed to stay in after his retirement. At the back of the garden is a small door leading directly to the factory. This is the way Jean-Denis goes to work. He came to live with his father when the latter –

wanting a successor and disappointed by the refusal of his eldest son, whom he had groomed for the job – turned towards the younger, who was beginning a career in banking. He overcame Jean-Denis's reluctance – his future was less promising in this career, but he had little liking for or ability in technical matters – by more or less formally promising him he would turn the company over to him once he knew the ropes: Xavier was hired to relieve him of technical responsibilities.

Jean-Denis still lives, with his wife and children in his father's house. The telephone on Jean-Albert's desk has a direct line to the factory. In my presence, the father asks his son for details concerning a technical point that arose during our conversation. But practically in the same breath Jean-Albert stresses that he does no wish to meddle in company affairs now that he is retired. Of course, his son keeps him informed about various problems and he is very upset, both for the company he founded and for his son, for whom he had greater hopes; he wonders if his son is not being unjustly treated. When he (Jean-Albert) first fell sick and was confined to his bedroom for several months, it was Jean-Denis who managed things and did very well.

Jean-Albert is a self-made man, hardworking and demanding; he has a rigid, hard, authoritarian character, which he has inherited from his Scandinavian ancestors. He dominated his son; at the factory, he used to go down to the shopfloor every day, knew all the workers, talked to them in dialect and yelled at them if they did the slightest thing wrong. He was feared, admired, respected and loved. Psychologically speaking, the company grew around him, through the power he had and the bonds each workman had with him; Robert, his right hand man, was the same sort of person.

This industrious man, this ego ideal, had unfortunately not kept up with the times; he had not known how to revise his economic and financial views, which were stuck in a routine. After having done well, the company was now in alarming financial difficulties. Worry contributed to the onset of Jean-Albert's first illness. He recovered, but had less physical and moral stamina; he could not arrest the worsening of the company's economic plight. An even more serious attack forced him to see what he did not want to see: his time was over, other ideas were needed, other men; he could only survive through his son.

Through all this there ran a common theme: although Jean-

Albert had officially retired and Bernard had replaced him, in everyone's mind, he was still the real boss.

Bernard, content to live in Paris with moderately heavy responsibilities and a high salary resulting from good sales, had no immediate ambition to take over the company. His allies on the board of directors had given him the post to save the company from ruin; he had accepted because his own financial interest was linked with that of the company. However, he felt guilty at having taken Jean-Denis's place. Because of this he left Jean-Denis as much independence as he could, though the latter, used to being firmly backed by his father, could only work well if he was given directions. With respect to most of the personnel, Bernard did not feel at ease: he was a Parisian and did not understand the people of northern France very well; he never went into the workshops. It is true that he had other things to do, as financial concerns took up most of his time. Above all, he knew that he lacked Jean-Albert's authority. He was afraid that the others would not forget Jean-Albert, that they would accuse him of usurpation, that the others would band together against him.

The ghost of Jean-Albert was just as lively in the minds of Robert and Xavier, but they reacted differently. For years Jean-Albert had tyrannized them. He had even wanted to impose his son on them, a shy, intellectual young man. Then, without realizing it, they had their revenge: they made the son pay for what they had suffered at the hands of the father. They humiliated the father now for having produced an incompetent, mediocre son. Jean-Albert also paid for something else: Robert's bitterness at having a newcomer as boss; he the oldest and most senior foreman had to take orders from a Parisian. Also, Xavier's bitterness at not having been made a director, as he would have, if Jean-Denis had not taken his father's place, did not come out openly as hostility against Bernard, but was displaced on to Jean-Denis.

Jean-Denis is a good example of ambivalence towards the paternal imago. In his interview with me, he expressed the phantasies underlying his behaviour far more spontaneously than I thought he would. He had believed his father's promise and had never doubted that he would take over the company. His father's compromise with the board of directors seemed to him to amount to personal treason and released latent hostility towards his father. From then on his attitude was:

(1) What is promised is owed; he did not accept being personnel

director, but really believed himself to be the real managing director; Bernard was a usurper; all his colleagues, Robert, Xavier, were potential usurpers, ready to take over the helm if they could and dispossess Jean-Denis of what was his by right.

(2) Consequently Jean-Denis was biding his time, when the truth would out, when his rights would be recognized and the usurpers, would prove themselves to be incapable of running the company; only Jean-Albert knew how to handle things and only his son would be able to go on doing so; as he (Jean-Denis) had been denied the post of managing director, he refused to act in his capacity as personnel director, his dignity was offended: he neglected his functions, brooded, complained and unconsciously sabotaged the company's functioning; he wanted to show that unless it had him as managing director, nothing could stop it from going to rack and ruin. But he did not realize that by doing nothing himself, he was actively contributing to its decline.

On the level of objective reality, it was in the interests of all of them to get together so that the factory could work better and the situation of each one of them could be maintained or bettered.

On the phantasy level, each of them still thought of Jean-Albert as the real boss; it was he who had proved himself and, despite his retirement, supervised everything from his adjacent house, knew everything, decided everything and no doubt pulled all the strings. From his control tower, linked to the factory by a network of telephone wires, the master listened in to them, and they always expected to hear his outbursts. The four members of the management committee all felt themselves to be heirs to this boss who could not die, either physically or in their phantasies; they fought over what he had left, each believing his should have the largest share. Officially, all were members of the management committee (there wasn't one in the days of Jean-Albert), but Bernard had the top job: this situation was not accepted, for objective reality cannot override an opposing phantasized reality. Bernard dared not use his power; Xavier, Robert, Jean-Denis used the power they had to show that Bernard was not in charge and, unconsciously, by disrupting the company, to oust the incompetent usurper.

The phantasies underlying this situation and shared by the four protagonists may be described as follows, in so far as an imago can be defined in words. For each of them the ideal leader is still Jean-Albert; but he is also hated for his rough way with people. All four implicitly understand that running things as he did is out of the question. Bernard is elected king; the feudal lords try to restrict his power and under the pretext of democratic leadership, they install anarchy. Jean-Denis is in his own eyes, and in the eyes of the others, the legitimate heir. Each one wants to take what is his and is afraid of the rule of a second Jean-Albert. There is only one solution: band together. Jean-Denis's life is thus made impossible; he is bullied; the other three take their revenge on him for his father's tyranny and for the tyranny of Jean-Denis, which they fear will come. In all this, the company, which is on the verge of economic collapse, is moving towards psychological collapse. Let the boat sink with everyone on board rather than try to save it! A collective suicide is better than the resurrection of Jean-Albert.

Everyone struggles with rational means against this shared phantasy, with the feeling that if they gave in, the result would be catastrophic. The managers stay late into the evening at the factory. They work on plans for the reorganization of the finances, growth and production. They discuss these matters at length, except with Jean-Denis. But there is no communication, despite the soundness and the relevance of these plans. The shared imago blocks them on a deeper level. It prevents their feeling the possibilities for agreement rationally and having confidence in them. Each one believes he is rational and judges what he believes to be phantasy in the others, without realizing that he is equally lured on by phantasies. All are depressed by the feeling that there is a heavy burden to carry, that energies are drained, that the situation is hopeless. This is an illustration of the slavery in which, according to Freud, the primary psychic processes hold the secondary processes.

In this atmosphere, my intervention was felt as a test of truth. This enabled me to proceed quickly: two meetings with Xavier, Robert and Jean-Denis, one with Jean-Albert and three with Bernard were enough in forty-eight hours to shed light on the imago, untie the knot and let the four decide for themselves how to function better in objective terms.

Bernard was made to realize that it was his job to chair the meetings of the management committee, to show his authority in a clear way. We explained that the problem of Jean-Denis was one of his feelings and reactions and not one of his intellectual capacity; we hinted that he treat Jean-Denis as the boss's son and not in the way a managing director would treat a departmental head. In short, we showed Bernard the need to recognize that he was now the new boss and to make others recognize it.

We gave Robert and Xavier a short psychology lecture: how Jean-Denis had been brought up, what ambitions had been encouraged, how he had been disappointed, how negatively he had reacted, and how their attitude only accentuated his negative reactions. How can someone who feels mistrusted and disdained by his colleagues avoid the trap they laid for him, keep his head, take his work to heart and avoid mistakes? Xavier was deaf to these arguments and exhibited in a quasi-cathartic fashion his implacable hostility towards Jean-Denis. So we drew up a list of all Jean-Denis's failures and mistakes and gave him the list. Jean-Denis had something to say on each point: the matter was not urgent, Xavier was abusing his power, he didn't see things as Xavier did and this divergence needed to be dealt with by Bernard (who hadn't dared to). We returned to Xavier and told him of Jean-Denis's answers. Some Xavier accepted; others he rejected. We left him, letting him draw his own conclusions: the real source of his conflicts with Jean-Denis was negligible compared with the emotional source, which magnified them out of all proportion; these conflicts could easily be resolved by a courteous discussion between equals, and where the difference of opinion remained there was a managing director there to settle the matter, even if he was not an engineering graduate and had not studied business management and human relations.

Robert, by contrast, soon caught on. He had watched Jean-Denis grow up. He had no trouble making out and understanding the elements of phantasy in the situation. Without speaking to me, he did two things to alleviate the crisis. Before dinner, he went to see Jean-Denis and behaved in a fatherly manner towards him, as an old employee who had shown the boss' youngest son the ropes would naturally do. This cleared up problems between their departments. Then, after dinner, he went to see Jean-Albert, his old friend, to whom he had not dared to speak for six months for fear that the old man would accuse him of conspiring against him. Robert went to see Jean-Albert, ostensibly about a town brass band, which they ran together. Delighted to see one another again, the two old friends had a relaxed chat that covered the general problems of the factory. Jean-Albert reiterated his intention to stay out of things so as not to get in the way of his successor. Robert gave him to understand that if his son went on brooding and reacting negatively he would prove his incompetence and inevitably be fired. Thus, having severed the ties of professional dependence on Jean-Albert, Robert was assured that from then on his boss would be Bernard; and Jean-Albert, prepared by his conversation with me, understood that instead of tacitly sympathizing with the injustices towards Jean-Denis, he had to confront his son with the reality, as he had himself a year before when he had handed over the reins to Bernard.

Our decisive conversation was with Jean-Denis. After showing him his behaviour (fixation on a dashed hope, bitterness and resentment towards his colleagues, whose superior he believed he ought to have been, and his vague wish to sabotage the factory of which he had been dispossessed), we described to him how the others saw his behaviour: as proof of his unfitness to be not only managing director but even personnel director. While thinking he was sabotaging the factory he was in fact sabotaging his own professional career. Things had reached a point of no return. Jean-Denis roundly defended himself against this truth, which had never been told him face to face and which, closed up in his phantasies, he had been able to see only vaguely. But the next morning he went to work, in the full sense of the word, and after going over with Bernard a list of things to be done in order of priority set himself a programme of action.

From then on, the management committee could meet again; Bernard took the chair and the change in the attitudes of Robert and Jean-Denis isolated Xavier, who was forced to stop playing the boss and to take up his real post. Still uneasy, Bernard asked us to come to the meetings as observer or even as monitor. In fact, he wanted support. In our last conversation with him, we refused his request, while reassuring him. The phantasized knot had been undone; it was now up to him to play the role of managing director and to resolve prolems rationally with his colleagues, who would now play the roles corresponding to their functions. For ethical and technical reasons, as a psychologist, I could not agree to take on the phantasized place that Jean-Albert's symbolic death had left empty.

At bottom the problem was that symbolic death. The retired boss kept power all the more insidiously because he no longer had any in reality. Often the absent, dead or idealized leader becomes all the more powerful because fascination with an imago of authority is stronger when the leader is not continually present in the flesh. A purely psychological power is greater than physical or social ones. At the same time because Jean-Albert had retired, the others could give free rein to their hatred of an often cruel and tough boss.

The 'Old Man's' sons, bastard or legitimate, did not bury this imago, towards which they still reacted with mingled admiration. The work of a psychologist consisted in resolving this situation solely on the phantasy level by making the four participants experience the myth Freud imagined in *Totem and Taboo*.

The management committee was able to function for eighteen months, time for the necessary economic steps to be taken. But the reader will have understood what I sensed at the time – that Bernard's personality was not suited to his position as managing director. This case proves once more the general law that group phenomena come from the collusion of collective phantasies with the individual psychological make-up of one of its members. The authority of the Old Man continued in the minds of his former subordinates not only because they were fascinated by it and because unconsciously he wanted to continue as boss, but also because Bernard, the newcomer, had not been able, given his personal make-up, to assume the authority of his position and to impose his authority. In turn, the strength of the unconscious fascination with Jean-Albert reinforced Bernard's uncertainty and timidity; for a time he muddled through, but only because I intervened. Once the group problem was solved, Bernard was increasingly faced with his personal problem. After eighteen months he had learned his lesson and turned in his resignation.

To conclude from this case that once phantasies are unknotted, groups can function rationally to obtain objective goals and become adaptable is a stereotyped explanation that has no real basis in fact. Our experience has shown otherwise. There are always phantasies in groups, whether objectively the group runs into difficulty or succeeds. To study group dynamics clinically it is necessary to recognize shared phantasies, analyse their structures, grasp their functions and establish processes by which they can be recognized.

## (B) A case of an obsessive in a group

In an earlier publication I gave an example of the 'active'

interpretation, in psychodrama, of a hysteric (the case of Irma (Anzieu, 1972)). Here I will deal with the case of an obsessive, observed during a diagnostic group lasting three days. The group was made up of eleven persons, five men and six women, aged between twenty-two and fifty. There was also an observer, with whom I had long, valuable conversations throughout the course.

Alex was about forty years old, an arts graduate, who had been seconded to a teacher-training centre in order to learn 'active' methods. He had already participated in a diagnostic group. During the introductions, he had listed his various diplomas and referred to his wealth of experience. Although there were doctors, psychologists, economists, directors of religious or educational organizations present, he soon convinced them that he had finished his training, whereas they were just beginning theirs.

One of Alex's traits was his impersonal manner. When he spoke, and he did so often, he always said 'one'. After several sessions, Désirée, a hysteric, hotly criticized him for this attitude: she ostentatiously said 'I' and vehemently challenged him to do the same, which he had difficulty doing.

Second, Alex rejected what he called 'sentimentality'. He criticized emotional expression in the group as counter to its goals. What was aimed at, he declared with such force that for a time the implicit collective norm prohibited any emotional display, was an exchange of ideas. He intellectualized and isolated emotions.

Third, he spoke often, commenting on, condemning, approving or contradicting the others. He did not allow free association to develop; and related everything to himself, the centre of conversation. I wrote in my notes: 'He is on the throne in the middle of the family circle and has everyone admire his faeces.'

He couldn't stand silence, no doubt fearing aggressivity; he continually broke it. Exhausted by his intellectualism and his narcissism, the other participants tended to speak less and less. This Alex criticized, as though they had given up and failed to respect the rules.

He also tried – in vain – to thwart references to childhood memories. His criticisms made one woman cry; she had just communicated with much emotion an important episode from her childhood which turned out to shed light on her attitude in the group.

For Alex the group and the group relations did not exist; what he perceived was a collection of individuals with whom he dealt one at a time. In these dyadic relations he acted either to get the other person to keep quiet, or to contradict what he had just said: he could not be satisfied until he had imposed a sado-masochistic relationship on his interlocutor.

Because Alex was convinced (and had convinced the others) that his experience and training were superior to theirs, he offered interpretations and acted like the real monitor of the group. His interpretations were always individualistic and hurtful. He criticized the group for its 'comatose' state, accused it of being dead, thus projecting on it his obsessional's lack of life, dominated by the death drive.

Unlike the other participants, he refused to communicate his own memories. However, after a period of psycho-analytic work (about which I shall speak shortly), the group became conscious of and less taken in by reactions to Alex himself and Alex himself became more flexible. He decided to express his gratitude to the group and demonstrate his confidence by communicating something very personal: not an old inadequate memory, but a phantasy that came to him during the session. The point of departure was a real fact related by two participants: the janitor of the building in which the session was being held had not been warned and expressed his surprise with ill humour when he saw people coming in on Saturday. Alex had imagined after the event what he might have replied: 'We have to work all weekend, because we are getting ready to hold up the Bank of France and we don't have much time to work out all the details.' And, he added, amused, half-an-hour later the police arrived. This phantasy was so unlike preceding secrets confided by the other participants that it fell flat. Nobody commented upon it, and Alex thought the group ungrateful in view of the efforts he had made.

I myself was wrong at the time to have also remained indifferent; I failed to understand the meaning rapidly enough and to use it to further psycho-analytic work. The symbol of anal power, money (robbing the Bank of France), which Alex continually tried to get for himself, and the superego, the permanent threat of the police, were there served up on a platter, so to speak. But this was not the problematic of the other participants, which revolved around the loss of a loved one or the demand for the phallus. My own counter-transference no doubt unconsciously made me reluctant to make Alex the centre of the group's attention by taking account of a phantasy that the group ignored. It was during a discussion with the observer that I realized this, too late to use my insight to stress the conflict within the group between anal and phallic representations of power. The group had by then moved on to other matters. But Alex, whose development was arrested by the absence of any response to his personal phantasy, fell back on his habitual position and began once again to hinder the group through provocation and excessive superego demands, although the intensity of these had diminished.

## The work of 'indirect' interpretation

Before the episode of this phantasy, a certain work of interpretation had been attempted. On the first day I had given an insufficient interpretation, explaining that the position of power was free, as I used non-directive methods, and that Alex had taken it. I noted that Alex behaved more as a monitor who provokes and criticizes than as a monitor who interprets, and that the rest of the group felt ill at ease before what they had no doubt sensed as usurpation. This interpretation, more psycho-sociological than psycho-analytic, was not accepted; it is, said participants, a common habit of monitors to try to relate to themselves and to transference everything that goes on in the group, whereas neither my role nor myself had until then been a problem; they felt neither dependence nor rivalry towards me.

On the second day I used the criticism that Désirée had aimed at Alex (he used the impersonal 'one') in order to be specific; I spoke of a conflict between persons rather than between hypothetical group phenomena. I was, nevertheless, careful to speak of roles, so as not to hurt individual participants and also to use references to individuals as illustrations of the group phenomena at work. I provided what may be termed an 'indirect' individual interpretation (contrary to the letter, but congruent with the spirit of Ezriel's rule). I described first the 'role' that Alex played in the group. In fact, I listed his character traits, as I did above, taking care to avoid psycho-analytic allusion and vocabulary. But I added that although these traits were probably related to his personal problems, these problems were not our concern as a group. What interested us was to know why and how Alex's 'role' gave rise to other 'roles' among other participants. And I described the aggressivity of some, the passivity of others and the unconscious wish of all to see others functioning like them.

This interpretation was more successful. Alex had ill digested the affective reactions of the others towards him, as these related to aggressivity and passivity, themes to which he was hyper-sensitive. He accepted the description that I gave of him because its tone and intent were objective and because he learned something about himself, which was what he had come for. For the rest of the group, the interpretation brought marked relief: I situated their problem where it really was, in the guilt feelings that Alex's attitude had aroused. They no longer felt guilty for their impatience, their irritation, their displeasure, or their paralysis. For whatever they were or were not when they came, Alex's superego attitude aroused strong guilt feelings. Each time it was needed they were able to talk things out with Alex, not in argumentative or inhibited fashion, but firmly and with humour. Each participant expressed what he expected of the group experience. From this time on childhood memories, painful episodes of mourning and moments of relieved emotion and individual experience could be discussed. The central role in the group was no longer taken by Alex, nor by Alex-Désirée, but by Thibaut, a young engineer whose wit, gaiety and negotiating talents rounded off the corners of interpersonal conflicts or tensions regarding Alex. Alex had played on the superego of the group members: Thibaut made them use their ego.

## On group problems stemming from individual psychopathology

(1) The formulation of rules at the beginning of the course must not overpower or crush the participants. For these rules are initially neglected, sometimes challenged and generally quickly forgotten. The monitor's function does not require prior explana-tion either: his essentially interpretative role will appear when he speaks for the first time, providing participants with a psycho-analytic interpretation. The only desirable directions at first concern the non-participation of the observer in group activities – symbol of the discretion used by seminar members in speaking about the seminar to outsiders – and the definition of the sort of activity participants are encouraged to engage in. Within this activity, participants may choose the subjects, themes and methods

they like. However, the participants should be reminded that they are free within the context of seminar activities, the condition of the realization of training goals, to communicate what they really feel.

(2) Interpretation may be meaningful and helpful to participants only on condition that they have been prepared and it may be given without aggressivity, even with a certain benevolence. Parenthetically, it may be remarked that helping participants may consist not in interpretation but in putting them face to face with their problems. Parsimonious, general and impersonal interpretations reflect a defensive attitude on the part of the interpreter and attenuate, even invalidate altogether, the effect of the interpretation. The very activity of interpretation is itself the foundation of all meaning: the monitor's presence, his receptivity, his wish to be there with others and his willingness to communicate.

(3) Another common error shared by participants as well as by monitors is to believe that interpretation is all powerful and consequently to be disappointed when it does not meet expectations. More generally, the monitor, like the other people engaged in training courses, must accept his own limitations, those of others, and those of the method with which he works. He must accept the fact that interpretation cannot solve all problems and is not always immediately successful, that it must be formulated later or reformulated; that changes only take place in a few members of the group; that participants are partially satisfied at the end of the seminar; that one knows nothing about what happens to participants after the seminar: all this is acquired only at the price of work on oneself, which is to be begun at virtually every course.

(4) In addition to accepting these limitations, the monitor must realize that a certain time is needed before he can arrive at understanding, recognize that it will take the group time to ripen, accept the diversity of the rhythms of change. Hence he must resist the temptation to interpret psychosociologically what is obscure to him in the unconscious dynamics of the group and must refrain from interpretation when the group gets bogged down.

(5) It may in fact appear difficult for the monitor to adjust to the considerable variety of individuals, if he restricts himself to group interpretation as Ezriel recommends (1950, 1966). Here the group-as-object is apt to come in the way of the monitor's understanding of individual unconscious activities. As I have already said, there is no such thing as a group phantasy; there are

predominant individual phantasies that preclude the manifestation of the phantasies of other individuals. When this happens, the unconscious dynamics of the group is to be interpreted as such; this cannot be done without the monitor's taking into account the relative positions, central or peripheral, of group members. When a group member with a strong personality and a distinctive type of psychopathological structure becomes the centre of group interest, the result is not a group phenomenon (unless there is quasi-unanimity to make this person a leader or a scapegoat), but rather a mosaic of individual reactions of identification-projection, defensive manoeuvres in reaction to this type of psychopathology. The whole of the course may be more or less totally devoted to the repetition of the same type of stimulation-response sequences, without doing anybody any good.

Experience with such cases has shown the ineffectiveness of interpretations centred on the group, particularly on a hypothetical group phantasy. It is a mistake to look for a group phenomenon where there are only individual phenomena in the group. Interpretation thus proves that character traits, defensive conflicts, and the economico-topographical organization of the central individual, as well as the unconscious reactions and attitudes of the other paricipants, have been understood.

(6) A participant whose psychopathology poses problems to all group members does not come to a training group to present his suffering or his problems, does not ask to be treated and the others do not necessarily feel inclined to help him. Or, if they do feel so inclined, it is not the monitor but the group or a part of it that carries out a brief psychotherapy (Missenard, 1971, 1972), for if the monitor agreed to treat a participant in difficulty during group sessions or on the side, he would only aggravate his state and worsen his breakdown. Obviously, if a participant has a break-down, appropriate therapeutic measures need to be taken at once. During a seminar one of the large group monitors is selected to take matters in hand, because they are not needed for the functioning of the small groups. In my very rare experiences with such instances one private meeting in depth may be enough to enable the participant either to return to the seminar or to get himself home. Generally, it turns out that such persons have already had psychiatric treatment.

In the case of François-Joseph (Missenard 1971, 1972), we have an instance of one whose choice of a career as training monitor was a defence against his own problems and those of others; his manifestly sociable, sympathetic and conciliatory attitude quickly became unbearable to the group. This loss of a narcissistic mooring on the others produced depression: he lost his bearings. But the women in the group realize this and function as co-therapists and allow him, in the Kleinian sense, to begin a reparative process in his depression. At the same time the group, which had dumped a number of problems on to François-Joseph, could deal with them through him.

In the case of Alex, events could not take the same course for, unlike François-Joseph, he was an obsessional. It was necessary to provide other participants with the opportunity of asking themselves questions concerning the prolems posed by his psychopathology and to learn something about dealing with such persons. Alex was given the opportunity of realizing how he affected others and of examining his reactions instead of repeatedly imposing his will on them. Where a fundamental unconscious phantasy of one person is at work, a training group cannot make him progress; only psycho-analytic treatment could do that.

The monitor needs to be firm when presenting this problem, for the central character tends to consider only the problems he speaks about 'true', and not the problems he presented for others. Thus both firmness and tact are required so that this person does not feel that he is being singled out by the monitor, as he inevitably is by certain participants. Moreover, if the monitor does not act in a clear and timely manner the group runs the risk of paralysis. In such cases one interpretation is not sufficient; clear interpretations are arrived at by real work and persistence. In the case of group members fascinated, irritated, inhibited or made passive by this pathological individual, work needs to be done to disengage their spontaneous reactions and to develop their awareness of this individual's effect on them. If the monitor does not provide an example of psycho-analytic work and if he does not help to create the conditions needed, such work will not be done by magic. This is, in fact, one of the forms of the 'psycho-analytic illusion' (Anzieu, 1973).

# Chapter 13
# Psycho-analytic group theory

## (A) An overview of unconscious group processes

The aim of this chapter is to consider unconscious group processes and organizing principles in the light of psycho-analytic theory. Clinical examples will be used to illustrate fundamental group processes.

The value of psycho-analytic explanation derives from the fact that it operates in terms both of forces and of meaning. Lewinean explanation, on the other hand, recognizes the group as a system of forces, but ignores it as an organization of unconscious meanings. The error of psycho-sociologists is to explain one manifest phenomenon, group functioning, on the basis of other manifest phenomena (common goals and norms, inter-individual relationships, etc.), whereas for the last three quarters of a century psycho-analysis has shown that manifest content is explained by latent content.

At present the only fruitful work being done with groups uses psycho-analysis; psycho-analytic practice and theory have demonstrated to us the inadequacies of the psycho-sociological approaches to groups. The remainder of this chapter will review in psycho-analytic perspective a certain number of key group processes.

### The group illusion

As we have said (see chapter 7), the group illusion is a feeling of group euphoria. The non-psycho-analytic monitor tends to participate in this illusion, which is gratifying for him: a good group has a good monitor.

In the group illusion the group itself is a libidinal object. Monitor and participants address the group in their discourse. 'The group' is to be told what 'the group' feels; the monitor suggests that 'the group' organize itself, analyse itself. In fact, an occasional, provisional group is no more than a collection of persons thrown together who hardly constitute a group in the psychological sense of the term and sometimes do not want to be one. To speak about this group-object, which does not exist, is to give participants the more or less explicit task of making it exist. Being a good group is a defensive displacement of the real goal: personal insight. The 'group' becomes the group's goal, a collective restoration of threatened individual narcissism. With hardly any experience, members set themselves up as monitors: they form groups in order to get others to share the euphoria and collegial ideology to be found in a group. The group thus functions in the minds of participants as an ideal ego.

This group process alternates with the process of identification with the leader as common ego ideal. Where the group situation mobilizes the ego ideal, the image of the leader, an all-powerful and benevolent father is cathected. Where it mobilizes the ideal ego, the group itself (narcissistic identification with the breast, associated with pleasure and fecundity) is cathected. Only a psycho-analytic type of interpretation can enable participants to recognize these processes instead of being taken in by them.

## Wish-fulfilment in groups

The group illusion is but one example of group phantasies produced by the group. This is why we have drawn an analogy between the group and the dream (see chapter 5): groups, like dreams, fulfil wishes.

As in dreams, the primary psychic processes, which, in the group, become objects of wishes shared by its members, are displacement, condensation, symbolization and reversal into the opposite. As in dreams, secondary elaboration re-arranges the results of the primary processes; in groups this takes the form of the production of myth-like narratives or intellectual constructions of an ideological type in which forbidden wishes are displaced. As Kaës (1971b, 1974b) has shown, myths and ideologies are compromise formations to be found only in group or social situations.

The group unconsciously creates illusions as individuals do dreams. Whether the group maintains pre-conscious phantasies by endless conversations or engages in reality-directed activities, participants 'stage' their common wishes in the 'theatre' of phantasized group space. In other words, in all groups, both natural and artificial, there is a process that incites participants to stage what Ezriel (1950) has called the lowest common denominator of their individual phantasies.

## Phantasized group space

Just as the nocturnal dream takes place against the backdrop of one's own derealized body image and perhaps, more primitively, the image of the breast-mouth, so group phantasies take place against the backdrop of phantasized group space.

In an informal small group, the spatial arrangement participants spontaneously adopt is a circle or oval. Underlying phantasies generally take the following forms. If participants are in a circle, the group is a mouth from which emerges coherent group discourse, a place where a multitude of mouths eat one another (phantasies of the group as hydra are almost always found in silent group members, later interviewed individually); the group may also be a vagina, a central hole in which the words of monitor or chairman-phallus penetrate and impregnate. If the form is oval, the group is a closed egg, the monitor the seed and the participants waiting to be born. In all cases, the circular or elliptical formations suggest a female, maternal image, whereas rows, such as are found in schools, function to loosen the hold of the female imago and to impose the paternal imago.

In the large group, participants tend first to stick together in what Turquet (1974) had called 'my neighbour's skin'. Then they sit side by side in a closed line (or two concentric lines) forming ovals or rectangles and delimiting an internal space. The central space is so anxiety-arousing that both participants and monitors feel the need to put tables in front of themselves and/or in the middle. Whether empty or filled with a table, this hole is phantasized as inhabited by the bad object (in the large group destructive drives are projected, not on to the outside, but on to the centre), or by the monitors (wherever they *actually* sit). Groups phantasize orifices and their functioning (though they *really* need to open doors and windows at certain times) and appendages or excrements (participants sitting behind others or off to one side).

The large group is then experienced as the inside of the mother's body. Correlative material deals with:

(a)  exploring the surface and inside of the body. Some sessions are like anthropologists' descriptions of mythical voyages in healing rites or giving birth; participants in training seminars say they have come to be cured or to be born. These amount to the same thing: becoming autonomous from the phantasized mother's body. Participants are ambivalent about this objective. They jealously defend their personal identity (their personal autonomy with respect to the group-mother); and, conversely, they are comfortable in the small group as in a mother's womb, and do not want to come out;

(b)  the acquisition of symbolism as the appropriation of the mother's body and the sublimation of the anxiety over losing her;

(c)  the rivalry of children (children-penis, children-excrement) in the mother's womb, destructive either for them or for her;

(d)  phantasies of joined parents and of the primal scene projected on to the team of monitors.

## Split transference in groups

Experience has shown that positive transference tends to concentrate on the small group and negative transference on the large group. The fixation of destructive fragmentation anxieties, as well as of persecutory or depressive anxieties on to the large group, hold the large group at a constant, archaic level of regression. This frees the evolutive libidinal processes that emerge in small diagnostic or psychodrama groups. These processes are: pregenital and genital sexual phantasies, intercourse, relation to authority and law, and to the double prohibition of incest and murder, the intermingling of masochism and narcissism, guilt feelings and their eroticization, the role of transgression, and the diversity and mobility of libidinal choices. In a seminar, the small group becomes the phantasized place of pleasure; the large group the phantasized place of death.

Not only the nature but also the object of transference differs in large and small groups. In a small group, the central transference is on to the monitor but there is also the lateral transference of participants on to one another. This is due to the fact that in a small group participants rapidly get to know one another. There is also a third type, much harder to discern, analyse and interpret: the transference of participants (and the counter-transference of the monitor) on to the small group as an object or entity.

Matters are quite different in a large group. In the first place lateral transference is minimal. In fact, participants who belong to different small groups hardly know one another. Our observations have even led us to the hypothesis that lateral transference in large groups is a displacement of central transference on to monitors. In small groups, by contrast, lateral transference of one participant on to another, while sometimes being displaced from the monitor, generally has meaning for the two persons (the object and subject of transference); it is the task of psycho-analytic work to shed light on and verbalize this double meaning.

In the second place, large group transference is directed at the team of monitors or one monitor as a member of the team. Material specific to large group transference includes the following themes: the monolithic solidarity or fragmentation of the 'staff', its cohesion or disagreements, its authoritarianism or 'laissez-faire', its knowledge or ignorance, its honesty or love of manipulation, its heterosexuality or homosexuality, its genital or perverse polymorphic character, the phantasized pleasure of staff members, the staff's intention to hide its wishes from participants in its womb without letting them out, etc.

Transference in the large group is complementary to that in the small groups. In a small group it is difficult to analyse the transference of participants on to the group as libidinal object because the small group is both subject and object of the transference. For example, it is difficult to analyse the group illusion, so frequently found in small groups, in a small group, even if the monitor is not duped by it. It may be analysed in the large group. Interpretation in such cases stresses the splitting of persecution and idealization (of the small group, monitors and group dynamics). More generally, interpretation needs to take into account group forms of the superego, the ego ideal and ideal ego.

*Manifestations of archaic anxieties*

Threats to the ego (breaking apart phantasies) mobilize archaic anxieties and defences against these anxieties. Related to the maternal imago, these are (1) anxieties of annihilation or emptiness, (2) anxieties of persecution and (3) depressive anxieties and (4) schizoid anxieties of breaking apart. Defences against these include (1) the splitting of the object into good and bad, (2) restoring the bond and (3) projective identification.

Depressive anxiety ('we aren't getting anywhere', 'we're no good', 'we're incapable of making the group function without a leader or monitor') is easier to tolerate and express than persecutory anxiety. One of the defence mechanisms to which it gives rise is identification with the monitors (trainees want to become, in turn, monitors and therefore in training groups speak as though they were monitors). Identification with the lost love object is in fact the surest and oldest way of overcoming the loss and reincorporating the love object.

Annihilation anxiety is the most trying because it threatens physical destruction and radical castration. Defence mechanisms in groups generally come in the following order: silence (certain participants are paralysed and do not manage to say a word), identification with the aggressor and with the victim (one participant presents himself to the group as its victim or does everything he can to be so treated; another reproduces the supposed narcissistic omnipotence of the monitor in sado-masochistic relations with other participants) and finally pairing. In pairing, one looks for a particular partner, whether of the same or the opposite sex, by whom one can be recognized as an individual; this counterbalance anxiety aroused by the 'bad mother' group who loves her children to keep them undifferentiated within herself without letting them be born: in this sense pairing is an escape from the group and at the same time a reparation of injuries incurred there.

## (B) The circulation of phantasies

Very broadly speaking, we can say that there are two opposite preconceptions concerning groups. The first, which may be called 'technical', makes the group out to be a mechanism that will work properly only with the right sort of know-how. Consequently, 'technical' preconceptions exclude phantasies or unconscious life. The second, which may be called 'phantasized', makes the group out to be a place where wishes come true, and where manipulations of reality are excluded. The second we have called the group illusion.

All human activity aims at satisfyng the needs of the living organism or of the social body by a mixture of phantasy and know-how. Those who are under what we might call the technical illusion resist phantasy; conversely those who are under what we might call the illusions of phantasy resist know-how.

Phantasizing is stimulated in two or three persons by love or deep friendship; in groups, this is done by joint activities like free discussion or dramatic improvisation (so long as group members have something at stake). Intermediary situations include hypnosis, psychoanalysis and relaxation. Moreover, the society itself provides three principal sources of phantasy: art, religion and science.

Phantasies are perhaps individual psychic reality *par excellence*, since the child becomes a subject when phantasies are organized: unconscious phantasies produce individuality. Thus it is not surprising that when participants in a training or therapeutic group feel their individuality threatened, they mobilize phantasies. More generally, in any encounter between several persons, an individual either turns in on himself to protect his threatened identity and his individual, unconscious phantasies, or he imposes these phantasies on others. Groups become paralysed if several competing individual phantasies cancel one another out. The apparent group unity may coalesce around such an individual phantasy thrust upon, for example, a scapegoat or deviant; sometimes there are endless abstract discussions, personal quarrels, prevarications, rationalizations, wild psychological analyses and even outbreaks of violence. Oppositions between two sub-groups may arise from the phantasized antagonism of two individual group leaders.

What is the psycho-analytic definition of individual phantasies in groups? It is a phantasized scenario between several persons, which the subject generally watches and does not take part in. It follows that this scenario has an *internal group organization*. In his behaviour, symptoms and nocturnal dreams, the subject tries to act out this scenario. His role and those he gives others are permutable; the scenario has variants but its structure remains the same. Each character in the scenario derives from the subject's identification with one or several real persons of importance to him and one or several representations of internal psychic processes. René Kaës (1976d) has drawn a homology between the internal group organization of phantasies and the group situation in which certain members are sometimes used as recognition points and sometimes as projective supports for their subjective topography and for their drives. We agree with Kaës that there is an internal group organization in individual phantasies. This is the basis of phantasy-resonance. Moreover, the homology of the group psychical apparatus with that of the individual is reversible: Freud conceived of the individual's organization (id, ego, super-ego) as an internalized group.

Phantasy-resonance is the grouping of certain participants around one group member who, through what he says and does, focuses the others on his individual unconscious phantasies. 'Grouping' means here not so much agreement as common, converging interests, echoes and mutual stimulation. As carriers of repressed desires; phantasies arouse horror, fascination or indifference, depending upon whether the wish arouses a violent condemnation by the superego, or a similar, hitherto latent wish now ready to break through, or effective defence mechanisms, particularly negation. Missenard (1971) describes the development of resonance thus:

> Group discourse may be understood as the staging of the phantasy of its 'bearer', to which other group members react. More exactly, each of the protagonists has an individual position in the phantasized scenario of the 'bearer'.
>
> This is possible for two reasons: first, the unconscious has only a limited number of themes; secondly each human being has to go through them in his own way.
>
> Other participants speak about these themes and thus can easily take one of the 'places' in the phantasy.
>
> Those who remain silent are nevertheless present – as 'spectator-listeners'. Thus they identify with those who 'act out' the phantasy; . . . some do it by identifying with another's wish, others by defending themselves against this same wish.

It is, then, an unconscious individual phantasy that 'organizes' the group's functioning. I would like to add an allusion to the organizing principles of the psychical life of infants and small children. Spitz distinguishes three successive ones: at three months, the infant smiles at a human being (this marks the transition from passive sensorial reception to active perception; there is elaboration of pre-object and pre-ego and the beginnings of social relationships); at eight months, the infant feels anxiety on seeing a strange face or anxiety at the loss of the love object (with differentiation between what is mine and what is unfamiliar, the structuring of the ego's boundaries with the id and with reality, the beginning of integration and adaptation); at about fifteen months, children begin designating things and persons (this is the condition for speaking, negation, judgment and communication at a distance).

The effect of 'unconscious resonance' in psychotherapeutic group has, since Foulkes (1948), become commonplace in psycho-analysis applied to groups, because a better term has yet to be found. The analogy with the physical phenomenon of resonance is particularly clear. Acoustic resonance was discovered about 1450. Helmholtz generalized the concept in 1862 after observing that the same phenomenon occurred in optics, in electro-magnetism, etc., in short, wherever there was a vibration. A physical system may be set in vibration even by a frequency unlike its own; this effect remains weak but strengthens as the stimulative frequency nears the natural frequency; it attains a high intensity vibration (volume) when it corresponds exactly with one of the natural frequencies (resonance frequency): the system is then said to be 'resonant'. The phantasy would appear to correspond therefore to one of those 'natural frequencies' of an individual and, when a phantasy in one subject sets one in another oscillating, their content may be qualitatively different but the frequency closest to the natural frequency makes it 'vibrate' at near maximum intensity. These are, of course, only metaphors.

Ezriel (1950, 1966) noted that in individual or group therapy, the thoughts and attitudes of the patient manifest themselves in the form of a wish to establish individual relationships with the psycho-analyst here and now. This comes from a need to find an outlet for unresolved unconscious conflicts by releasing the tension they have created in the subject. In everyday life, in groups and in individual therapy transference is one of the patient's efforts to establish such relationships with those around him. When several persons meet, each tends to project his unconscious phantasies on to the others and tries to make them act as he wants. If this corresponds to their own phantasies, the others will play the role expected of them. If enough members of the group find enough mutual response (phantasy-resonance), a 'group tension' will result unless a majority of participants get together to use unconscious defence mechanisms against this tension. What the group psycho-analyst tries to understand is 'what the attitude and thoughts of one group member mean for the others and how each one reacts in a specific manner to a common group problem'. The analyst's interpretations concern a latent problem, revealed by the manifest content of the discussions, 'the common denominator of the phantasies of the group'. Resistances to the common group tension may take the form, for example, of a general silence, autobiographical accounts, inconsequential chat about jobs or literature or jokes, refusal to speak in front of others, or speaking for others.

This theory of intra-group phantasy-resonance is the basis of the technique of group psycho-analysts. The interpretation applies to the here-and-now situation only (whereas in individual analysis it links the individual's past to his present). It aims, not at an individual's problems, but at the common denominator of the unconscious phantasies of group members, or at collective mechanisms mobilized against common group tension. Finally, it only takes into consideration *central* transference on to the psycho-analyst – *lateral* transferences between members is considered as displacement of central transference. (It is true that for Ezriel, as for most British Kleinian psycho-analysts of groups, one psycho-analyst is enough to run a group.)

André Missenard (1971) has observed that the origin of phantasy-resonance is to be found in the dual, symbiotic relationship between the child and his mother. He proposes the metaphor of the plasmodium to describe the wishes common to participants and monitor(s). 'At this level of its functioning the group may be described as a living tissue called plasmodium, composed of a set of nuclei in a single cytoplasm. The group may be represented as oscillating between this image of itself and another, that of a tissue made up of differentiated cells, each having a certain unity.'

Thus one unconscious organizing factor of the group tends to construct the group psychic apparatus around that of an individual. This is 'isomorphy' (Kaës, 1976d), which Kaës believes is one of two group tendencies and can lead to the fusion of individual psychic apparatuses with the group psychic apparatus.

The second factor is what Kaës calls increasing 'homophormy'. By this expression Kaës means that the group apparatus is propped up by the individual psychical apparatus, but is differentiated from it.

*Organizing principles: (1) a dominant individual phantasy*

When a group is manifestly organized around the unconscious phantasy of one of its members, how does this affect its latent structure? I think that the members unconsciously delegate to one leader the role of arbitrator between the ego and the id, between the ego and reality; they get rid of their own psychical conflicts by dumping them on to him; this leader is central to the group's latent structure and acts as an ego to the group.

In his 1971 article, Missenard gives us an example of the first principle: the organization of group phantasies around the phallic claims of Dominique, a female participant. The group of Cythera (or Paradise Lost), which I described when dealing with the group illusion, was organized around Léonore's phantasies of narcissistic omnipotence. The triumphantly egalitarian ideology corresponds to an isomorphic tendency. On the other hand, failure of the first organizing principle involves risks of a breakdown if the group refuses to fuse with the central (individual) phantasy: it is no coincidence that the breaking-apart phantasy is the counterpart of the group illusion.

The unconscious individual phantasy also functions in natural groups when, for example, an enterprise or organization institutionalizes the phantasy of their founders. In the eyes of an ill-informed observer, these organizations seem to function around the image of their leader. A boss who succeeds in such an organization is one who, dealing effectively with external reality, controls the phantasy-resonance within the group. There are serious difficulties, however, when there is dissonance between the phantasies of the official leader and those of the group. In such cases informal leaders appear, or the formal founder disappears, leaving its organization with resonances none the less present because the founder has 'retired'.

By contrast, in training groups predominant individual phantasies are generally less stable. Because the phantasies of group members are not compatible, some bar the way for others and thereby impede phantasy-resonance. In a group where all members are equal, no one phantasy can predominate. Thus the group goes adrift and has to look for another organizing principle.

## Organizing principles: (2) the imago

Bion here sets us on the right track, providing one thinks out more rigorously several of his intuitions. His notion of unconscious basic assumptions is an interesting and significant attempt to find what the second organizing factor does. Bion's contribution follows in the Freudian tradition, showing how members of a collectivity find a sense of unity, each one substituting for his ego ideal the same ideal image, that of the leader. For Freud, it is not the prevalent phantasy of an individual but the imago of a leader that gives a group coherence. The imago belongs to the same order of unconscious reality as the phantasy, with two important differences: a phantasy is the representation of an action – which implies *several* protagonists personifying drives and defences – whereas the imago is the representation of nobody, a representation constituting a nucleus of regulatory psychical agencies of the ego, such as the superego, the ego ideal and the ideal ego. Secondly, phantasies develop with the individual. At least for Freud, the imago was constituted during the development of the species and exists potentially in all children at birth. Hence the universal character of imagos and their predisposition to provide groups (organizations) with a profound psychical unity. Hence also, the greater stability that imago organization confers on a group: the same imago may support several individuals and the imago-based group may follow more easily the changes encouraged by the leader than if it is organized around the phantasy of an individual member.

The imago, then, is the second organizing unconscious principle in groups. Jung used the term imago to refer to three domains: paternal, maternal, fraternal. In chapter 8, I showed, for example, that the collective oral phantasies derive from the organization of a group *around* the alternatively good and bad maternal imago. In chapter 12, I interpreted the difficulties in a company's management committee as being due to conflicts organized around the massive presence of a *paternal* imago.

The inventory of imagos remains an open question. The

existence of a maternal or paternal imago (the object of ambivalence) is obvious and beyond question. Should the imago of the phallic mother be added to this list? The phallic mother and the bad mother are undoubtedly two quite different psychical realities. But the former seems to me to be more a phantasy than an imago. The notion of a fraternal imago needs to be taken into consideration. Béjarano (1974) successfully studied it in a large group and called it a 'societal' imago.

Imagos tend to give a group a balance between isomorphy and homomorphy. Their function in groups illustrates particularly well the articulation between organization and structure. The imago emerges as the manifest organizing principle of the group when the underlying structure of the group is dominated by the ego ideal (see Freud, 1921), the ideal ego (e.g. the Cythera group), or the superego.

Although an imago may guarantee the unity of a group, the bivalence of imagos, which Freud was the first to stress, facilitates sudden reversals (in general the good imago becomes bad), which leads to upheaval, disorders or transformation in the internal organization and functioning of the group.

*Organizing principles: (3) primary phantasies*

Primary phantasies may be classified and related structurally:

(1) To the individual's origins; these are phantasies of intra-uterine life, of the child-to-be-born in the womb of his mother, of the coitus of his parents, in short, of the primal scene; these phantasies underlie the infantile sexual theories by providing children with ways of answering the question of where children come from.

(2) To the origin of sexual differences; these are castration phantasies. The child imagines a unisex penis, the preservation or disappearance of which defines men and women respectively in his eyes.

(3) To the origins of sexuality: these are phantasies of seduction, the sexual emotions of the child, which he explains as the effect of the seduction of the desired object. (See Laplanche and Pontalis, 1964).

I treated intra-uterine phantasies in the section devoted to phantasized space and in my discussions of the large group. I also alluded to group phantasies of exploring symbolically the inside of the mother's body.

Primal scene phantasies may be observed in several forms in groups. Scaglia (1976b) shows that the triadic situation – monitor, observer, group – allows for all possible permutations of this phantasy. The observer may feel himself and be felt as the outsider, excluded by monitor and group. But the group may equally feel excluded from monitor-observer relations. In certain large groups meetings between monitors and observers are phantasized as collective coitus, as a primal scene that tempts participants to spy (peeking through the keyhole, coming in to disturb).

Castration phantasies assume rather specific forms in T groups, as I have mentioned in my chapter on breaking-apart phantasies (chapter 9). Here one finds both phallic castration anxiety and oral anxiety at being separated from the other. Primal phantasies usually remain unexpressed at first and are then communicated with great difficulty, after several sessions. Confronting these phantasies is a risk that trainee members must take in group situations: it is unconsciously felt as the 'real'-ization of a threat. In the psycho-analytic sense, the group dynamic operates between the two poles of wish-fulfilment (participants go to groups as they enter a dream) and of the realization of a threat (once the group has begun, they will experience the situation as a persecutory machine, see the analysis of group machine phantasies. In psychodrama groups, primal castration phantasies may be expressed in the themes of deformed children unable to walk or talk.

Seduction phantasies seem to correspond to Bion's third basic presupposition. The phantasy of the group machine, discussed in chapter 10, illustrates the transition from persecution by the bad-mother imago to a primary seduction phantasy.

Primal phantasies are also aroused in monitors. Inter-transferential analysis is necessary when such phantasies too strongly dominate counter-transference.

With primal phantasies the group psychic apparatus acquires a more elaborate and varied system of oppositions than it does with the bivalence of the imago: for example container-contained (intra-uterine phantasies), actor-observer (primal-scene phantasies), active-passive (castration phantasies), initiator-initiated (seduction phantasies). These differences tend to cancel out the group illusion (see chapter 7), which for this reason I have considered as a primal counter-phantasy. The group organized around a primal phantasy may accept differences between its members because it is assured of sharing something definite, namely, the origin. Individual psychic apparatuses are recognized in their relative autonomy and in their transitive character. They may occupy antagonistic, symmetrical or complementary positions on different vectors of the group apparatus. Some identifications are accepted; others are refused. Codes of exchange and codes for classification of internal and external realities come into being with primary phantasies, the third organizing principle; the group tends towards homomorphy, which counterbalances the tendency towards isomorphy. The organization of the group unconscious around a primal phantasy seems to me to correspond to a group psychical structure in which the prevalence of one particular psychical element (e.g. the ego) is not stable: different individuals may, depending on circumstances and the particularities of their subjective topographical organizations, occupy different positions in the group. There is thus a certain variety and variability in drives, defence mechanisms and the perceptions of rules and values.

## The Oedipus complex and the organization of the family

Freud's position is well known. The Oedipus complex is the psychic nucleus of culture and social life, as it is of child-rearing and of neurosis: the mythical scenario of the collective murder of the father would appear to constitute the group or social version of Oedipal phantasies. This thesis raises several objections.

My first argument is that the organizing principles are not necessarily the same in individuals as in groups. Certainly, groups are made up of individuals. Thus, although they deal with the same psychic material, these processes are organized differently. Three principles of homomorphic organization are: the inter-individual imago, the resonance of an individual's phantasy and the universality of what we may call the 'collectivization' of a primal phantasy. The group imago is inter-individual; it occurs in relations between two or more persons. The resonance of an individual's phantasy is one specific to groups, institutions and crowds. The collectivization of a primal phantasy is specific to informal groups, large or small.

My second argument derives from everyday observation. Supposing a group is made up of individuals who have dealt adequately with their Oedipal problems and behave in accordance with the genital phase of libidinal development. Once in a group such persons will have considerable difficulty feeling, thinking and reacting at an Oedipal or post-Oedipal level. Every informal group, large or small, provides those who participate in it, observe it or interpret its acts, with a demonstration of the existence of a *pregenital* psychic life. Precisely the same thing is true of institutional groups, but the phenomenon is partly hidden by the institutional framework (institutions are a defence against pregenital regression). If the pleasure of understanding what is happening in groups is a largely Oedipal pleasure (see Anzieu, 1976a), the attraction or the pleasure of being in a group consists of sharing or of hoping to share with others pregenital experience relegated to the back of one's mind or repressed at the genital stage.

My third argument, formulated in France by Lacan and in England by Foulkes (1972), is the following: the Oedipal situation is a family complex. Oedipal attitudes and feelings, in real families as in the legend, are the product of parents as well as children. Laius, frightened by the new-born Oedipus, turns him out and mutilates him; Jocasta, who probably recognized her son when he returned as conquerer, consorts with him knowingly; the Oedipus complex of children towards their parents is often a reaction to the Oedipal complex of the parents towards their children. As Foulkes observes, the same drama may centre on any member of the family group.

My final argument, suggested by Annie Anzieu, is that the genital stage presupposes that sexual differences have been recognized, thus allowing *triadic* rather than dual relationships. However, only individuals have a sex. A group does not, nor can it have one.

There is a natural tendency for all groups to level out the sexual difference of its members. I have not noticed any fundamental difference in the unconscious dynamic of the group, whether it be composed of members of one or of both sexes, or if of both whatever the proportions of each may be.

The group is a psychic reality that precedes sexual difference. Pregenital, homosexual, unconscious bonds are stronger in groups. They constitute a good defence against the potential aggressivity of its members. This is not the case in the family, where heterosexual relationships are dominant.

It is common knowledge that the group situation enables members to let off steam they could not let off within the family on account of sexual prohibitions. It is no coincidence that incest prohibitions exist universally. Freud in *Totem and Taboo* uses the clan as at once the group and the family. This confusion of group and family led Freud to attribute to groups a characteristic specific to the family. I prefer to think that Freud's proto-group-horde represents a phantasy of collective life, a sort of primal group phantasy.

In conclusion, the Oedipus complex is one of the organizing principles of the unconscious in families; it is not so in groups. Oedipal aspects of actions or free associations in groups may be explained by the other three organizing principles: (1) the resonance of an individual's phantasy (in which the Oedipal element is important), (2) emotional reactions to a central imago (see chapter 12), and (3) a primal phantasy (in which case one is dealing with early forms of the Oedipus complex, which Melanie Klein brought to our notice).

I am even tempted to go further; groups often use the Oedipus complex as a pseudo-organizing principle. It is hardly necessary to add that this is a pseudo-Oedipal defence against pregenital regression; forming a group is for some participants a way of adopting a pseudo-Oedipal façade (Anzieu, 1976a).

My hypothesis that the structural organization of the unconscious of the family and of the group is different sheds light on the fact that Oedipal organization may be obtained only within the family; no other social reality, whether informal or institutional, can take its place. The failure of free communities – in which so many of our youth have participated – is clear. However, once groups are unified by unconscious organizing principles, they really act on the basis of the intellectual and affective resources of their members. A work group, for example, manages to function according to common rules, a division of labour, reality-testing and self-regulation, if most of its members have got beyond the Oedipus complex.

Studies of so-called primitive societies attest to the coexistence, on the one hand, of an extended family (clan) ruled by a chief, and in which sexual relations are regulated and, on the other, the group in which the bands of young heterosexual peers functions temporarily as a mother substitute. We find the maternal imago as organizing principle of the first peer groups.

The psychotherapeutic group has an intermediate status: like the family, it mobilizes the Oedipus complex in members individually. Several patients individually re-experience incestuous or parenticidal drives. Group therapy can only treat the individual Oedipus complex *indirectly*: in groups, it operates regressively in transference by means of late (delayed) substitutions and displacements (Foulkes, 1972, p. 61). As Foulkes observes (p. 68): 'Generally speaking I have the impression that the glimpses we have of the conflictual Oedipal situation come to us in groups like the beacon of a distant light-house, each patient behaving as though the signal were his.'

## Organization, pseudo-organization and disorganization

In addition to the psychological organizing principles I have mentioned there are economic, sociological and historical ones. Ethologists have even found chemical principles in insect societies. Moreover, groups may try to find substitute principles.

For example, the individual phantasy may be unconscious (dream, symptom, etc.) or conscious (daydream), as Spitz has noted. The same holds for groups. In chapter 6, I cited the daydream of the animals in the Camargue. Max Pagès (1968) analyses the 'whale' group, so named because of the group's whale phantasies. However agreeable such phantasies may be, their training or therapeutic effect is virtually null; they were pseudo-organizing principles. Nocturnal dreams that participants relate during sessions are quite another matter. Pontalis (1972) has analysed a group on the basis of dreams related by its members, and dream material is important for the analyses of monitors and observers. The similarity of the dreams of different members of the same group is sometimes striking. In one instance, two members dreamed of a scene in George du Maurier's *Peter Ibbetson* (1891). This is but another illusration of phantasy-resonance.

In a group, as in an individual, a phantasy may also function as a disorganizing factor, depending upon the nature and intensity of the anxiety connected with it. The group-as-machine phantasy reflects a fragmentation anxiety; certain silences may express the anxiety of being devoured. The group illusion is constituted around a denial of the loss of the love object; it is a collective defence against the anxiety of this loss. Breaking-apart anxiety is more difficult to define: at times I have explained it as a phantasized castration, at other times as the loss of the object. It is always accompanied by the projection of destructive envy. This is to say that the phantasy may be related to three very different levels of anxiety. Its frequency is no doubt due to its position as common denominator of the various disorganizations possible by which participants in a group may feel threatened: thus it appears as the primary factor in the disorganization of the group's psychic apparatus.

In training or psychotherapeutic groups the appearance of disorganizing phantasies and anxieties leads participants to resort to primary defence mechanisms or to breakdowns. In natural groups, the institutional framework constitutes more stable collective defences against such phantasies and anxieties (see Jaques, 1955). To understand the constructive or destructive influence of resonating phantasies one has to consider notions of the body image and what we have called the psychic 'envelope'.

### The group's body imago, its 'envelope', its imago

It seems appropriate to add another organizing principle to those already mentioned, the group's body imago (see Kaës, 1976d and Gori, 1974). Freud's fundamental hypothesis that all psychical functions are related to organic ones does not apply to groups. Groups suffer from not having a body and consequently imagine one. As I noted in chapter 5, metaphors of the group as a 'body' and individuals as 'members' express this wish. A group does not exist as such until it has acquired an 'esprit de corps'.

I am not sure these metaphors should be taken literally. Like the nocturnal dream, they are wish-fulfilments. Whether allegorical or mystical, the body thus designated is not more than an *ersatz*, a substitute for the biological body that doesn't exist. From the foregoing it may be supposed that:

(1)    the supposèd imago of a group body is in fact a pseudo organizing principle;
(2)    it corresponds to a nostalgic dream of symbiosis between group members.

However, the psychic apparatus, whether of individuals or groups, constitutes a containing envelope; it is delimited and protected by what I have called an ego-skin (Anzieu, 1974b). A number of authors have observed similar phenomena.

Pierre Turquet (1974) has shown that besides the projection of destructive envy on to the out-group or on to an individual (the monitor or a deviant, who are not considered as really belonging to the group), there is a projection on to the centre, particularly in the large group. The group centre symbolizes the interior of the body by becoming the place where the bad object is. Another Kleinian psychoanalyst, Donald Meltzer (1967), discovered that in addition to the three imagos (the good breast, which nourishes and heals; the bad breast, which frustrates and destroys; and the idealized breast phantasized as all-powerful, omniscient and immortal), there is a more primitive toilet-breast. Here the anal function of expulsion is primal and constitutes the earliest representation of the mother as part object.

For Meltzer, the resolution or non-resolution of projective dependency on the toilet-breast establishes the boundary between psychotic and normal mental development.

Argentinian psychoanalysts were the first to apply this notion to groups, by stressing their function as a waste depot. Scaglia (1976a) believes this role is attributed in groups to the monitor. Unconsciously, for participants and even for the monitor, the observer in a training group is effectively present and silent: one can say anything in front of him, for, on the one hand, he will not tell anyone outside and, on the other, the disagreeable wishes participants project on to him will not boomerang. As Elliott Jaques has observed, the participants 'shit on' the observer. André Missenard (1971), in the observation of the case of François-Joseph, also uses the notion of a garbage can, a dump: while attacking François-Joseph for defensively avoiding regression and free speech, most participants dumped their problems on to him and were able subsequently, by treating his, to treat their own indirectly. Gear and Liendo (1976) have applied these views to an understanding of the unconscious dynamic of families one member of which is psychotic, and to overall psycho-analytic work with such families.

The breast-toilet functions as a dump; it receives without reacting, is neither loved nor hated; like Pandora's box in Greek mythology, which enclosed the principal evils of humanity unleashed as winds, it is a container. It is imperceptible and for this reason highly regulatory. It is also a dumping process that liberates phantasies, creativity and the wish to know (epistemophilia) in participants and monitors.

I can now return to the distinction I made earlier between structure and organization. The individual or primal phantasy and the imago can 'organize' the group's psychic structure on condition that it is to some extent structured. This structure, or rather pre-structure, is provided by the psychic agencies described by Freud and developed by his successors: the id, the ego, the ideal ego, the superego, the ego ideal. But the identity of the group is not one of perception of thought, as in primary and secondary processes respectively, but an enveloping identity. In fact, what tends to dominate in the psychic organization of the group tends to be not so much the centre, the nucleus, but rather the enveloping 'ego skin', which guarantees its unity, its continuity, its integrity, the differentiation between inside and outside, in which one finds areas of selective exchanges, implications and things forgotten. An adequate understanding of the psychic group envelope calls for further study.

# Chapter 14
# Conclusions

## (A) Short history of dynamic and psycho-analytic group theories

There have been two major currents in the study of small groups. The first uses a model borrowed from physics (electro-magnetism) and from mathematics (topological algebra). The group is defined as a field of forces working within social institutions, the principal elements of which are sub-groups, members, communication channels and barriers. Group behaviour is the result of the combination of these forms according to the particular laws of psycho-sociology or the more general laws of *Gestalt-theorie*: for example, by acting on one single element it is possible to change the structure of the whole. The system of these forces may be graphed. Kurt Lewin (1890-1947) was able to deduce certain specific laws from general field theory: the frustration of group members arouses either regression or aggression; groups function according to a fixed balance and resist more-than-minimal changes. This 'physicalist' model also enabled Lewin to test his laws in laboratory situations and on artificial groups. Lewin posited that a group cannot be reduced to the individuals who compose it, however alike they may be; he defined the group as a system of interdependence between its members and the variables of the field. However, shortly before his death, his successors at Betheal developed group techniques and theories. Group training methods, influenced also by Rogers and Moreno, spread throughout the West. Other 'naturalist', 'cognitive' or mathematical models have since been proposed, but none has had the same public success or scientific impact.

The second current influencing group theories and techniques comes from psycho-analysis. Whereas the 'physical' model implies an experimental method, psycho-analysis implies a clinical one. For Lewin's disciples, the amelioration of individual and social efficiency is the primary goal. For the psycho-analyst, the group is a means by which individuals may learn truths about themselves and learn to recognize those of others.

Let us sum up the contributions of psycho-analysis.

Freud invented psycho-analysis between 1895 and 1900 by comparing the observations of his hysterical patients with the self-analysis of his own dreams. His first theory concerned the individual psychic apparatus (conscious, preconscious, unconscious). Three factors led him to take into consideration the role of the unconscious in collective life:

(a)  sociological/anthropological work on totemism, primitive promiscuity, and crowds;
(b)  experience with groups and conflicts with his first disciples within the earlier psycho-analytic institutions;
(c)  the memory of three families living in symbiosis when he was very young. Before he was three, his father's family, that of his half-brother (twenty years older than he) and that of the locksmith who rented a room and shop (and who was related to Freud's nanny) lived together in the same house. Between 1912 and 1932 Freud developed the concepts of group solidarity and ambivalence on the basis of his own personal memories.

We have already mentioned *Totem and Taboo* (1912-13), written when Jung was expelled from the psycho-analytic movement. In this work Freud's thesis is that the Oedipus complex is not only the nucleus of neurotic conflicts; it is also the nucleus of education and culture.

Another consequence of Freud's position was suggested by Lacan in 1938: the Oedipus complex constitutes the psychic organization of the unconscious of the family.

With *Group Psychology and the Analysis of the Ego* (1921) Freud took a decisive step towards his second theory of the psychic apparatus (the id, the ego, and the superego). This model is not part optical (real and potential images) and part electroneurological (energy transfer), as was the first. Rather it is grounded in group experience. Freud considers sub-groups, leaders, affinities, alliances, tension between members and the constant negotiation of compromises with a view towards goals acceptable to all. Mental functioning is only *apparently* individual; in fact, it is an inner theatre where characters come face to face, where parents are internalized and drives and defence mechanisms organized in sub-systems. Certain psychic processes take the form of imaginary, unconscious plays, phantasies in which the subject is assigned the role of spectator. This is a key point for an understanding of the way groups work: participants try to get others to play various roles dictated by their unconscious.

Freud's successors continued work on these psychic agencies derived from identifications. The superego (system of rules and prohibitions) is the result of internalizing relations of authority between parents and children. The ego ideal (system of personal values) is the result of internalizing relations of respect and esteem between parents and children. The ideal ego (infantile ideal of narcissistic omnipotence) reinforces and perpetuates the archaic identification with the omnipotent maternal breast.

In *Group Psychology and the Analysis of the Ego* Freud analyses the processes of identification and shows that it is the foundation of all social life. He compares identification with hypnotic suggestion or being in love. In the army and the church, two large organizations, one finds two complementary types of identification. On the one hand, the leader is internalized and his imago substituted for the ego ideal of each individual. Consequently a group ego ideal comes into being and guarantees the unity of the group. On the other hand, a network of mutual identifications between members is established. These function at the level of the ego and foster, not group unity, but rather group cohesion. Moreover, although members identify with the leader who is phantasized as a good, all-powerful father (as in the theme of *Totem and Taboo*) identification of members with one another is symbolic: they feel like brothers of the same father. Mutual identification protects the group against the dangers of breaking apart and maintains intra-group aggressivity at a low level. The admired imago of the good, all-powerful leader, on the contrary, has negative as well as positive aspects; sooner or later he becomes feared, indifferent and cruel, in which case the aggressivity of group members is mobilized and expressed in the group. Unity can then be maintained only by sacrificing the leader (or a scapegoat, deviant or minority in his stead).

Although Freud did not make this explicit, Melanie Klein in her 'Group Psychology', demonstrates the fundamental interaction between identification and projection. Like individuals, groups incorporate what is 'good', to have it for themselves, and reject what is 'bad' outside. Idealization always has, as a corollary, persecution. This balance is precarious. For groups, as for individuals, what is good is easily lost, what is bad invades everything; the process of their permutations is endless.

The applications of these insights to small groups are numerous and important. Psycho-analytically, the psychical reality of a group is a more or less stable system of identification-projections. Here is an essential difference between psycho-analytic work with individuals and with groups. In the first case, the work may 'flush out' the individual phantasy. In the case of groups (where there are only resonances and antagonisms between individual phantasies which, generally speaking, cannot be analysed), the work aims at understanding the identification-projections. Moreover, changing identification constitutes the principal benefit to be had from group participation.

Melanie Klein's contributions to group psycho-analysis have been substantial, although she never published anything on groups as such. In addition to her distinctions between the good and bad mother, the good and bad object or identification and projection, she described psychotic anxieties of being torn to pieces and devoured. She developed the hypothesis that a child between the ages of six months and a year goes through paranoid, then schizoid, then depressive and finally restorative phases. This conception of ontogenesis, together with her work on splitting (dissociating the libido from aggressivity) provided guidelines for observing group phenomena.

As a result of Klein's work, it became clear that although Freud was correct in stressing the role of the paternal imago and Oedipal relationships in social organizations, in temporary, non-directive training or psychotherapeutic groups, regression led subjects to experience anxieties on a psychotic level and to feel the group situation theatened their personal identity.

Following Klein, Bion (1961) demonstrated that a group meeting functions on two levels: that of secondary processes (the 'working group' centred on the perception of reality and rational action) and that of primary processes (which in groups assume the form that Bion calls 'basic presuppositions'). Bion believes there are three such basic assumptions:

(1)   the dependence of the group on the monitor, or leader;
(2)   the hit-and-run dialectic; and
(3)   the constitution of a couple, by which the rest of the group is fascinated. Thus the second two basic presuppositions correspond to the aggressive and sexual drives respectively, whereas the first reproduces the infant's state of distress and his need for motherly love and care. A group cannot function as a working group by rationally analysing external reality, as long as the underlying basic presupposition has not been elucidated. Moreover, one basic assumption may fulfil a defensive role against the appearance of another.

Ezriel (1950, 1966) has stressed the patient's wish to establish a particular object relationship with the psycho-analyst. In groups this relationship is related to the resonance that it provokes in other group members, to the tensions as well as the collective defence mechanisms against which the interpretation is focused in the here-and-now situation. It is also related to the common denominators of the unconscious phantasies of group members.

Elliott Jaques (1951, 1955) has specialized in psycho-analytic work with industrial organizations. He discovered that rules, codes and institutions play a valuable role in defence against two types of archaic anxiety (persecutive and depressive). These same anxieties hinder the exercise of authority and the acceptance of responsibilities. The larger the group (when we go from the 'small' diagnostic group to the 'large' plenary meeting), the more intense are these anxieties and the more difficult it is to avoid them without organization and rules.

Turquet (1974), influenced by Bowlby and Winnicott, as well as by Klein, showed that in large groups one finds strong and prolonged attachment drives (described by Bowlby), the need to establish a group skin. From this fact, it follows, as I have said, that monitors of a large group must be supportive (in Winnicott's sense of holding), must create a transitional space between group members and monitors and also between the group and external reality.

In France, Pontalis (1963) described non-directive group situations in which participants struggle to impose an unconscious ideal representation of the life, organization and functioning of a group.

Group members can invest drives and project unconscious individual phantasies on to the group as they can on to the monitor. The dreams of group participants are an illustration of this (Pontalis, 1972). The zeal of group enthusiasts (participants and certain monitors) expresses libidinal over-investment in the group-object.

In 1965 I worked with common group metaphors (the group represented as a 'body') and interpreted group defences against breaking-apart anxiety. I also observed that the group is not the result of a symbolic order; it functions as a sort of crowd in which each member threatens to devour the others. Then, in 1966, I proposed an analogy between the group and the dream (see chapter 6). Individuals expect to have their wishes come true in groups; hence the themes of Paradise Lost, the conquest of the Holy Land, the voyage to Cythera – a Utopia. Correspondingly, the anxiety and the feeling of guilt are intensified. Hence the paralysing silence so frequently found in situations where participants are encouraged to speak freely (i.e. of repressed wishes).

I was led therefore to analyse the group illusion. To the manifest content (we are a good group) corresponds the latent content (incorporation of breast as good part object, participation in an ideal of narcissistic omnipotence projected on to the group-mother, manic defences against the archaic fear of the destruction of rival siblings in their mother's womb).

From this time on it seemed necessary to me to concentrate on work with Freud's second model of the psychic apparatus (id, ego and superego), the one grounded in group experience. I attempted to demonstrate that as soon as a group is 'formed', it ceases to be an agglomeration of individuals and becomes a projection. In the group illusion, the group takes the place of the ideal ego of each of its members, in the same way as in hierarchical organizations the leader takes the place of the ego ideal of each of the members, as Freud observed.

A group may be organized around a persecutory-seductive superego: this is the phantasy of the group as machine. It may be organized around oral wishes and the bond of symbiotic dependence of the child on the mother: this is the phantasy of the group as breast and mouth or toilet-breast. It may be organized around the wish to destroy the object (the breaking-apart phantasy) or that of self-destruction (paradoxical resistance). This work has been devoted largely to this topographical hypothesis and to a description of phantasies appearing only in group situations.

Béjarano (1971) has studied the splitting of transference that inevitably occurs in small groups (eight to twelve persons), and to a still greater extent in large ones (30 to 60 persons). Positive feelings are concentrated in the group illusion. Negative feelings, split off, tend to crystallize on one particular individual (leader, scapegoat), a rival group or on external reality (for example, on society as a whole). Béjarano's work led him the following year (1972) to add that transference in group situations is generally towards one or several of the following: the monitor psycho-analyst, the group, one member of the group, the out-group. He also hypothesized that group situations produced a fraternal and social imago.

Missenard (1971) has also studied psycho-analytic work in training groups. This involves a loss of old phantasized identifications that is seen as a threat to psychic unity and which is reacted to with depression and fear of a breakdown. Simultaneously, however, new phantasized identifications are constructed around relations between one group member and the others. These enable the group member to adopt new attitudes in his private and social life.

Continuing from there, Missenard (1972, 1976, 1979) distinguished the work of participants from that of psychotherapists or monitors, and analysed their identification-projections in the group. He described the group's narcissistic role and relationships between prefusional primary narcissism and secondary narcissism, which follows the creation of a phantasized specular double.

René Kaës showed that all training activities have underlying unconscious phantasies: he described the phantasies of self-training and of anal or oral omnipotence that reappear in adult training groups, in education and in initiation rites. The very terms 'seminar' and 'session' set various phantasies resonating. Kaës has also hypothesized that in groups compromise formations appear in specific forms: myths, Utopias, ideologies. In small groups these may be observed *in status nascendi*. He classifies ideologies according to their relations to the psychic apparatus. There are two kinds of ideologies related to the ideal ego: (1) persecutory (struggles against the image of the devouring mother projected on to nature, the city, society, idealizing the 'cause' that one is dedicated to and on which one projects an image of narcissistic omnipotence), and (2) depressive (nostalgia for a lost paradise, feelings of guilt for having destroyed what was good, negation of differences between human beings). Only ideologies relating to the ego ideal can bring about a reparative sublimation; it fulfils the same role in thought that the production of fetish objects does in the economy of the neurotic's wishes. Kaës (1975) stressed the need in psycho-analytic groups to consider not only transference and counter-transference, but also inter-transference between psycho-analysts. The latter may protect psycho-analysts from the group or shed light on the unconscious displacements of group members on to them. More generally by the term transitional analysis, Kaës designates group relationships that provide participants with the opportunity of breaking their habits, of assuming inner crises and interpersonal conflicts and then of changing and becoming more creative.

However, Kaës' most significant theoretical contribution is the hypothesis of a group psychic apparatus that complements my own of unconscious psychic organizing principles. A group is a trans-individual reality that has to be constructed. Members do this by homomorphic tendencies (exemplified in psychotic families and which encourage the fusion or symbiosis of individual and group) and isomorphic tendencies (which introduce a creative gap between individual and group). As we have said, whereas the individual psychic apparatus is intimately bound up with the body, the group psychic apparatus has no body and consequently must produce substitutes. One of the objectives of psycho-analytic work in groups is to understand how the group apparatus compensates for this lack.

Hector Scaglia (1974a, 1974b, 1976a, 1976b) has shown that all non-directive groups begin with a persecutory phase. Then persecutory anxiety is displaced on to the observer, whose presence is subsequently forgotten. Scaglia also found that for the group, the monitor and the observer, two get along well but the third is excluded.

Roland Gori (1973a, 1974, 1976) noticed a particular form of resistance among participants: speaking for the sake of breaking silence is a sort of 'wall of sound'.

Psycho-analytic work with groups aims at affecting not only perceptive and cognitive, but above all *unconscious* processes. The group is not so much a system of forces, but the object of investment, accompanied by effects and phantasies. The ease or difficulty of communication between members depends on the phantasy-resonance already described (see chapter 13). Whereas Lewin stressed leadership, psycho-analysis has shown that group leaders can, in fact, function as spokesmen for group or subgroup resistance (unconscious wishes). The climate of a group, its successes, failures, obstacles and momentum are due to phantasy-resonance (or phantasy-dissonance) between members or sub-groups. Group life may be understood in terms of conflictual tension between three poles: one 'neurotic', a second 'narcissistic' and the third 'psychotic'.

The psycho-analyst observes the resistance and transference of the group's various sub-groups: psychoanalysts, observers, rival sub-groups composed of members. The interpretation of individual reactions is generally the work of group members, who function as co-therapists. Group psycho-analysts generally provide interpretations of group, not individual, reactions. This leaves group members free to interpret their reactions individually. If the group is run by a team of psycho-analysts, interpretation is polyphasic; each one interprets the unconscious processes to which he is sensitive. If there is only one psycho-analyst, he diversifies his interpretations to try to cover the range of unconscious processes at work in the group.

There are four sorts of explanation: (1) dynamic (what wish corresponds to what defence?); (2) economic (what identifications, what investments and counter-investments are involved?); (3) topographical (what is functioning primarily: the ego, the super-ego, the ego ideal or the ideal ego?); (4) genetic (what stage in ego development is being regressed to?). To explain group life using all four means either drawing on existing psycho-analytic concepts that can be transposed from the vertical unconscious encountered in individual therapy to the horizontal unconscious encountered in groups or inventing new psycho-analytic concepts suitable to understanding the unconscious processes of groups. Psycho-analytic training group methods seek to give participants greater inner freedom and to enable them to realize their possibilities more fully, to be more attentive to unconscious phantasy-resonance.

Because the group situation produces regression to what Klein has called psychotic positions, psycho-analytic group training methods are particularly appropriate for persons who intend to work with psychotic adults or children or for psycho-analytic work with institutions the organization of which functions (more or less successfully) as defences against psychotic attitudes. In such cases the psycho-analyst encourages and stimulates symbolization on four levels: intra-individual, inter-individual, group and institutional.

Experience in artificial groups also provides an enriching contact with human narcissism: its different forms, structures, and ego investment; its fragility (different for every individual); predispositions to its wounds or narcissistic anger and defensive counter-cathexis; a play of phantasized identifications (projective, specular, ideal, masochistic-heroic, symbolic); longing for a primary collective narcissism, etc.

In natural groups individuals want – and eventually find – basic narcissistic security. A psycho-analytically orientated group may not only provide each individual with such security but may enable him to recognize this need in others, while reducing the cost of his defence mechanisms. Responses to groups vary; for some persons an intensive course of several days is enough: for others, repeated groups or alternation with individual psychotherapy is needed; for others, a slow open group is effective. Psycho-analysts foster this security by creating the rules and styles of interpretations in groups; once narcissistic security is guaranteed, the group becomes a container for the drives, affects and phantasies that circulate among members. Thus it facilitates the constitution of a psychic envelope, which each group member may internalize in the place of an overly rigid or inadequate ego-skin. Furthermore, participants are provided with an opportunity to relive and recover fundamental human relationships: that of the baby at the breast (group-mouth phantasies), that of the dependent child (phantasy of the group as machine) and so forth. Winnicott's transitional analysis, discovered in his work with young children (and applied to groups by Kaës) actually structures the group; structures its cumulative trauma, its ruptures as well as those of members and restores the activity of symbolization.

A gathering is not a group. As Kaës has shown, a group displays a particular sort of psychic reality, which is many-layered: the group psychic apparatus is constructed on those of individual members and a specific socio-cultural environment. As we have pointed out in this work, the group psychic apparatus tends to be formed around the superego, the ego ideal, the ideal ego, libidinal, aggressive or self-destructive drives, on the one hand,

and around a leader or subgroup that polarizes its attention, on the other. I have hypothesized that phantasies play a mediating role between group members and the particular psychic agency that happens to be dominant. Thus I described three unconscious organizing principles of groups: (1) the individual phantasy of a founder who produces phantasy-resonance in most other members; (2) a primal phantasy which, since it belongs to nobody in particular, gives members who share it an unconscious footing (a historical genealogy, myth or legend); (3) an imago of an outstanding individual (e.g. the paternal imago represented by the leader), or of the group (e.g. the imago of the bad mother incarnated by the wild crowd, or the imago of the 'body', which gives the group its *esprit de corps*).

The group strives to acquire an ego, i.e. an instrument whereby it can deal with external, physical and social reality, on the one hand, and the phantasies that provide it with its internal coherence, on the other. As Bion observed, the work of the group (at the perceptive-conscious level, i.e. that of secondary processes) can only be accomplished when the group is unconsciously united on the level of primary processes.

Freud dealt with the phantasy of collective murder, Bion with three 'basic assumptions' (primary processes), and I have described several other group phantasies: phantasies of the fulfilment of impossible or prohibited wishes, the group illusion, phantasies of the group-mouth or toilet-breast, phantasies of breaking-apart, fantasies of the group as machine, the group-superego, the group paradox.

Group participants may use the group as an artificial limb or a defensive screen in order to deny or avoid dealing with the individual unconscious or the unconscious aspects of the culture (or its values, customs, beliefs and rites). For example, members may use the group for *anaclitic* support and have it deal with their difficulties and rely on it for the satisfaction of their wishes. The group psycho-analyst must be careful to analyse artificial group defences and to encourage adequate training and therapy. Otherwise, when the group sessions come to an end, there is a risk of breakdowns.

## (B) Collective representations and phantasy-resonance

As in the case of the individual unconscious, the group is a projective surface for society. It is a two-sided mirror. Like Freud's ego, it has a double surface, one external the other internal, sensitive at once to collective representations and to unconscious individual phantasies. Whereas natural groups hide culturally supported phantasies from their members, psycho-analytic training groups sound the social unconscious resonance and seek to shed light on it.

Group monitors know to what extent they can take the pulse of public opinion by listening to what is said spontaneously in groups, especially in training groups using psychodramatic methods. In France in the 1960s, one encountered the following themes: opposition to the death penalty, opposition to the Algerian war and enthusiasm for contraception and women's right to decide whether or not she wants a child. Subsequently, in the 1970s, common themes were the desire for workers' control, growing intolerance of the increasing number of human beings, the quantities of manufactured goods and information, a desire for a way of life which over and above productivity, allowed for greater personal contact and disenchantment with language (a feeling of glut and of the emptiness of conversations at school, in professional or social gatherings and, generally speaking, disillusionment with linguistics). Finally, more recently and with considerable conta-gion, the theme of the body as at once the basis of the subjective existence and instrument of contact and communication has appeared (men, for example, are much less hesitant to speak of homosexual experiences, whereas in the past in this sort of training group they spoke only of their heterosexual lives).

Disenchantment with language and the importance attributed to bodily existence have had important consequences. Whereas up to the 1960s public opinion was reflected in training groups in the choice of themes for discussion and in the organization of conversation, thereafter the very conception of the activities, ends and functioning of non-directive groups was open to question. The result was the multiplication of sessions, the blurring of rules, goals and temporal and spatial limits, and the predominance of physical and emotional self-expression and physical contact with others. One can recognize in these themes reactions to the industrial society where manufactured objects are over-cathected as compared with natural and human factors.

This is the first example of the way in which phantasy-resonance in small groups reflects collective representations: these representations appear at a given time and in a given culture and are picked up by the sounding boards of small groups.

Socio-cultural changes are also picked up by the social sciences, whose concepts and theories often correspond to attempts to deal with socio-cultural crises. This is the case with group dynamics, invented by Kurt Lewin during the war in 1944. For Lewin, who had emigrated from Germany to the USA fifteen years earlier, individualism and explanations of individual behaviour and the dynamics on which he had worked seemed inadequate when Hitler came to power. For American democracy, struggling against both Germans and Japanese, it was indispensable to understand how fascism and Nazism had been psychologically possible. Laboratory research with small artificial groups conducted by Lewin together with Lippitt and White in 1939 demonstrated the superiority of democratic as opposed to authoritarian or laissez-faire group methods. When the war was over, research with 'small groups' was believed highly important to the US, and consequently in other democratic countries. The first T group and live-in seminar was held in France. It was run by French monitors trained at Bethel, with American assistance.

The attention lavished on small groups was justified by two principal themes. On the one hand, the group appeared as the antidote to social impersonality. The sense of belonging, of solidarity, the sharing of ideals, norms and objectives believed to be inherent in small groups, restored human relationships distorted by the scientific division of labour, mass communications, the anonymity and manipulation of urban industrial civilization and bureaucratic social organization. On the other hand, groups collectively learn truths about themselves and about their society. Thus the Quakers believed that God reveals his truths only to gatherings of men. The small group whose members share an ideal is perceived as the leaven of society, an ideal projected by the Greeks on to the twelve gods of Olympus and by the early Christian church on to the twelve apostles. This is Kurt Lewin's model of the small group.

Having seen how socio-cultural changes are reflected in the dynamics of small groups (e.g. themes in France in the 1960s and 1970s) and even in the conceptual models of the group (e.g. Kurt

Lewin's attempts to understand Hitler and Nazism in psychological terms) let us now turn to a third example of cultural values or 'collective representations' and the dynamics of small groups: Russian group psychology.

During the 1960s and 1970s, despite de-Stalinization, the USSR and other Communist countries remained sceptical about group dynamics. They claimed that it was a capitalist science or an arm in the hands of those within the Soviet Union who imprudently wanted to liberalize the communist regime. Such doctrinaire criticism is rooted in the old suspicion of centralized states towards groups. This suspiciousness may be characterized as follows: if individuals want to isolate themselves they are clandestine, in which case it may be deduced that they are conspiring against the government or are morally suspect (engaged in perverse sexual practices or socially delinquent activities). Group activities are acceptable only if they confirm belief in the authority of the state.

The following is a description by Isidore Ziferstein of psycho-therapeutic groups in the Soviet Union observed over a period of months: 'For example, in one group that I observed, a married woman announced her intention never to have any children. She explained her decision thus: (1) Several years of experience in children's summer camps had convinced her that all children are monsters and that one can expect no joy out of having them; (2) Life is hard. The world is unjust. And she saw no point in bringing children into such a world. The group promptly united to persuade this patient that her views were erroneous, that children were the future of the nation and of mankind, that we all have a responsibility to procreate and give our children the best we are capable of, and that surely she must be mistaken in her evaluation of the children in summer camps. When asked for my opinion (I was not permitted by the group to be a non-participant observer), I suggested that perhaps the patient should be granted the right not to have children, that perhaps there are people who can have a better life without children than with them. The group considered this a provocative statement and reacted to it by turning on me. They accused me of introducing an anti-therapeutic note, which, instead of helping the patient overcome her unhealthy stereotype, encouraged and reinforced it. They declared that this was particularly reprehensible coming from a psychiatrist, whose word is a powerful stimulus because it comes from a person with the authority of "learning" '.

Another way of articulating collective representations and the phantasy-resonance of individuals is through the effect of the phantasies of a single individual on phantasy-resonance in a small or large gathering. This is the *Bund* with its prescribed, 'elected' leader, a charismatic individual prominent in German sociology. In 1921 in his *Group Psychology and the Analysis of the Ego*, Freud showed that there is a double identification of members with one another and with the leader (or army or church) as group (social) ego ideal. This thesis consequently reminds us of Freud's links with the German sociological tradition of charismatic leaders and foreshadows Nazism. In this work he obliterates distinctions between small groups, large groups, crowds and peoples – which to me, are absolutely fundamental. His thesis is therefore a throwback to the nineteenth-century French '*psychologie intermentale*' of Tarde and the crowd psychology of Le Bon: a creative individual does something creative and the masses follow. Making these distinctions is, it seems to me, an essential methodological point for social psycho-analysis: it must distinguish analytically and empirically between the unconscious phantasies of the individual, the phantasy-resonance of the group and the collective representations of society.

My final example of the inter-relation of group phantasy-resonance and collective representations is that of May 1968 in France. I observed the events of May 1968, both as a teacher at the University of Paris (Nanterre) and as a resident of the Latin Quarter, and described them in a book which was published in mid-July 1968 under the pseudonym of Epistemon (*Ces idées qui ont ébranlé la France*). The immediate effect of these events was well expressed in one of the many slogans written on the walls of the French capital: '*L'Imagination au pouvoir*' (Power to the Imagination). As a result of intense phantasizing in groups, verbal expression was unleashed in French universities as well as in many occupational and social milieus. But this freedom did not last long. It seems to me that what succeeded in May 1968 depended upon imagining what was real but latent. Thus, great discoveries are made by representing what is potential in order to actualize it. On the other hand, what failed in 1968 failed because it had no basis in reality. When imagination shuns reality, reality resists and subsists. Those who were disappointed by the aftermath of 1968 and felt short-changed, rejected ready-to-hand possibilities for innovation. They refused to *take* Utopias whose incoherence and isolation from the course of events appeared more and more inescapable.

Let us now analyse in more detail the events leading to May 1968.

From November 1967 to May 1968 the campus at Nanterre was increasingly a spontaneous theatre where authors acted out their plays. Free entry into girls' and boys' rooms in the residence, the contempt for university officials and for knowledge in general, protests against programmes designed to stuff students with facts, the freedom of unauthorized political meetings, the examination and collective discussion of the social presuppositions of courses given the abandonment of academic boundary lines, the break-down of academic hierarchies, student participation in deciding exam procedures, open access to university positions, and the right to jobs – such were the more common themes of the strikes and demos at Nanterre during the academic year 1967-8.

Three factors put oil on the fire: the ineffective, authoritarian reactions of the vast majority of the teaching staff and administration, whose pride was hurt and whose ambition to make the Nanterre campus a pilot university was thwarted; the growing number of student groups swept up in the course of events and ready to participate whatever the situation, even though their ideologies of Utopias were different; the growing curiosity of students in what the 'actors' were doing, the curiosity of students about the psychodramatic activities that transformed them from mere spectators into members of a chorus as in Greek drama and even into active participants.

The themes of discussions and improvised psychodramas outside Nanterre (in Paris and in most of France) changed too, becoming more general (critical analysis of the functioning of society, critiques of institutions, affirmation of human equality, etc.) or more specific (dealing with marginal groups: social workers, homosexuals, prisoners, etc.).

Behind this collective dramaturgy was a series of conflicts between established collective representations and new ideas and beliefs. Established beliefs that could not summon up active phantasy-resonance in enough Frenchmen lost out. New ideas won the day as long as they produced phantasies of sufficient intensity in numerous groups, and as long as they did not lose touch with reality.

In my opinion this explains why the events of 1968 had virtually no economic or political effect: the old systems were not radically altered. In fact, they were often strengthened. Those sociologists who believed that 1968 marked the beginning of a new revolutionary class in hyper-industrialized societies were mistaken: history does not repeat itself twice.

Collective representations, however, were affected by the events of 1968, particularly in three areas.

First, in the style of relationships. After 1968 one carried out one's responsibilities, while consulting, explaining to, seeking the opinions of others, even if this style was neither universal nor acquired once and for all. Minorities were recognized as different and as having the right to express themselves.

Second, customs and mores changed. Women affirmed their right to think, write, love, to be respected as women and protected against being raped or beaten, to have jobs, salaries and responsibilities equal to those of men. The liberalization of contraception and abortion, and the removal of censorship on erotic books and films was officially accepted. Disapproval of homosexuality declined. Generally speaking, freedom for each person to find suitable pleasure with a consenting partner gained public acceptance, whereas prior to 1968, this freedom had not existed.

Third, May 1968 affected conceptions of society. Today such themes as self-management, neighbourhood life, the quality of daily living, reactions against the sheer size and impersonality of economic or administrative organizations are common, but were not before 1968. The disillusionment that followed the failure of Utopias born and bred in 1968 has also brought to light other themes: the incompatibility of social organization and individual wishes, the irreducibility of moral and political affairs, the permanence and ubiquity of the figure of the Master or the Prince and the continual need to 'de-mystify' it.

The Utopias of 1968 may also be compared to the group illusion which spread like wildfire in France and which I identified in the following years. The group illusion and the phantasy of the group-machine were phantasies fostered by the events of 1968 in France.

What happened seems to me to conform to the theory that Vernant (1972) and others have proposed to account for Greek tragedy. In ancient Greece, one finds tragedy staged in the fifth century B.C. and only then. One can assume that it met a collective need that ceased when tragedy ceased. But what need?

That of abandoning old beliefs inherited from monarchies that had long presided over the destiny of the major Greek cities and of enabling new conceptions of man and of the world to come into being, conceptions that corresponded to new forms of political, social, scientific and cultural activity and aspiration. Conflict between old and new ideas was personified and dramatized in these tragedies, which show either the struggle of a legendary hero who succeeds in imposing a new morality or sensibility, but at the price of death or exile, or catastrophic delusions of pride that lead to stalwart traditionalism.

The spectators who came to see fifth-century tragedies experienced the drama by means of cathartic phantasy-resonance, which contributed to the decisive change in collective representations.

Group participants in 1968-70 also experienced the conflict between the old and new orders in terms of phantasy-resonance. Moreover, the group illusion and group-as-machine phantasies may be seen as versions of major social currents 'transposed' to group dynamics, just as the utopias and themes of impersonal (machine-like) social organization may be seen as versions of the group illusion and group-as-machine phantasies 'transposed' to French society as a whole.

The social psycho-analytic empirical observation of group functioning and conceptions (and perceptions) of the small group is thus capable of analysing both individual phantasies and collective representations.

But, as we have seen throughout this book, to grasp phantasy-resonance in groups, to sense intuitively the ways in which reality and phantasy are intermingled, to apprehend the reality of phantasies, requires constant self-examination and continual readiness to revise theories and extend one's field of perceptions. Indeed, psycho-analytic group theories may continue to be fruitful only if methods of alternating groups and inter-transferential analysis are interpreted flexibly, if theories of psychic group functioning are subordinated to careful, attentive, observation, if group leaders recognize that not only is every group different, but group themes and reactions reflect wider socio-cultural changes, which in turn influence the theory and perception upon which the rules of group functioning are predicated.

# Bibliography

AFAP (1961), *Evaluation des résultats de la formation*. no. 3, 'La représentation sociale du groupe', roneo.

Anzieu, A. (1974), 'Emboîtements', *Nouvelle Revue de Psychanalyse*, no. 9, pp. 57–71.

Anzieu, D. (1956), *Le psychodrame analytique chez l'enfant*, Paris, PUF.

Anzieu, D. (1964), 'Introduction à la dynamique des groupes', *Bulletin de la Faculté des Lettres de Strasbourg*, 49, no. 7, pp. 393–426.

Anzieu, D. (1965), 'Intragroup Communications', in Geldard, F., *et al.*, *Communication Processes*, Oxford, Pergamon Press.

Anzieu, D. (1966), 'Œdipe avant le complexe ou l'interprétation psychanalytique des mythes', *Les Temps modernes*, no. 245, pp. 675–715.

Anzieu, D. (1969), 'Difficulté d'une étude psychanalytique de l'interprétation', *Bulletin de l'Association psychanalytique de France*, 5, pp. 12–32.

Anzieu, D. (1970a), 'Eléments d'une théorie de l'interprétation', *Revue française de Psychanalyse*, 34, nos. 5–6, pp. 3–67.

Anzieu, D. (1970b), 'Freud et la mythologie', *Nouvelle Revue de psychanalyse*, no. 1, pp. 114–45.

Anzieu, D. (1972), 'Le moniteur et sa fonction interprétante', in Anzieu, Béjarano, *et al.*, *Le travail psychanalytique dans les groupes*, Paris, Dunod.

Anzieu, D. (1973), 'La fantasmatique de la formation psychanalytique', in Kaës, Anzieu, Thomas *et al.*, *Fantasme et formation*, Paris, Dunod.

Anzieu, D. (1974a), 'Vers une métapsychologie de la création', in Anzieu, Mathieu, Besdine, Guillaumin, and Jaques, *Psychanalyse du génie créateur*, Paris, Dunod.

Anzieu, D. (1974b), 'Le moi-peau', *Nouvelle Revue de Psychanalyse*, no. 9, pp. 195–208.

Anzieu, D. (1974c), 'Introduction', special number, 'Groupes: psychologie sociale clinique et psychanalyse', *Bulletin de psychologie*, pp. 1–13.

Anzieu, D. (1975), 'Le désir de former des individus', *Connexions*, no. 16, pp. 29–36.

Anzieu, D. (1976a), 'Oedipe supposé conquérir le groupe', in Kaës R., Anzieu D., Béjarano A., Scaglia H., Gori R., *Désir de former et formation du savoir*, Paris, Dunod.

Anzieu, D., Béjarano, A., Kaës, R. and Missenard, A. (1974), 'Thèses sur le travail psychanalytique dans les groupes', *Bulletin de Psychologie*, special number, 'Groupes: psychologie sociale clinique et psychanalyse', pp. 16–22.

Anzieu D., Béjarano A., Kaës R., Missenard A. and Pontalis J.-B. (1972), *Le travail psychanalytique dans les groupes*, Paris, Dunod.

Anzieu D., Martin J.-Y. (1968), *La dynamique des groupes restreints*, Paris, PUF, 4th edition, revised and expanded, 1973.

Anzieu, D., Mathieu, M., Besdine, M., Guillaumin, J. and Jaques, E. (1974), *Psychanalyse du génie créateur*, Paris, Dunod.

ARIP, (1966), *Pédagogie et psychologie des groupes*, Paris, Editions de l'Epi; new edition 1972.

Ayel, M.-H. and Villier, J. (1974), 'Transfert et contre-transfert dans un groupe thérapeutique. De quelques aspects le spécifiant comme groupe en psychanalyse', *Bulletin de Psychologie*, special number, pp. 327–8.

Balint, M. and Balint, E. (1961), *Psychotherapeutic Techniques in Medicine*, London, Tavistock.

Basquin, M., Dubuisson, P., Samuel-Lajeunesse, B. and Testemale-Monod, G. (1972), *Le Psychodrame: une approche psychanalytique*, Paris, Dunod.

Béjarano, A. (1966), *Ecoute psychanalytique et transfert en dynamique de groupe*, paper presented to APF (roneo).

Béjarano, A. (1971), 'Le clivage du transfert dans les groupes', *Perspectives psychiatriques*, no. 33, pp. 15–22.

Béjarano, A. (1972), 'Résistance et transfert dans les groupes', in Anzieu, Béjarano, *et al.*, *Le travail psychanalytique dans les groupes*, Paris, Dunod.

Béjarano, A. (1974), 'Essai d'étude d'un grope large', *Bulletin de Psychologie*, special number, pp. 98–122.

Béjarano, A. (1976), 'L'analyse du contre-transfert comme source de créativité', in Kaës, R., Anzieu, D., Béjarano, A. *et al.*, *Désir de former et formation du savoir*, Paris, Dunod.

Bernard, J. (1957), 'L'étude sociologique des conflits', in *Unesco* (1957), pp. 37–130.

Bérouti, R. (1973), 'Du groupe: limites de l'intervention du psychanalyste dans les groupes', *Connexions*, no. 5, pp. 115–52.

Besançon, A. (1967), *Le Tsarévitch immolé*, Paris, Plon.

Besançon, A. (1969), 'Vers une histoire psychanalytique', *Annales*, no. 3, pp. 394–416, and no. 4, pp. 1011–33.

Bettelheim, B. (1967), *The Empty Fortress*, New York, Free Press.

Biffe, M. and Martin, J.-Y. (1971), 'A propos de l'imaginaire dans les groupes de diagnostic', *Perspectives psychiatriques*, no. 22, pp. 53–7.

Bion, W.R. (1961), *Experiences in Groups*, London, Tavistock.

Bion, W.R. (1962), *Learning from Experience*, London, Heinemann.

Bléandonu, G. (1973), 'Groupes psychothérapiques, orientation analytique et hôpital de jour', *Perspectives psychiatriques*, no. 41, pp. 25–34.

Bléandonu, G. (1974), 'Thérapie multiple et processus groupal', *Bulletin*

264    *Bibliography*

*de Psychologie*, special number, pp. 75–9.

Bourbon-Busset J. de (1962), *La grande conférence*, Paris, Gallimard.

Braunschweig, D., Diatkine, R., Kestemberg, E. and Lebovici, S. (1968), 'A propos des méthodes de formation en groupes', *Psychiatrie de l'enfant*, 11, no. 1, pp. 71–180.

Burner, M. (1974), 'Le psychothérapeute et les psychothérapies analytiques de groupe. L'expérience lausannoise, 1954–1974', *Bulletin de Psychologie*, special number, pp. 37–44.

Dautremont, D. (1974), 'Du corps dans le groupe', *Bulletin de Psychologie*, special number, pp. 164–6.

Decobert, S. and Soulé, M. (1972), 'La notion de couple thérapeutique', *Revue française de psychanalyse*, 36, no. 1, pp. 83–110.

Deleuze, G. and Guattari, F. (1972), *L'anti-Oedipe, Capitalisme et Schizophrénie*, Paris, Editions de Minuit; English translation, *Anti-Oedipus, Capitalism and Schizophrenia*, New York, Richard Seaver Books, 1977.

Dorey, R. (1971), 'La question du fantasme dans les groupes', *Perspectives psychiatriques*, no. 33, pp. 22–6.

Dubuisson, P. (1971), 'Notule concernant les mécanismes de défense à la fin du groupe', *Perspectives psychiatriques*, no. 33, pp. 79–80.

Eiguer, D. Litovsky de and Chanoît, P.F. (1974), 'Une expérience de techniques asociées: expression corporelle et psychothérapie de groupe', *Bulletin de Psychologie*, special number, pp. 167–73.

Eiguer, D. Litovsky de and Eiguer, A. (1974), 'Introduction à la théorie sur les groupes d'E. Pichon-Rivière', French trans. in *Bulletin de Psychologie*, special number, pp. 45–60.

Ezriel, H. (1950), 'A psycho-analytic approach to group treatment', *British Journal of Medical Psychology*, 23, pp. 59–75.

Ezriel, H. (1966), 'Le rôle du transfert dans le traitement psychanalytique de groupe', French trans. in Schneider (1968).

Favez, G. (1971), 'L'illusion et la désillusion dans la cure psychanalytique', *Nouvelle Revue de Psychanalyse*, 4, pp. 43–54.

Fornari, F. (1971), 'Pour une psychanalyse des institutions', French trans. in *Connexions*, 1973, no. 8, pp. 91–122.

Foulkes, S.H. (1948), *Introduction to Group Analytic Psychotherapy*, London, Heinemann.

Foulkes, S.H. (1964), *Therapeutic Group Analysis*, London, Allen & Unwin.

Foulkes, S.H. (1966), 'De l'interprétation en analyse de groupe', French trans. in Schneider (1968).

Foulkes, S.H. (1971), 'L'accès aux processus inconscients dans le groupe d'analyse de groupe', French trans. in *Bulletin de Psychologie*, 1974, special number, pp. 31–6.

Foulkes, S.H. (1972), 'L'Oedipe et la régression dans les psychothérapies de groupe', French trans. in Schneider (1972).

Foulkes, S.H. and Anthony, E.J. (1967), *Group Psychotherapy: the Psychoanalytic Approach*, Harmondsworth, Penguin.

Freud, S. (1895), *Project for a Scientific Psychology*, *Standard Edition*, vol. 1.

Freud, S. (1908), 'On the Sexual Theories of Children', *Standard Edition*, vol. 9.

Freud, S. (1912–13), *Totem and Taboo*, *Standard Edition*, vol. 13.

Freud, S. (1921), 'Group Psychology and the Analysis of the Ego', *Standard Edition*, vol. 18.

Freud, S. (1929), *Civilization and Its Discontents*, *Standard Edition*, vol. 21.

Freud, S. and Breuer, J. (1895), *Studies on Hysteria*, *Standard Edition*, vol. 2.

Gear, M.C. and Liendo, E.C. (1976), 'Psychanalyse, sémiologie et communication familiale', *L'Evolution psychiatrique*, no. 2.

Geissmann, P. and Durand De Bousingen, R. (1968), *Les méthodes de relaxation*, Brussels, Dessart.

Genevard, G. and Jordi, P. (1968), 'Essai d'évaluation des concepts de statut et de fonction des cothérapeutes en groupe', in Schneider (1968).

Gifotiahn, M. (1974), 'Retour du refoulé dans la famille psychanalytique', *Bulletin de Psychologie*, special number, pp. 71–4.

Gori, R. (1973a), 'L'objet-parole dans les groupes de formation', *Bulletin de Psychologie*, 1972–1973, 305, 26, nos. 10–11, pp. 634–48.

Gori, R. (1973b), 'Les théories sexuelles spiritualistes', *Bulletin de Psychologie*, 1972–1973, 306, 26, nos, 12–13, pp. 681–97.

Gori, R. (1974), 'Parler, dans les groupes de formation', *Bulletin de Psychologie*.

Gori, R. (1976), 'Sur le savoir préalable dans les groupes de formation. A Corps perdu dans le langage', in Kaës, R., Anzieu, D., Béjarano, A. *et al.*, *Désir de former et formation du savoir*, Paris, Dunod.

Grunberger, B. (1971), *Le narcissisme*, Paris, Payot.

Herbert, L. (1959), 'L'utilisation des techniques de groupe dans la préparation de l'enseignement', *Bulletin de Psychologie*, 12, no. 16, 10 June, pp. 969–79.

Herbert, L. (1961), 'La dynamique de la situation scolaire', *Bulletin de Psychologie*, 14, 10 May, no. 14, 194, pp. 801–6; reprinted with revisions in *La situation scolaire*, ARIP, 1966–1972.

Hermann, I. (1930), *L'instinct filial*, French trans. by G. Kassai, with an Introduction to Hermann by N. Abraham, Paris, Denoël, 1973.

Isaacs, S. (1943), 'The Nature and Function of Phantasy', in Klein, M., Heimann, P., *et al.*, *Developments in Psycho-Analysis*, London, Hogarth Press, 1952.

Jacobi, B. (1974), 'Position et fonction de l'observateur dans les groupes de formation', *Bulletin de Psychologie*, special number, pp. 253–9.

Jaques, E. (1948), 'L'utilisation du groupe d'évolution comme méthode de facilitation du changement social', French trans. in *Connexions*, 1972, 1, no. 3, pp. 95–115.

Jaques, E. (1951), *The Changing Culture of a Factory*, London, Tavistock.

Jaques, E. (1955), 'Des systèmes sociaux comme défenses contre l'anxiété dépressive et l'anxiété de persécution', French trans. in Lévy (1965), ch. 35.

Kaës, R. (1970a), 'Interprétation, fondation, séduction' (roneoed).

Kaës, R. (1970b), 'La référence à un tryptique judéo-chrétien: Paradis perdu, Babel, Pentecôte. Contribution à l'étude des fantasmes et des mythes dans les groupes – 1. Propositions pour une étude psychanalytique des mythes dans la vie des groupes' (roneo).

Kaës, R. (1971a) 'Travail et illusion dans la formation', *Mouvement psychiatrique*, 2, pp. 34–6.

Kaës, R. (1971b), 'Processus et fonctions de l'idéologie dans les groupes', *Perspectives psychiatriques*, no. 33, pp. 27–48.

Kaës, R. (1971c), 'Hypothèses concernant le concept d'appareil groupal' (roneo).

Kaës, R. (1972), 'Les séminaires "analytiques" de formation', in Anzieu D. *et al.*, *Le travail psychanalytique dans les groupes*, Paris, Dunod.

Kaës, R. (1973a), 'Aspects de la régression dans les groupes de formation: Réadolescence, perte de l'objet et travail du deuil', *Perspectives psychiatriques*, no. 41, pp. 43–65.

Kaës, R. (1973b), 'Quatre études sur le fantasmatique de la formation et le désir de former', in Kaës, *et al.*, *Fantasme et formation*, Paris, Dunod.

Kaës, R. (1974a), 'Séminaire. Le mot, la chose et l'usage dans la pratique formative. Contribution à l'étude de la fantasmatique de la formation', *Bulletin de psychologie*, special number, pp. 187–203.

Kaës, R. (1974b), 'Le groupe large, l'espace et le corps', in *ibid.*, pp. 123–32.

Kaës, R. (1974c), 'Le fantasme du groupe embroché et le conte des sept suabes', in *ibid.*, pp. 273–82.

Kaës, R. (1974d), 'L'archigroupe. Puissance et pouvoir dans les petits groupes', *Nouvelle Revue de Psychanalyse*, no. 8, pp. 207–21.

Kaës, R. (1974e), 'Représentations du groupe. La geste du groupe héroïque', *Etudes philosophiques*, no. 1, pp. 45–58.

Kaës, R. (1974), 'Situation et dispositif psychanalytique de groupe: pour une méthode d'étude des productions idéologiques', *Cahiers de Psychologie*, 17, pp. 169–80.

Kaës, R. (1975), '"On (dé)forme un enfant": fantasme originaire, processus et travail de la formation', *Connexions*, no. 16, pp. 37–49.

Kaës, R. (1976a), 'Désir de toute-puissance, culpabilité et épreuves dans la formation', in Kaës *et al.*, (1975).

Kaës, R. (1976b), 'L'analyse inter-transférentielle', in *ibid*.

Kaës, R. (1976c), 'Analyse inter-transférentielle, fonction alpha et groupe conteneur', *L'Evolution psychiatrique*, no. 2.

Kaës, R. (1976d), *L'appareil psychique groupal. Constructions du groupe*. Paris, Dunod.

Kaës, R. and Anzieu, D. (1976), *Chronique d'un groupe: observation et présentation du groupe du 'Paradis perdu'*, Paris, Dunod.

Kaës R., Anzieu D., Thomas L.V., Le Guérinel N. and Filloux J. (1973), *Fantasme et Formation*, Paris, Dunod.

Kaës, R., Anzieu, D., Béjarano, A., Gori, R. and Scaglia, H. (1975), *Le désir de former et la formation du savoir*, Paris, Dunod.

Kestemberg, E. (1972), 'A propos des méthodes de formation en groupe', in Schneider (1972).

Kestemberg, E. and Kestemberg, J. (1966), 'Contribution à la perspective génétique en psychanalyse', *Revue française de psychanalyse*, 30, nos. 5–6, p. 569–713.

Kestemberg, J. and Decobert, S. (1964), 'Approche psychanalytique pour la compréhension de la dynamique des groupes thérapeutiques', *Revue française de Psychanalyse*, 28, no. 3, pp. 393–418.

Khan Masud, R. (1969), 'Vicissitudes of being, knowing and experiencing in the therapeutic situation', in *The Privacy of the Self*, London, Hogarth Press, 1974.

Klein, M. (1921–45), *Contributions to Psycho-Analysis*, London, Hogarth Press, 1948.

Klein, M. (1930), 'The Importance of Symbol-Formation in the Development of the Ego', in *Contributions to Psycho-Analysis*, Hogarth Press, 1932.

Klein, M., Isaacs, S., Heimann, P. and Rivière, J. (1952), *Developments in Psycho-Analysis*, London, Hogarth Press.

Lagache, D. (1965), 'Le modèle psychanalytique de la personnalité, in *Les modèles de la personnalité en psychologie*, Paris, PUF, pp. 91–117.

Lagache, D. (1967), 'Pour une étude sur le changement individuel au cours du processus psychanalytique', *Bulletin de l'Association psychanalytique de France*, no. 3, pp. 7–43 and *Documents et débats*, 1975, no. 11, 7–26.

Lai, G. (1974), 'Les groupes d'apprentissage et les systémes relationnels', *Bulletin de Psychologie*, special number, pp. 61–70.

Lajeunesse, B.S. and Missenard, A. (1971), 'Le psychodrame analytique en groupe', *Perspectives psychiatriques*, no. 33, pp. 69–78.

Laplanche J. and Pontalis J.B. (1964), 'Fantasme originaire, fantasmes des origines, origine du fantasme', *Les Temps modernes*, no. 215, pp. 1833–68.

Le Bon, G. (1895), *La psychologie des foules*, Paris, Alcan.

Lebovici, S. and Diatkine, R. (1962), 'La dynamique du groupe', *Psychiatrie de l'enfant*, 5, no. 1.

Lebovici, S., Diatkine, R. and Kestemberg, E. (1958), 'Bilan de dix ans de pratique du psychodrame analytique chez l'enfant et l'adolescent', *Psychiatrie de l'Enfant*, 1, pp. 63–179.

Lemoine, G. and Lemoine, P. (1972), *Le psychodrame*, Paris, Laffont.

Lévi-Strauss, C. (1949), *Les structures élémentaires de la parenté*, Paris, PUF, republished Mouton; English translation, *The Elementary Structures of Kinship*, London, Eyre & Spottiswoode, and Boston, Beacon Press, 1969.

Lévi-Strauss, C. (1958), *Anthropologie structurale*, Paris, Plon; English translation, *Structural Anthropology*, London, Allen Lane, 1968.

Lévy, A. (1965), *Psychologie sociale. Textes fondamentaux anglais et américains*, French trans. Paris, Dunod.

Lewin, K. (1931–1947), *Psychologie dynamique* (collection of articles) French trans. Paris, PUF, 1959.

Lewin, K. (1948), *Resolving Social Conflicts: Selected Papers on Group Dynamics*, New York, Harper.

Mathieu, M. (1973), 'Contribution à l'étude du transfert dans les groupes

268    *Bibliography*

Mathieu, M. (1974), 'Groupe de diagnostic à Nanterre, ou l'Inconscient-La-Folie', *Bulletin de Psychologie*, special number, pp. 337–8.

Meltzer, D. (1967), *The Psycho-analytical Process*, London, Heinemann.

Métraux, A., Lowie, R.M. and Moraze, C. (1963), 'Compromis et résolution des conflits', *Revue internationale des sciences sociales*, 15, no. 2, pp. 173–263.

Missenard, A. (1969), 'Note sur l'identification dans les groupes et les séances plénières dans les séminaires' roneo.

Missenard, A. (1971), 'Dépression et petit groupe, dépression en petit groupe, groupe déprimé?' *Perspectives psychiatriques*, no. 33, pp. 59–68.

Missenard, A. (1972), 'Identification et processus groupal', in Anzieu, Béjarano *et al.*, *Le travail psychanalytique dans les groupes*, Paris, Dunod.

Missenard, A. (1974), 'Note sur le corps, dans les groupes et ailleurs', *Bulletin de Psychologie*, Special number, pp. 161–3.

Missenard, A. (1976), 'A propos du narcissisme dans les groupes', *L'Evolution psychiatrique*, no. 2.

Missenard, A. and Gelly, R. (1969), *L'identification dans la formation du médecin*, Rapport du colloque de Psychologie médicale de langue française, Barcelona.

Monod, M. and Testemale, G. (1974), 'Une session de psychothérapie analytique de groupe à l'Institute of Group Analysis de Londres', *Bulletin de Psychologie*, special number, pp. 329–36.

Morissette, L., Baltrami, E., Laurendeau, D., Crombez, J.C. (1968), 'Métacommunication et communication paradoxale', *Interprétation*, 2, no. 4, pp. 59–72.

Muller, J. (1965), *Dépendance et formation*, roneo, Faculté des lettres et sciences humaines, Strasbourg.

Muller, J. (1971), 'Les résistances dans les groupes de diagnostic', *Perspectives psychiatriques*, no. 33, pp. 49–59.

Muller, J. (1974), 'Groupes de formation: quelques idées reçues contestées peut-être constables', *Bulletin de Psychologie*, special number, pp. 23–30.

Napolitani, D. (1972), 'Signification, fonctions et organisation des groupes dans les institutions psychiatriques', *Mouvement psychiatrique*, 12, pp. 16–32.

Netter, M. (1974), 'Interventions psychologiques et interprétations psychanalytiques dans les groupes restreints', *Bulletin de Psychologie*, special number, pp. 260–72.

Ngufulu-Basuluka, I. (1974), 'Fantasme et transfert en psycho-palabre', *Bulletin de Psychologie*, special number, pp. 294–303.

Pagès, M. (1968), *La vie affective des groupes*, Paris, Dunod.

Perelman, C. and Olbrechts-Tyteca, L. (1958), *Traité de l'argumentation*, Paris, PUF, 2 vols.

Pilon-Podhorski, A. (1976), 'Quelques réflexions sur les dimensions extraverbales dans le psychodrame analytique', *Perspectives psychiatriques*.

Pons, E. (1974), 'L'effet organisatuer du fantasme de scène primitive dans les groupes institutionnels', *Bulletin de Psychologie*, special number, pp. 314–25.

Pontalis, J.B. (1959), 'Réflexions naïves sur quelques expériences de groupe: phénomènes et idéologie,' *Bulletin de Psychologie*, special number, pp. 6–9, pp. 352–358; republished under the title: 'Des techniques de groupe de l'idéologie aux phénomènes' in *Après Freud*, Paris, Gallimard, 1968.

Pontalis, J.B. (1963), 'Le petit groupe comme object', *Les temps modernes*, no. 211, pp. 1057–1069; republished in *Après Freud*, Paris, Gallimard, 1968.

Pontalis, J.B. (1972), *Rêves, dans un groupe*, in Anzieu, Béjarano *et al.*, *Le travail psychanalytique dans les groupes*, Paris, Dunod.

Rice, A.K. (1965), *Learning for Leadership*, London, Tavistock.

Rogers, C. (1970), *Encounter Groups*, London, Allen Lane, and New York, Harper & Row.

Sapir, M. (1972), *La formation psychologique du médecin*, Paris, Payot.

Sapir, M., Reverchon, F., Prévost, J.J., Canet-Palaysi, C., Philibert, R., Cornier, A., Cohen-Léon, S., Fédida P. (1975), *La relaxation: son approche psychanalytique*, Paris, Dunod.

Sartre, J.-P. (1960), *Critique de la raison dialectique*, Paris, Gallimard; English translation Alan Sheridan, Critique of Dialectical Reason, London, New Left Books.

Scaglia, J. (1974a), 'La période initiale', *Bulletin de Psychologie*, special number, pp. 227–44.

Scaglia, H. (1974b), 'L'esprit et les liens du groupe', in *ibid.*, pp. 245–52.

Scaglia, H. (1976), 'La position fantasmatique de l'observateur d'un groupe', in Kaës, R., Anzieu, D., Béjarano, A., Scaglia, H. and Gori, R., *Désir de former et formation du savoir*, Paris, Dunod.

Schindler, R. (1963), 'Psychothérapie didactique de groupe avec des psychanalystes', in Schneider (1965).

Schindler, R. (1964), 'Personnalisation du groupe', French trans. in *La Personnalisation. Etudes sur la psychologie d'Igor Caruso*, Paris, Desclée de Brouwer, 1971, pp. 91–107.

Schneider, P.B. (1965), *Pratique de la psychothérapie de groupe*, collected papers from the first international seminar on group psychotherapy, Lausanne, 1963; Paris, PUF, et Florence, Giunti.

Schneider, P.B. (1968), *Pratique de la psychothérapie de groupe. II. Les techniques*, collected papers from the second international seminar on group psychotherapy, Lausanne, 1966; Paris, PUF, and Florence, Giunti.

Schneider, P.B. (1972), *Pratique de la psychothérapie de groupe. Problèmes actuels de la psychothérapie de groupe analytique et de groupes de discussion*, collected papers from the third international seminar on group psychotherapy, Lausanne, 1971; Paris, PUF, and Florence, Giunti.

Serraf, G. (1974), 'Les méthodes de développement de la créativité', *Bulletin de Psychologie*, special number, pp. 174–85.

Slavson, S.R. (1950), *Analytic Group Psychotherapy*, New York,

Columbia University Press.

Springmann, R. (1976), 'La fragmentation en tant que défense dans les grands groupes', *L'Evolution psychiatrique*, no. 2.

Tausk, V. (1919), 'De la genèse de "l'appareil à influencer" au cours de la schizophrénie', trans. in *La Psychanalyse*, 1958, no. 44, pp. 227–65.

Turquet, P.M. (1974), 'Menaces à l'identité personnelle dans le groupe large', trans. in *Bulletin de Psychologie*, special number, pp. 135–58.

Valabrega, J.-P. (1967), 'Le problème anthropologique du fantasme', in *Le désir et la perversion*, Paris, Seuil, pp. 165–89.

Watzlawick, P., Helmick-Beavin, J., Jackson, D. (1967), *Pragmatics of Human Communication*, London, Faber & Faber.

Widlöcher, D. (1970), *Freud et le problème du changement*, Paris, PUF.

Winnicott, D.W. (1953), 'Transitional Objects and Transitional Phenomena', in *Playing and Reality*, London, Tavistock, 1971.

Winnicott, D.W. (1967), 'The Location of Cultural Experience', in *Playing and Reality*, London, Tavistock, 1971.

Wolfson, L. (1970), *Le shizo et les langues*, Paris, Gallimard.

# Index

Abbey of Thélème, 130
abortion in France, liberalization
  after 1968, 260
abstinence, rule: in groups, 8, 9,
  11, **23-7**, 29, 31, 32, 33, 34; in
  psychodrama, 51, 57; of psycho-
  analyst and subject, 1, 12, 37
acted-out interpretations in
  psychodrama, 51, 60
acting as mode of transgression, 33
acting out: in large groups, 76; in
  psycho-analysis, 33
active-passive oppositions in
  castration phantasies, 237
actor-observer oppositions in
  primal-scene phantasies, 236
adaptive functions, effect of
  psychodrama, 50
AFAP, 130
affective commitment: increased
  by physical contact, 57
affective maturation, effect of
  psychodrama, 50
affective states combining
  individuals, 110
affective tonality of psychodrama,
  57
affects: in psychodrama, 43; of
  group-as-machine phantasy, 189
affinities, network of, between
  group members, 24
aggressive cathexis in diagnostic
  group, 24
aggressive drives: in groups, 75,

136, 140; in psychotics, 192;
  related to hit-and-run dialectic,
  248
aggressive transference in large
  groups, 85
aggressivity: collective, interpretation by monitor, 70; externalization of, in psychodrama, 61, 201;
  fending off, in psychodrama, 63;
  intra-group, maintained by
  mutual identification, 246; laws
  governing, 39; of group
  members, defence against, 239;
  of groups, 114
Agrippa (Menenius Agrippa), 124
Alexander the Great, 133
Algerian war, French soldiers in,
  **95-8**, 255
Alsace, diagnostic group in, 38,
  **152-4**
alternating groups, alternation of
  groups: group illusion, 154-5;
  identity in, 73
ambivalence: towards authority,
  externalization, 61; towards
  parental imagos, 235
American housewives, changes in
  dietary habits, 104-5, 116-17
American marines, training, 173
analytic psychodrama, 43-67
animals (*see also* 'reflective bull'):
  as machines, Cartesian theory,
  127; themes in collective free
  associations, 167

271

body metaphor, 118, 249
bonds: child-mother, 249; group metaphor, 154; homosexual, in groups, 239; search for, in groups, 75
Bowlby, J., 75, 248
Bread and Puppet Theater, 47
breaking-apart phantasies, 74, 171-87; see fragmentation
breast: baby, child, at: 93, 160, 253; equivalences of, 169; group as, 3, 159, 161, 224, 249; imago of, 242; source of pleasure, 144, 158, 169, 224; 'training', 169
Breuer, J., 13
brothers, society of, Freud's myth, 39; *see also* murder of father
Buddha, 202
'buddies', group of, 117
'bull, reflective', *see* 'reflective bull'
*Bund*, 258
Buñel, L., 167

Cartesian theory of animals as machines, 127
case material in psychology training, 53
castration anxiety: collective, difficulty in identifying, 174; denial of, by neurotic, 33; egalitarian ideology as defence against, 154; in groups, 171, 186, 236; in mythical model, 135; oral, 162, 165, 187, 236; particular case of death drive, 204; related to what is forbidden, 24
castration phantasies: accompanying speaking, 163; active-passive oppositions in, 237; in groups, 236; related to origin of sexual differences, 235
cathexis: in groups, 24, 143; narcissistic, 108; of rules, in psycho-analysis, 3
Cau, J., 107
censorship of erotic books and films in France, removal after 1968, 260

*Ces idées qui ont ebranlé la France*, 258
changes, changing (*see also* resistance to change): and training, 183, 184, 194; in bodily psychodrama, 49; in dietary habits, 104-5, 116-17; individual and institutional, 41; phantasies and anxieties about, 173
Chanoît, P.E., 49
Charcot, J.-M., 195
child, children: autistic, in psychodrama, 49; bonds with mother, fear of breaking, 187; deformed, theme related to castration phantasies, 236; dependent, related to group phantasies, 249, 253; invalid, theme in psychodrama, 62; mirror stage in, 121; relations with parents, forming superego and ego ideal, 246; rivalry of, 79, 226
childhood: appearance of paranoid and depressive anxieties, 113, 247; repressed wishes from, 133
childhood anxiety and trauma of monitors, 89, 98
Christian myths, biblical myth, 38, 39, 167, 180
church: communal mystique in, 125; group ego ideal in, 140; identification in, 246
cinema, *see* films
clans: as group and family, 239; in primitive societies, 240; within large groups, 68
closed Jewish communities, 108-9
cohesion: fight-flight as sign of, 111; in paranoid-schizoid group, 114; of gathering, guaranteed by ego ideal, 101
collective aggressivity, interpretation by monitor, 70
collective analytic psychodrama, 52-67
collective anonymity of large groups, 73
collective castration anxiety, difficulty in identifying, 174

136, 140
libidinal object, group as, 143
libidinal processes, freeing in large
  groups, 84
libido: circulation of, 81; division
  of, 193; dualism of, 192;
  equilibrium between object and
  ego, 143; mobility, in diagnostic
  group, 19; object, transformed
  into narcissistic, 92
Liendo, E.C., 242
Lippitt, R., 256
live-in seminar, 256: case history,
  171-87
living organism, group metaphor,
  123, **124-6**
Living Theater, 47
logical paradoxes, 203-5
logic, pathogenic communication,
  199-201
*Lord of the flies*, 16
lover, theme in psychodrama, 64

machine(s): animals as, Cartesian
  theory, 127; body as, phantasy,
  192; group as, metaphor, 126-8,
  **188-94**, 260, 261
madness (*see also* mental illness):
  theme in psychodrama, 63-4
Maisonneuve, J., 163
*Maîtres fous, Les*, 47
management committee difficulties, 119-20; phantasy of father's
  murder in, 206-16
manifest content: explained by
  latent content, 223; in psychodrama, 63; in tangentialization
  and disqualification, 199; of
  dreams, symptoms, creative
  works, 23; of phantasy, 186, 191
man-woman relationship, in
  psychodrama, 62
*Marines, The*, 173, 184
marines, training, 173
Martin, J.-Y., 7
maternal imago (*see also* parental
  imagos): organizing principle,
  234, 235, 240

maturation, effect of psychodrama,
  50
Mauriac, F., 108
May 1968, France, events of, 47,
  52, **258-61**
Mayo, E., 103
Mead, G., 45
meaning(s): in group, 223; latent,
  199; of psychodrama performance, 59; relation to words,
  183
*Medea*, 167
Meltzer, D., 242
Menenius Agrippa, 124
mental illness (*see also* madness):
  as disturbance in communication, 199; dismemberment of
  body image in, 118
messianic hope in group, 112
metaphors, group, 118-19, 123,
  **124-8**, 188, 232, 241, 249
Métraux, A., 130
military, *see* army
mime in psychodrama, 56, 197
mime plays, inspired by psychodrama, 47
mimo-drama, 46
minorities in France, recognition of
  after 1968, 260
mirror: as theme, 17; group as,
  118, 255; Morenian psychodrama procedure, 46; stage, of
  childhood, 121, 158
Missenard, A., 5, 25, 41, 48, 76,
  92, 166, 221, 230, 232, 233, 242,
  250
*Moi, un noir*, 47
Molière, 117
monitor(s): Bion's view of, 112-13;
  childhood traumas of, 89, 98; in
  large groups, 70-3, 91-3, 98-9; in
  psychodrama, 61-2, 63, 64, 65,
  66, 221, 222; in relation to group
  problems, 219, 220, 221, 222; in
  small groups, 177; of alternating
  groups, 87; oral phantasies of
  169-70
Monod, M., 50

Welles, Orson, 158
White, R.K., 256
Wilson, Bob, 47
Winnicott, D.W., 5, 6, 93, 95, 159, 248, 253
wish-fulfilment: group as, 4; in groups, **129-42**, 224-5
wish to know, learn, understand (epistemophilic drive): frust-ration of, in diagnostic groups, 25; in large groups, 90, 93; liberation of, by dumping process, 243; removal of inhibi-tions concerning, 67; rooted in infantile sexual curiosity, 26
Wolfson, L., 190
woman, women: crowd as, 118-19,

139; in France, affirmation of rights after 1968, 260; of own group, prohibition of sexual relations with, 25; predominance in psychodrama groups, 59
woman-man relationships, in psychodrama, 62
words (*see also* language; speech; verbs; vocabulary): as objects, 190; relation to meanings, 183
work group: function, in relation to Oedipus complex, 239; threat to individual freedom, 117

Ziferstein, I., 257
Zola, E., 119